JUDAISM AND VEGETARIANISM

Richard Schwartz
RSCHW12345@ aol.com
jewishveg. com/schwartz

JUDAISM
AND
VEGETARIANISM

Richard H. Schwartz, Ph.D.

Lantern Books
A Division of Booklight Inc.

2001
Lantern Books
One Union Square West, Suite 201
New York, NY 10003

Printed in the United States of America

Library of Congress Cataloging-in-Publication Data

Schwartz, Richard
  Judaism and vegetarianism / by Richard Schwartz—[New and rev. ed.].
    p. cm.
  Includes bibliographical references and index.
  ISBN 1-930051-24-7
    1. Vegetarianism—Religious aspects—Judaism. 2. Ethics, Jewish. I. Title.

BM538.V43 S38 2001
296.3'693—dc21

00-054577

STATEMENTS OF SUPPORT

It is to be hoped that this major publication will not only adorn the bookshelf of many a Jewish home, but will also become a guide to an ever-increasing movement of Jews toward vegetarianism, born out of sincere religious conviction rooted in our most sublime teachings.—**David Rosen**, former Chief Rabbi of Ireland

My own view is that a vegetarian diet may in fact hasten the coming of Moshiach (the Messiah). The more we live as if this were the messianic age the closer we are to it. Richard Schwartz's *Judaism and Vegetarianism* is a powerful guide to moving self and society closer to Moshiach.—**Rabbi Rami Shapiro**, author, *The Way of Solomon*, and founder and director of The Virtual Yeshiva and Simply Jewish

Richard Schwartz is changing the world and I am proud to be his friend. You do not have to be a Jew to read and enjoy *Judaism and Vegetarianism*. Richard has brilliantly written a most fascinating book, no matter what your religion. I found it to be one of the best books I've ever read.—**Howard F. Lyman**, President, EarthSave International; author, *Mad Cowboy*

Why, I have wondered, are so many Jews today shifting toward a more vegetarian diet? In his scholarly and thoughtful style, Richard Schwartz demonstrates the profound imperatives at the heart of the Jewish faith that lead inexorably in a vegetarian direction. He shows us that to be a *mensch* today, to be a whole and healthy and fully human being, you have to bring your food choices into alignment with your ethics, and that means, for anyone who aspires towards peace and compassion, eating a plant-based diet.—**John Robbins**, author, *Diet for a New America* and *The Food Revolution: How Your Diet Can Help Save Your Life and Our World*

Thank God, and Professor Richard Schwartz, for a very accurate, very readable, very stirring book! The author's intellectual integrity, moral passion, and simple human warmth help illustrate a hitherto almost unexplored, yet vastly important territory. His Jewish commitments are as profound as his ethical concerns are universal. The work is a challenge to mind and soul, a call to the conscience, and a guide for practical, necessary action. There must be much acclaim for this brave, pioneering, shiningly humane achievement.—**Dr. Andre Ungar**, Rabbi of Temple Emanuel, Westwood, New Jersey; former chairman of the Hebraic Studies Department, Rutgers University

Jews like me who have (so far) not become full vegetarians will still (like me) find Schwartz's analysis of the problems of meat-eating to be serious food not only for thought but for action to eat far less meat. And those who are drawn to explore the deeper meanings of Torah will find Schwartz a good and careful guide in this aspect of Jewish tradition. For us who are all the People of the Mouth—whether it is food in or words out—this is an important book.—**Rabbi Arthur Waskow**, author, *Down-To-Earth Judaism: Food, Money, Sex, and the Rest of Life, Godwrestling—Round 2,* and several other books

Search no further, Richard H. Schwartz has covered all the conceivable aspects of non-meat-eating and the Jewish religion.
—**Marc Leepson**, *The Vegetarian Voice*

EXCERPTS FROM PUBLISHED REVIEWS OF EARLIER EDITIONS

Schwartz makes his most original contribution by showing that for each of the standard arguments in favor of vegetarianism, there is a specifically Jewish approach which underpins the vegetarian position.—*The Vegetarian Activist*

A brilliant book of outstanding merit....A classic that should find its way into every Jewish bookcase and certainly of interest to all others who love to widen their knowledge of the ancient and compassionate philosophies.—**Victor Ruben**, *Jewish Vegetarian*

This is a convincing, compassionate, and comprehensive argument...marshals overpowering evidence...amply documented.... [We] will be compelled to think most seriously about the issues raised in this provocative book.—**Harry Essrig**, *The American Rabbi*

Professor Schwartz has presented us with impressive material supporting his thesis that a practical, healthy, and Torah way of eating is through vegetarianism.—*Emunah*

Dr. Schwartz's work should find a place in the home library of every thinking individual, religious or not. It should become required reading for high schools, and certainly in pre-marriage counseling....—"Nutrition for Better Health," **Shirley Mandel**, *The Jewish Press*

By any standard of measurement, this is an extraordinary book; it covers a field never before explained. When you get through its pages, you might shake your head in bewilderment and say, "This is all so true, why hasn't it been said before?"—Health Page, **Simon Bloom**, *American Jewish Ledger*

It would be hard for anyone ethically sensitive—Jew or non-Jew—to read this book and not take up the vegetarian cause.—**Paul Peabody**, Fellowship of Reconciliation

A titan in its glorification of the Jewish faith and spirit.—**Rabbi Marcus Kramer**, *Staten Island Advance*

TABLE OF CONTENTS

FOREWORD

TURN FROM EVIL AND DO GOOD SAYS THE PSALMIST
(Psalms 34:15). As Professor Richard Schwartz effectively
demonstrates in this excellent book, meat-eating today—more
than ever before—is harmful in a variety of ways. Conversely, we are able
to personally enhance well being for ourselves, our society, and our
environment through maintaining a vegetarian diet.

I believe that there are compelling arguments to advocate
vegetarianism even in an ideal human society, just as the late Chief Rabbi
Abraham Isaac Hakohen Kook envisaged the messianic age as a vegetarian
era on the basis of biblical texts. However, I recognize as an Orthodox Jew
that these compelling arguments are not conclusive.

Nevertheless, under present day conditions in modern society,
involving, on the one hand, so much damage and danger as well as cruelty
in the consumption of animals, and, on the other, the possibilities to have
a healthy balanced diet without meat, perhaps as never before it is
apparent that the consumption of animal flesh has become halachically
unjustifiable.

Those who seek to live in accordance with the most sublime values of
Judaism will find Richard Schwartz's book an inspiration and guide for an
authentic modern Jewish life that fulfills the above mentioned injunction
to "turn from evil and do that which is good, seek peace and pursue it."

Rabbi David Rosen
Former Chief Rabbi of Ireland, President for Israel of IJVS
Director of Israel Office of the Anti-Defamation League

PREFACE TO
THE FIRST EDITION

J UDAISM AND VEGETARIANISM? CAN THE TWO BE RELATED? After all, what is a *simcha* (Jewish celebration) or holiday dinner without gefilte fish, chopped liver, *cholent*, roast beef, chicken, and chicken soup? And what about passages in the Torah referring to Temple sacrifices of animals and the consumption of meat?

Because of these factors, this book is the result of a leap of faith, an intuition that a religion that has such powerful teachings about compassion for animals, preserving health, feeding the hungry, helping the poor, and conserving resources must be consistent with vegetarianism. As I probed for appropriate Jewish teachings and concepts, I became increasingly convinced that to be more completely involved with the glorious goals and values of Judaism, one should be a vegetarian.

While Judaism emphasizes *tsa'ar ba'alei chayim*, the prohibition against causing needless suffering for animals, animals are raised for food today under cruel conditions, in crowded, confined cells, where they are denied fresh air, exercise, and any natural existence.

While Judaism mandates that we be very careful about preserving our health and our lives, animal-centered diets have been linked to heart disease, several forms of cancer, and other degenerative illnesses.

While Judaism stresses that we are to share our bread with the hungry, seventy percent of the grain grown in the United States and over one-third of the grain grown worldwide is fed to animals destined for slaughter, as millions of people die annually because of hunger and its effects.

While Judaism teaches that "the earth is the Lord's" and we are partners with God in preserving the world and seeing that the earth's resources are properly used, a flesh-centered diet requires the wasteful use of food and other resources, and results in much pollution.

While Judaism stresses that we must seek and pursue peace and that violence results from unjust conditions, flesh-centered diets, by wasting valuable resources, help to perpetuate the widespread hunger and poverty that eventually lead to instability and war.

There are many indications in the Jewish tradition that point toward vegetarianism. The first dietary law (Genesis 1:29) allowed only vegetarian foods. When permission to eat meat was given as a concession to people's weakness, many prohibitions and restrictions were applied to keep alive a sense of reverence for life. After the Exodus of the Children of Israel from Egypt, a second non-flesh diet was introduced in the form of manna. When the Israelites cried out for meat, God was angry. He finally relented and provided meat, but a plague broke out and many Jews died. According to Rabbi Abraham Kook, the first chief rabbi of pre-state Israel, based on the prophecy of Isaiah ("...the lion will eat straw like the ox..."), people will again be vegetarians in the time of the Messiah.

Many difficult questions are asked of vegetarians who take the Jewish tradition seriously. These include: Don't we have to eat meat on the Sabbath and to celebrate joyous events? Isn't it a sin not to take advantage of pleasurable things like eating meat? Weren't we given dominion over animals? What about sacrificial Temple services? These and other questions are considered in this book.

There have been several recent examples of increased Jewish interest and involvement in vegetarianism. In this book I cite Jewish vegetarian groups and activities in the United States, Britain (where the Jewish Vegetarian Society has its international headquarters), and Israel. I also include biographies of famous Jewish vegetarians such as Shlomo Goren, the late Ashkenazi Chief Rabbi of Israel, Franz Kafka, Isaac Bashevis Singer, and I. L. Peretz. Finally, there is an annotated bibliography with many relevant sources for those who wish more information on such issues as vegetarianism, nutrition, recipes, and ideas relating Judaism and vegetarianism.

Judaism has much to say about solutions to the critical problems that face the world today. This volume attempts to show how vegetarianism is consistent with Jewish ideals and can play a role in reducing global problems such as hunger, pollution, resource depletion, poverty, and violence.

This book is only a beginning of the study of an issue that must be considered in depth by the Jewish community.

PREFACE TO THE REVISED EDITION

WHY A NEW EDITION OF *JUDAISM AND VEGETARIANISM*? There are several reasons: Never before have the problems and threats related to animal-based diets and agriculture been so urgent. It is becoming increasingly clear that a shift toward vegetarianism is a planetary imperative. The epidemic of degenerative diseases linked to animal-based diets continues to expand. Costs related to treating diseases have been soaring, and these have caused major changes in health care systems, with decisions being made often for economic rather than medical reasons. Modern livestock farming is contributing substantially to much environmental damage, including the destruction of tropical rain forests and other habitats, soil erosion and depletion, and air and water pollution. There are frequent media reports of record temperatures, droughts, severe storms, melting of glaciers and polar ice caps, bleaching of coral reefs, and other negative effects of global climate changes. With increasing human population and greater consumption of animal products, some experts on food sustainability are warning of future scarcities.

In view of the many negative effects of animal-based diets and agriculture and the Jewish teachings they contradict, it is essential to bring to the attention of the Jewish community the connections between Judaism and vegetarianism. We need to continuously research and discuss these questions, which connect to so many basic Jewish values.

While Judaism has very beautiful and powerful teachings about acting with compassion to animals, protecting human health, preserving the environment, conserving resources, sharing with hungry people, and pursuing peace, the realities of animal-based diets and modern intensive livestock agriculture are completely contrary to each of these values. Hence, if Jewish teachings are to be taken seriously, it is important that there be a comprehensive discussion of the many moral issues related to current typical Jewish diets, along with appropriate resolutions and actions.

Many changes have been made in this new edition, including the following:

- All material has been carefully reviewed, and revised and updated, where appropriate.

- Many new developments and much new research on the impacts of animal-centered diets on health and ecology have been added.

- Major changes in the Jewish vegetarian world, such as the opening of a Jewish Vegetarian Center in the heart of Jerusalem and recent activities of Jewish vegetarian groups, are discussed.

- The bibliography has been updated, expanded, and reorganized by subjects.

- The question-and-answer section has been expanded from seventeen questions in the first edition and thirty-seven in the second edition to sixty-two in two chapters (one on Jewish issues, and one on general issues) in this edition, with the addition of many new questions related to health, the treatment of animals, and some recent vegetarian-related issues. Responses to previous questions have also been reviewed and modified for added clarity.

- In many cases, updated sources and more scholarly authorities have been cited to give greater credibility to the thesis.

- Topics that are new or discussed in significantly greater detail include: global warming; high protein diets; the heart disease–reversal diet of Dean Ornish, M.D.; the Cornell/China/Oxford study ("grand prix of epidemiology"); protein and calcium myths; recent shifts of China to animal-based diets; early puberty among girls due to animal-based diets; questions for respectfully challenging meat-eaters; "Why I am a vegetarian"; a Jewish vegetarian resolution; suggestions for couples when one person is vegetarian and one is not; organic vegetarian food; and important Internet websites, including some containing vegetarian recipes, restaurants, and cyberstores.

This book argues that:

1. Jews have a choice with regard to their diets, and that choice should not be based only on habit, convenience, and tradition, but should consider basic Jewish values and the realities of the modern intensive livestock agriculture that produces today's animal products.

2. There is no inconsistency between Judaism and vegetarianism, since basic Jewish values point to vegetarianism as the ideal diet.

3. It is a *mitzvah* to be concerned about both animals and people. When animals are mistreated on factory farms and then eaten, there are negative effects, including damage to human health, pollution, the destruction of ecosystems, increased hunger, and the misuse of scarce resources.

As with previous editions, it is hoped that the present edition will lead to a long overdue respectful dialogue in the Jewish community and beyond on the many moral issues related to our diets, and that thereby it will help speed the arrival of that vegetarian time when "...no one shall hurt nor destroy in all of God's holy mountain...." (Isaiah 11:9)

And God said: "Behold, I have given you every herb yielding seed which is upon the face of all the earth, and every tree that has seed-yielding fruit—to you it shall be for food."
(Genesis 1:29)

RABBINIC ENDORSEMENT

CONGRATULATIONS TO MY ESTEEMED COLLEAGUE AND friend, Professor Richard Schwartz. May G-d bless him, for he has worked hard and composed a wonderful work which describes the ideal of vegetarianism and peace of our prophets and sages of Israel as an absolute ideal toward which the laws of our codes of *kashrut* lead.

We look at the vegetarian way of life as a special path of worship and as a step forward toward the "Great Day," i.e., the coming of the Messiah, the day where "Nation shall not lift up sword against nation, neither shall they learn war any more." (Isaiah 2:4) Bloodshed will cease, and a "Suckling child shall play on the hole of the asp, and the weaned child shall put his hand on the adder's den." (Isaiah 11:8)

During the messianic era, when "The lion shall eat straw like the ox," (Isaiah 11:7) people will certainly return to the first stage, in the generations of Adam to Noah, before the eating of meat was sanctioned, and the consumption of fruits and vegetables was indeed sufficient. Then there will be total, perfect peace among people as well as between human beings and the animal kingdom. "And the calf and the young lion and the fatling (shall be) together; and a little child shall lead them." (Isaiah 11:6) Israel and the rest of the world will be blessed, as our Rabbis observed, "Peace was the source of blessings which the Almighty gave to Israel"— may it be restored in the Days to Come.

Great scholars of Israel, namely the late Chief Rabbi, Harav Abraham Isaac Hakohen Kook, and his outstanding disciple, my own great father [Rabbi David Cohen, "the Nazir of Jerusalem"], of blessed memory, preached and taught vegetarianism.

May it be the will of the A-mighty that the number of noble souls who make vegetarianism their way of life will increase. Blessed they will be because they will be observing the dictum of our Rabbis, "Sanctify yourself with that which is permitted unto you." May they abstain from eating the flesh of living animals and may they be satisfied with the blessings which G-d provided the earth; "And the work of righteousness shall be peace." (Isaiah 32:17)

May the knowledge of G-d be spread in this way and may the words of the prophet Malachi be realized: "Behold, I will send you Elijah the Prophet before the coming of the great and awesome day of the L-rd. And he shall turn the heart of the fathers to their children and the children to their fathers." (Malachi 3:24)

Rabbi Shear Yashuv Cohen
Ashkenazic Chief Rabbi and Rosh Bet Din, Haifa

Translated from the Hebrew by Atara Perlman

ACKNOWLEDGMENTS

FIRST, I WISH TO EXPRESS MY THANKS TO GOD BY RECITING the traditional Jewish blessing for when a person reaches a milestone in his or her life or that of the Jewish people: "Blessed are you, Lord our God, King of the universe, Who has kept us alive and sustained us and brought us to this season."

While a switch toward vegetarianism is both a societal and a Jewish imperative, and it is essential that the issues discussed in his book be put on the Jewish agenda, I recognize my limitations in presenting this information. However, I have been very fortunate to have had input and suggestions from a wide variety of dedicated, very knowledgeable individuals.

The following (in alphabetical order) reviewed the entire final draft of the manuscript and made valuable suggestions:

1. Rabbi Yonassan Gershom: Breslov Chassid; author of *Jewish Tales of Reincarnation* (Jason Aronson, 1999); he and his wife, Caryl Rachel, are ovo-lacto vegetarians who live on a hobby farm in Minnesota, sharing the land with numerous dogs, cats, geese, chickens, and wildlife that all live to a ripe old age. His practical experience with animals was most appreciated in reviewing the manuscript, as was his help with the section on Chassidism and "raising sparks."

2. Jay Lavine, M.D.: opthalmologist with a specialty in medicine, including preventive nutrition; has articles in several professional journals; his first book, *The Eye Care Sourcebook*, contains much information on the nutritional prevention and treatment of eye disease; he is beginning work

on a nutrition sourcebook. He provided valuable suggestions related to diet and health.

3. Mark Nagurka, Ph.D. (MIT): Associate Professor of Mechanical and Biomedical Engineering at Marquette University in Milwaukee, Wisconsin. His lifelong passion is love of Jews, Judaism, and Israel. Although he resides in Glendale, Wisconsin, his heart and soul are in Jerusalem.

4. Charles Patterson, Ph.D: author of *Anti-Semitism: The Road to the Holocaust and Beyond* and eight other books. His most recent books are *Angel on My Shoulder: From Concentration Camp to Carnegie Hall* and *Eternal Treblinka: Our Treatment of Animals and the Holocaust*. His experience as a copy editor was very valuable in sharpening my writing.

5. Rabbi Dovid Sears: Breslov Chassid; author of many books, including *Compassion for Humanity in the Jewish Tradition: A Source Book* and *The Path of the Bal Shem Tov: Early Chassidic Teachings and Customs*. His research for his latest writing project, tentatively titled *The Vision of Eden: Animal Welfare and Vegetarianism in Jewish Law and Mysticism*, provided valuable sources and concepts that made his review of this book especially valuable.

6. Jonathan Wolf: his course, "Judaism and Vegetarianism," at Lincoln Square Synagogue provided the original impetus for this work. Several sections of this book reflect his ideas and those of his students with whom I have had the pleasure of studying. His thorough review of every edition of this book was extremely valuable.

Yosef Ben Shlomo Hakohen, a long time friend, has been a constant source of sensible advice and encouragement, which is much appreciated. He reviewed much of an early draft and suggested additional Judaic sources that have been incorporated into the book.

A prime source of ideas and inspiration has been *The Jewish Vegetarian*, the magazine of the Jewish Vegetarian Society, edited for many years by the late Mr. Philip Pick, the honorary president. Without the existence of this group and its quarterly publication, this project might never have been started.

People who made major contributions to specific parts of the book include: Emanuel Goldman (Professor of Microbiology and Molecular Genetics, New Jersey Medical School, University of Medicine and Dentistry of New Jersey) and Lewis Regenstein (author of *Replenish the Earth: The Teachings of the World's Religions on Protecting Animals and Nature, America the Poisoned*, and *The Politics of Extinction*; president of the Interfaith Council for the Protection of Animals and Nature in Atlanta, an affiliate of the Humane Society of the United States).

I wish to thank John Robbins (author of *Diet for a New America* and several other books, and founder of EarthSave, a national group devoted to promoting vegetarianism), for permitting me to see an advance copy of his manuscript, *The Food Revolution: How Your Diet Can Help Save Your Life and Our World*, which provided valuable information. John is one of my heroes because, as the only son of Irving Robbins, the co-founder of the Baskin-Robbins ice cream empire, he gave up a very lucrative future in order to help educate people about the many negative effects of animal-based diets and agriculture.

The excellent work done by Erica Weisberg in designing the cover is most appreciated.

Others who reviewed parts of the book and made valuable suggestions or made other significant contributions include: Dr. Erv Bloom (President of Israeli vegetarian moshav *Amirim*); Janine Bronsome; Robert Cohen (author of *Milk: the Deadly Poison*; founder of the Anti-Dairy Coalition; Executive Director, Dairy Education Board); Bruce Friedrich (vegetarian coordinator for People for the Ethical Treatment of Animals); Zev Gelbendorf (neighbor and friend); Aaron Gross (a vegetarian and animal rights activist); Ronald Halweil (M.D., practicing physician for thirty-five years and author of Eat *This!*; Rev. J. R. Hyland (author of *God's Covenant With Animals* and editorial director for Humane Religion publications); Eva and Israel Mossman (coordinators of the Jewish Vegetarians of North America—JVNA—and editors of its newsletter); Sandra Kahler; Roberta Kalechofsky (founder and director of Jews for Animal Rights (JAR), author of *Vegetarian Judaism* and several other books on vegetarianism and animal rights, editor and publisher, head of Micah Publications, Inc.);

Stephen Kaufman (Co-chair of the Medical Research Modernization Committee; Director of the Christian Vegetarian Association); Nina Natelson (founder and coordinator of Concern for Helping Animals in Israel); Danila Oder (Food Irradiation Coordinator for the Organic Consumers Association); Kate Palmer (long-time Jewish vegetarian, vegan, environmental, and animal rights activist); Murray Polner (former editor of *Present Tense* magazine, co-chair of the Jewish Peace Fellowship, and editor of *Shalom: The Jewish Peace Letter*); Mindy Ribner (author of *New Age Judaism*; Jewish meditation instructor); Rabbi David Rosen (former Chief Rabbi of Ireland and current director of the Jerusalem office of the Anti-Defamation League); Don Seeman (lecturer in anthropology, Hebrew University); Charles Stahler (co-coordinator of the Vegetarian Resource Group); Lara Denis Werthheimer (Assistant Professor of Philosophy, University of California, Irvine); Yossi Wolfson (Coordinator of Anonymous, Israel's largest animal rights organization).

I am very grateful to Gene Rasmussen and Joseph Roccombli for running drafts of the manuscript. The excellent work done by Martin Rowe at Lantern Books in editing and producing this volume is much appreciated.

I apologize to any contributors whom I inadvertently omitted.

I wish to express deep appreciation to my wife, Loretta, our children, Susan (and David Kleid), David, and Deborah (and Ariel Gluch), and our grandchildren, Shalom Eliahu, Ayelet Breindel, Avital P'nina, and Michal Na'ama Kleid, and Eliyahu, Ilan Avraham, and Yosef Gluch, for their patience, understanding, and encouragement as I took time away from other responsibilities to gather and write this material.

Although all of these people have been very helpful, the author takes full responsibility for the final selection of material and interpretations.

Finally, I wish to thank in advance all who will read this volume and send me ideas and suggestions for improvements so that this book can help lead toward that day when "none shall hurt nor destroy in all My holy mountain" (Isaiah 11:9).

In loving memory of my mother- and father-in-law Bessie and Edward Susskind, whose guidance and devotion were always an inspiration.

1: A VEGETARIAN VIEW OF THE BIBLE

And God said: "Behold, I have given you every herb-yielding seed which is upon the face of all the earth, and every tree that has seed-yielding fruit—to you it shall be for food." (Genesis 1:29)

GOD'S INITIAL INTENTION WAS THAT PEOPLE BE vegetarians. The foremost Jewish Torah commentator, Rashi (1040–1105), says the following about God's first dietary law (above): "God did not permit Adam and his wife to kill a creature and to eat its flesh. Only every green herb shall they all eat together."[1] Most Torah commentators, including Rabbi Abraham Ibn Ezra (1092–1167), Maimonides (1135–1214), Nachmanides (1194–1270), and Rabbi Joseph Albo (d. 1444), agree with this assessment. As Rabbi Moses Cassuto (1883–1951) in his commentary *From Adam to Noah* notes:

> You are permitted to use the animals and employ them for work, have dominion over them in order to utilize their services for your subsistence, but must not hold their life cheap nor slaughter them for food. Your natural diet is vegetarian....[2]

These views are consistent with the Talmud, which says that people were initially vegetarians: "Adam was not permitted meat for purposes of eating."[3]

The great 13th-century Jewish commentator Nachmanides claims that one reason behind this initial human diet is the kinship between all sentient beings:

> Living creatures possess a soul and a certain spiritual superiority which in this respect make them similar to those who possess intellect [human beings] and they have the power of affecting

their own welfare and their food, and they flee from pain and death.[4]

Fifteenth-century Jewish philosopher Rabbi Joseph Albo, adds that "in the killing of animals there is cruelty, rage, and the accustoming of oneself to the evil habit of shedding innocent blood."[5]

God's original dietary plan represents a unique statement in humanity's spiritual history. It is a spiritual blueprint of a vegetarian world order. Yet many millions of people have read this Torah verse (Genesis 1:29) and passed it by without considering its meaning. After stating that people must adhere to a vegetarian diet, the Torah indicates that animals were not initally intended to prey on one another but to also subsist on purely vegetarian food:

> And to every beast of the earth, and to every fowl of the air, and
> to every thing that creeps upon the earth, wherein there is a living
> soul, [I have given] every green herb for food. (Genesis 1:30)

Immediately after giving these dietary laws, God sees everything He has made and "behold, it was very good" (Genesis 1:31). Everything in the universe is as God wanted it, in complete harmony, with nothing superfluous or lacking.[6] The vegetarian diet is consistent with God's initial plan.

There are other indications in the early chapters of Genesis that people originally were to be sustained on vegetarian diets:

> And the Lord God commanded the man, saying: "of every tree
> of the garden, you may freely eat...." (Genesis 2:16)

> "...and you shall eat the herbs of the field." (Genesis 3:18)

Chapter 5 of Genesis tells of the long lives of people in the vegetarian generations from Adam to Noah. Adam lives 930 years; Seth (Adam's son) 912 years; Enosh (Seth's son) 905 years; Kenan (Enosh's son) 910 years, and so on, until Methuselah, who lives 969 years, the longest life recorded in the Torah. After the flood, people live for much shorter periods. Abraham, for example, lives only 175 years.

Why the tremendous change in lifespans? A partial explanation may be that the change in diet contributed to the change in lifespans. Before the flood, people were forbidden to eat meat; after the flood it was permitted (Genesis 9:3). This view that meat-eating shortened lives was held by Nachmanides.[7] Recent evidence linking heavy meat consumption with numerous diseases reinforces this point of view (see Chapter 3). Of course, a shift to sensible vegetarian diets would not increase lifespans to anywhere near those attributed to early biblical people, but recent medical evidence indicates that it would lead to an increase in the average span and quality of life.

The strongest support for vegetarianism as a positive ideal in Torah literature is in the writing of Rabbi Abraham Isaac Hakohen Kook (1865–1935). Rav Kook was the first Ashkenazic Chief Rabbi of pre-state Israel and a highly respected and beloved Jewish spiritual leader. He was a mystical thinker and a great Torah scholar. He spoke powerfully on vegetarianism, as recorded in A Vision of Vegetarianism and Peace (edited by Rav Kook's disciple, Rabbi David Cohen, "The Nazir of Jerusalem").

Rav Kook believed that the permission to eat meat was only a temporary concession; he felt that a God who is merciful to His creatures would not institute an everlasting law permitting the killing of animals for food.[8] He states:

> The progress of dynamic ideals will not be eternally blocked. Through general moral and intellectual advancement...shall the latent aspiration of justice for the animal kingdom come out into the open, when the time is ripe.[9]

People are not always ready to live up to God's highest ideals. By the time of Noah, humanity had morally degenerated. "And God saw the earth, and behold it was corrupt; for all flesh had corrupted their way upon the earth" (Genesis 6:12). People had sunk so low that they would eat a limb torn from a living animal. As a concession to people's weakness,[10] permission to eat meat was then given: "Every moving thing that lives shall be food for you; as the green herb have I given you all." (Genesis 9:3)

According to Rav Kook, because people had descended to such an extremely low spiritual level, it was necessary that they be taught to value human life above that of animals, and that they first emphasize the improvement of relationships between people. He felt that if people were denied the right to eat the flesh of animals, some might eat the flesh of human beings instead, due to their inability to control a lust for flesh. He regarded the permission to slaughter animals for food as a "transitional tax," or temporary dispensation, until a "brighter era" dawns, when people will return to vegetarian diets.[11]

Rabbi Joseph Albo suggests that, in the era before the flood, some people developed the mistaken idea that the reason they were not permitted to eat meat was that human beings and animals were on the same moral level—so human beings were no more responsible for their actions than were animals. Albo indicates that such a view led to moral degeneracy and ultimately to the great flood. He states that the prohibition against eating meat was removed after the flood so that human beings would realize they were on a higher level than animals, and that they therefore had a greater degree of responsibility.[12] However, the laws of *kashrut* later greatly limited the conditions under which Jews could eat meat.

Isaak Hebenstreit, a Polish rabbi who wrote *Kivrot Hata'avah* (*The Graves of Lust*) in 1929, contends that God never wanted people to eat meat, because of the cruelty involved; people shouldn't kill any living thing and fill their stomachs by destroying other life. He asserts that God temporarily gave permission to eat meat because of the conditions after the flood, when all plant life had been destroyed.[13]

Just prior to allowing Noah and his family to eat meat, God says:

And the fear of you and the dread of you shall be upon every beast of the earth, and upon every fowl of the air, and upon all wherewith the ground teems, and upon all the fish of the sea; into your hands are they delivered. (Genesis 9:2)

Now that there is permission to eat animals, the previous harmony between people and animals no longer exists. Rabbi Samson Raphael Hirsch (1808–1888), the outstanding German neo-Orthodox Torah commentator, argued that the attachment between people and animals was broken after the flood, a rift that initiated a change in the relationship of people to the world.[14]

The permission given to Noah to eat meat was not unconditional. There was an immediate prohibition against eating blood: "Only flesh with the life thereof, which is the blood thereof, shall you not eat." (Genesis 9:4) Similar statements are made in Leviticus 19:26, 17:10 and 12 and Deuteronomy 12:16, 23, and 25, and 15:23. The Torah identifies blood with life: "...for the blood is the life" (Deuteronomy 12:23). Life must be removed from the animal before it can be eaten, and the Talmud specifies an elaborate process for doing so.

A modern Conservative rabbi, Samuel Dresner, commenting on the dietary laws, indicates:

> The removal of blood which *kashrut* teaches is one of the most powerful means of making us constantly aware of the concession and compromise which the whole act of eating meat, in reality, is. Again it teaches us reverence for life.[15]

Biblical commentator Rabbi Moses Cassuto states:

> Apparently the Torah was in principle opposed to the eating of meat. When Noah and his descendants were permitted to eat meat this was a concession conditional on the prohibition of the blood. This prohibition implied respect for the principle of life ["for the blood is the life"] and an allusion to the fact that in reality all meat should have been prohibited. This partial prohibition was designed to call to mind the previously total one.[16]

Immediately after permission is given to eat meat, God says, "And surely, the blood of your lives will I require" (Genesis 9:5). The rabbis base the prohibition of suicide on these words.[17] The fact that this statement comes directly after flesh is permitted perhaps also hints that eating meat is a slow form of suicide. Maybe God is warning us: "I prefer that you do not eat meat. But if you choose to eat meat, there will be a penalty—your life blood will I require."[18] In other words, if people choose to live amid violence, by slaughtering and eating animals, they must pay a penalty—their lives will be shortened. This speculation is consistent with the decrease in biblical lifespans that occurred after permission to eat meat was given, and also with modern research in health and nutrition.

According to Rabbi Isaac Arama (1420–1494), author of *Akedat Yitzchak*, after the Israelites left Egypt, God tries to establish another non-meat diet: manna.[19] The Torah introduces the story of the manna with the following Divine message, which Moses conveys to the Israelites in response to their concern about what they will eat in the desert:

> God said to Moses, "Behold! I shall rain down for you food from heaven; and the people shall go out and gather a certain portion every day...." (Exodus 16:4).

Manna is described in the Torah as a food that does not come from animals and that tastes, "like coriander seed" (Numbers 11:7). The rabbis of the Talmud held that the manna had whatever taste and flavor the eater desired at the time of eating. It must also have had sufficient nutrient value because Moses says that "it is the bread which the Lord has given you to eat" (Exodus 16:15). Rabbi J. H. Hertz (1872–1946), former Chief Rabbi of Great Britain, comments on God's beneficence in providing the manna to sustain the Israelites: "God in His ever-sustaining providence fed Israel's host during the weary years of wandering in His own unsearchable way."[20]

The manna teaches the Children of Israel several lessons, which are significant from a vegetarian point of view.

(1) God provides for our needs; sufficient manna is available for each day's requirements. In the same way, vegetarian diets can result in enough food for all. A meat diet leads to scarcity of food for some and the potential for violence (see Chapters 4 and 6).

(2) We should be content with what we have.[21] In the Bible, each person was to gather one omer (a measure) of manna, but some gathered more and some less. When they measured it out, they found that whether they had gathered much or little, they had just enough to meet their needs. As it is written, "They gathered out an omer, and he that gathered much had nothing left over, and he that gathered little had no lack; everyone according to his eating had they gathered" (Exodus 16:18). Again, a vegetarian diet provides enough for everyone's needs. With a meat-centered diet, some eat more than they need, and many are malnourished.

(3) Enough was provided on Friday morning so that there was no need to gather manna on the Sabbath. The people were commanded to rest on the seventh day. (See Exodus 16:5, 22–30.) With a vegetarian diet, people do not need to continually struggle for their means of subsistence. They are able to truly rest, to have a peaceful Sabbath, knowing that their needs are being met and thus there is no reason to struggle for necessities.

The Israelites are not satisfied, however, with the simple diet of manna that sustained them in the desert. They complain, "Would that we were given flesh to eat." (Numbers 11:4) God is angry and Moses is displeased. God reluctantly provides meat in the form of quail, which is brought by a wind from the sea. While the flesh is still in the mouths of the Israelites, even before it is chewed, the anger of God is kindled against the people and He strikes them with a great plague (Numbers 11:4–33).

Note the following key points from a vegetarian point of view:

1. God wanted the people to be sustained on manna. He was displeased when they cried for flesh to eat.

2. Perhaps the many deaths due to the plague were intended to teach the Israelites that they should not eat meat, and, if they did, it would have dire consequences.

3. The place where this incident occurred was named "The Graves of Lust," to indicate that the strong desire for flesh led to the many deaths (Numbers 11:34). While manna, their staple food in the desert, kept the Israelites in good health for forty years, many deaths occurred when they deviated from this simple diet.

When the Israelites were in the wilderness, animals could only be slaughtered and eaten as part of the sacrificial service in the sanctuary (Leviticus 17:3–5). The eating of "unconsecrated meat"—meat from animals slaughtered for private consumption—was not permitted. Every meat meal, therefore, had to be an integral part of a sacrificial rite. Maimonides states that the biblical sacrifices were a concession to the primitive practices of the nations at that time.[22] (The sacrifices will be discussed in more detail in Chapter 7, Question 5.)

Finally, God permitted people to eat meat even if it was not part of a sacrificial offering:

> When the Lord your God shall enlarge your border as He has promised you, and you shall say: "I will eat flesh," because your soul desires to eat flesh; you may eat flesh, after all the desire of your soul. (Deuteronomy 12:20)

This permitted meat was called *basar ta'avah*, "meat of lust," so named because rabbinic teachings indicate that meat is not considered a necessity for life.[23]

The above verse does not command people to eat meat. Rabbinic tradition understands it as indicating people's desire to eat flesh, not God's dictum that people must do so. Even while arguing against vegetarianism as a moral cause, Rabbi Elijah Judah Schochet, author of *Animal Life in Jewish Tradition*, concedes that "scripture does not command the Israelite to eat meat, but rather permits this diet as a concession to lust."[24] Similarly, another critic of vegetarian activism, Rabbi J. David Bleich, a noted contemporary Torah scholar and professor at Yeshiva University, states: "The implication is that meat may be consumed when there is desire and appetite for it as food, but it may be eschewed when there is not desire and, *a fortiori*, when it is found to be repugnant."[25] According to Rabbi Bleich, "Jewish tradition does not command carnivorous behavior...."[26]

Commenting on the above Torah verse (Deuteronomy 12:20), the respected Torah scholar and teacher Nehama Leibowitz (1905–1997) points out how odd the permission is and how grudgingly the permission to eat meat is granted. She concludes that people have not been granted dominion over animals to do with them as they desire, but that we have been given a "barely tolerated dispensation" to slaughter animals for our consumption, if we cannot resist temptation and must eat meat.[27] Rav Kook also regarded the same Torah verse as clearly indicating that the Torah did not regard the slaughter of animals for human consumption as an ideal state of affairs.[28]

Rabbi I. Hebenstreit points out that God did not want to give the Israelites who had left Egypt permission to return to a meat diet because it involved cruelty to animals. However, the "mixed multitude" (other slaves who left Egypt with the Jews) lusted for meat and inculcated this desire among the Jewish people. Hence, God reluctantly gave permission once again for the consumption of meat, but with many restrictions.[29]

The Talmud expresses this negative connotation associated with the consumption of meat:

> The Torah teaches a lesson in moral conduct, that man shall not eat meat unless he has a special craving for it...and shall eat it only occasionally and sparingly.[30]

The sages also state that eating meat was not for everyone:

> Only a scholar of Torah may eat meat, but one who is ignorant of Torah is forbidden to eat meat.[31]

Some authorities explain this restriction in practical terms; only a Torah scholar can properly observe all the laws of animal slaughter and meat preparation. While there are few conditions on the consumption of vegetarian foods, only a diligent Torah scholar can fully comprehend the many regulations governing the preparation and consumption of meat. However, master kabbalist Rabbi Isaac Luria explains it in spiritual terms: only a Torah scholar can elevate the "holy sparks" trapped in the animal.

How many Jews today can consider themselves so scholarly and spiritually advanced to be able to eat meat? Those who do diligently study the Torah and are aware of conditions related to the production and consumption of meat today would, I believe, come to conclusions similar to those in this book.

Rav Kook writes that the permission to eat meat "after all the desire of your soul" was a concealed reproach and an implied reprimand.[32] He argues that a day will come when people will detest the eating of the flesh of animals because of a moral loathing, and then people will not eat meat because their soul will not have the urge to eat it.[33]

In contrast to the lust associated with flesh foods, the Torah looks favorably on vegetarian foods. In the Song of Songs, the divine bounty is mentioned in terms of fruits, vegetables, vines, and nuts. There is no special *bracha* (blessing) recited before eating meat or fish, as there is for other foods such as bread, cake, wine, fruits, and vegetables. The blessing for meat is a general one, the same as that over water or any other undifferentiated food. Typical of the Torah's positive depiction of non-flesh foods is the following:

> For the Lord your God brings you into a good land, a land of brooks of water, of fountains and depths, springing forth in valleys and hills; a land of wheat and barley, of vines and fig trees and pomegranates; a land of olive trees and honey; a land wherein you shall eat bread without scarceness, you shall not lack anything in it....And you shall eat and be satisfied, and bless the Lord your God for the good land which He has given you. (Deuteronomy 8: 7–10)

> I will give you the rain of your land in its due season, the first rain and the latter rain, that you may gather in your corn, and your wine, and your oil. (Deuteronomy 11:14)

Among many similar statements by the prophets are:

> I shall return my people from captivity, and they shall build up the waste cities and inhabit them, and they shall plant vineyards and drink the wine from them, and they shall make gardens and eat the fruit from them, and I shall plant them upon their land. (Amos 9:14–15)

Build houses and dwell in them, and plant gardens and eat the fruit of them. (Jeremiah 29:5)

Rabbi Yonassan Gershom, a Chassidic rabbi from Minnesota, remarks: "Concerning the priority given to blessings, meat is on the bottom of the hierarchy." He notes that on Sabbaths and festivals, wine comes first. Otherwise, bread comes first, and a blessing over bread covers all other foods except wine. If there is no bread, foods are blessed in the following order: (1) wine, (2) baked grains, (3) tree fruits, (4) vegetables, (5) all other foods, including fish, meat, etc. In other words, meat has the lowest priority in the *bracha* (blessing) system. Also, when bread is eaten, a full *Birkat Hamazon* (grace after meals) is to be recited. After eating the grains and fruits (the seven species) mentioned in the Torah (Deuteronomy 8: 7–10), there is a shorter blessing recited (*al hamichya*). But if only other foods such as meat or fish are eaten, only one sentence is to be recited (*borei nefashot*). Since, as our sages taught, words have replaced sacrifices today, apparently flesh foods are least honored.

The permission to eat meat is circumscribed by many laws and restrictions (the laws of *kashrut*). Rav Kook suggests that the reprimand implied by these regulations is an elaborate apparatus designed to keep alive a sense of reverence for life, with the aim of eventually leading people away from meat-eating.[34] Rav Kook is not the only Torah authority to voice such sentiments. Torah commentator Rabbi Solomon Efraim Lunchitz comments in his classic work *Kli Yakar*:

What was the necessity for the entire procedure of ritual slaughter? For the sake of self discipline. It is far more appropriate for man not to eat meat; only if he has a strong desire for meat does the Torah permit it, and even this only after the trouble and inconvenience necessary to satisfy his desire. Perhaps because of the bother and annoyance of the whole procedure, he will be restrained from such a strong and uncontrollable desire for meat.[35]

Pinchas Peli, a 20th-century Orthodox rabbi makes a similar statement:

Accordingly, the laws of *kashrut* come to teach us that a Jew's first preference should be a vegetarian meal. If, however, one cannot control a craving for meat, it should be kosher meat, which would serve as a reminder that the animal being eaten is a creature of God, that the death of such a creature cannot be taken lightly, that hunting for sport is forbidden, that we cannot treat any living thing callously, and that we are responsible for what happens to other beings [human or animal] even if we did not personally come into contact with them.[36]

Rav Kook argued that the high moral level involved in the vegetarianism of the generations before Noah was a virtue of such great value that it cannot be lost forever.[37] In the future ideal period, he thought, people and animals would again not eat flesh.[38] People's lives would not be supported at the expense of animals' lives. Rav Kook based these views on the prophecy of Isaiah:

> And the wolf shall dwell with the lamb,
> And the leopard shall lie down with the kid;
> And the calf and the young lion and the fatling together;
> And a little child shall lead them
> And the cow and the bear shall feed;
> Their young ones shall lie down together,
> And the lion shall eat straw like the ox....
> They shall not hurt nor destroy in all My holy mountain....
> (Isaiah 11:6–9)

In his booklet summarizing many of Rav Kook's teachings, Joseph Green, a 20th-century South African Jewish vegetarian writer, concludes that Jewish religious ethical vegetarians are pioneers of the messianic era; they are leading lives that make the coming of the Messiah more likely.[39]

The Jewish tradition asserts that one way to speed the coming of the Messiah is to start practicing the ways that will prevail in the messianic time. For example, the Talmud teaches that if all Jews properly observed two consecutive Sabbaths, the Messiah would immediately come.[40] This means symbolically that when all Jews reach the level when they can fully observe the Sabbath in terms of devotion to God and compassion for people and animals, the conditions would be such that the messianic period would have arrived. Hence, based on Rav Kook's teaching, if all became vegetarian in the proper spirit, with compassion for all animals and human beings, and concern about preserving and honoring God's world, this might very well hasten the arrival of the Messiah.

Although most Jews eat meat today, the high ideal of God, the initial vegetarian dietary law, stands supreme in the Torah for Jews and the whole world to see—an ultimate goal toward which all people should strive.

2: *TSA'AR BA'ALEI CHAYIM* —JUDAISM AND COMPASSION FOR ANIMALS

> *While our teacher Moses was tending the flock of Jethro in the wilderness, a kid ran away from him. He ran after the kid until it reached Hasuah. Upon reaching Hasuah, the kid came upon a body of water and began to drink. When Moses reached him he said, "I did not know that you were running because [you were] thirsty. You must be tired." He placed the kid on his shoulder and began to walk. The Holy One, blessed be He, said, "You are compassionate in leading flocks belonging to mortals; I swear you will similarly shepherd my flock, Israel."* (Midrash *Exodus Rabbah* 2:2)

ANIMALS ARE PART OF GOD'S CREATION AND PEOPLE are given special responsibilities toward them. The Jewish tradition clearly indicates that we are forbidden to be cruel to animals and that we are to treat them with compassion. These concepts are summarized in the Hebrew phrase *tsa'ar ba'alei chayim*, the biblical mandate not to cause "pain to any living creature." This Torah-based teaching is found in all strata of Jewish texts and history and occupies a central place in Jewish ethical practice. It is part of the Jewish vision of what it means to be a *tzaddik* (righteous individual) and to imitate God's ways. In ancient times the mandate of not causing unnecessary suffering to animals led to highly regulated meat-eating. This chapter aims to demonstrate that the modern realities of raising animals severely violate Jewish teachings and present major *halachic* and moral questions.

Psalms 104 and 148 show God's close identification with the animals of the field, creatures of the sea, and birds of the air. Psalm 104 pictures God as "giving drink to every beast of the field," and "causing grass to spring up for the cattle." Sea animals and birds are given the same blessing/injunction as are people: "Be fruitful and multiply" (Genesis 1:22). Animals are initially given a vegetarian diet similar to that of people (Genesis 1:29–30). The Hebrew term *nefesh chaya* (a "living soul") is applied in Genesis (1:21, 24) to animals as well as people. In contrast to the way people regard and treat animals today, these teachings show the very high regard that God has for them and wants people to have for them.

Although the Torah states that people are to have "dominion over the fish of the sea, and over the fowl of the air, and over every living thing that creeps upon the earth" (Genesis 1:28), there is to be a basic relatedness, and the rights and privileges of animals are not to be neglected or overlooked. As indicated previously, people's dominion over animals is immediately limited by God's first (completely vegetarian) dietary law (Genesis 1:29), and this is quickly followed by God's statement that all of creation is very good (Genesis 1:31), showing that this vegetarian diet is consistent with the stewardship that God wants people to practice.

While the Torah states that only human beings are created "in the Divine Image" (Genesis 5:1), animals are also God's creatures, possessing sensitivity and the capacity for feeling pain. Hence God is very concerned that they be protected and treated with compassion and justice. In fact, to be created in the Divine Image, state the sages, means that people have the power to emulate the Divine compassion to all creatures. "As God is compassionate," they teach, "so you should be compassionate."[1]

In his classic work *Ahavat Chesed* (*The Love of Kindness*), the revered Chafetz Chayim discusses this teaching at length, and he writes that whoever emulates the Divine love and compassion to all creatures "will bear the stamp of God on his person."[2] Rabbi Hirsch also discussed this concept:

> You can know God only through His acts of love and justice; and, in turn, you too are called upon to act with love and justice, not merely to indulge or endure.[3]

In this spirit, Rabbi Hirsch states, we human beings were created to "serve (work) and safeguard the Earth" (Genesis 2:15), and this limits our rights over other creatures and all living things. He writes:

> The earth was not created as a gift to you. You have been given to the earth, to treat it with respectful consideration, as God's earth,

and everything on it as God's creation, as your fellow creatures—
to be respected, loved, and helped to attain their purpose
according to God's will....[T]o this end, your heartstrings vibrate
sympathetically with any cry of distress sounding anywhere in
creation, and with any glad sound uttered by a joyful creature.[4]

God even makes treaties and covenants with animals, as He did with
humans:

"As for me," says the Lord, "behold I establish My Covenant with
you and with your seed after you, and with every living creature
that is with you, the fowl, the cattle, and every animal of the earth
with you; of all that go out of the ark, even every animal of the
earth." (Genesis 9:9–10)

And in that day will I make a covenant for them with the animals
of the field and with the fowls of heaven and with the creeping
things of the ground. And I will break the bow and the sword and
the battle out of the land and I will make them to lie down safely.
(Hosea 2:20)

In contrast to modern law, which generally considers animals as material
possessions and thus permits them to be cruelly treated, Divine law in the
Bible as reflected in God's covenants considers animals worthy of
recognition and committment.

Ecclesiastes examines the kinship between people and animals. Both
are described as sharing common fates of mortality:

For that which befalls the sons of men befalls animals;
even one thing befalls them;
as the one dies, so dies the other;
yes, they all have one breath;
so that man has no preeminence above an animal;
for all is vanity.

All go to one place; all are of the dust.
who knows the spirit of men whether it goes upward;
and the spirit of the animal whether it goes
downward to the earth? (Ecclesiastes 3:19–21)

God considers animals, as well as people, when he admonishes Jonah, "and should I not have pity on Nineveh, that great city, wherein are more than six score thousand persons...and also much cattle? (Jonah 4:11)

The psalmist indicates God's concern for animals in declaring: "His tender mercies are over all His creatures" (Psalms 145:9). This statement serves as a cornerstone of rabbinic teachings on compassion to animals. The author of Psalms also pictures God as "satisfying the desire of every living creature" (Psalms 145:16), "providing food for animals and birds" (Psalms 147:9), and, in general, "preserving both people and animals" (Psalms 36:7)

The Talmud describes God providing animals with the attributes necessary for survival in their environment. For example, the camel has a short tail so it won't become ensnared when she feeds upon thorns; the ox has a long tail so he can protect himself from gnats when he feeds in the plains; the antennae of locusts are flexible so they won't break against trees and blind the locusts.[5]

Perhaps the Jewish attitude toward animals is best summarized by the statement in Proverbs 12:10, "the righteous person regards the life of his or her animal." This is the human counterpoint of "The Lord is good to all, and His tender mercies are over all His creatures" (Psalms 145:9). One who is cruel to animals cannot be regarded as a righteous individual! In his explanation of Proverbs 12:10, the Malbim, a 19th-century biblical commentator, explains that the righteous person understands the nature of his or her animal, and hence gives the animal food at the proper time and according to the amount needed. He is also careful not to overwork the animal. For, according to the Malbim, "the *tzaddik* (righteous person) acts according to the laws of justice; not only does he act according to these laws with human beings, but also with animals."[6]

Torah Laws Involving Compassion for Animals

1. It is forbidden to cause pain to any animal.

Maimonides[7] and Rabbi Judah ha-Hasid[8] (1150–1217) state that this is based on the biblical statement of the angel of God to Balaam, "Wherefore have you smitten your ass?" (Numbers 22:32). This verse is used in the Talmud as a prime source for its assertion that we are to treat animals humanely.[9] The *Shulchan Aruch* (Code of Jewish Law) is more explicit and specific:[10]

> It is forbidden, according to the law of the Torah, to inflict pain upon any living creature. On the contrary, it is our duty to relieve the pain of any creature, even if it is ownerless or belongs to a non-Jew.

> When horses, drawing a cart, come to a rough road or a steep hill, and it is hard for them to draw the cart without help, it is our duty to help them, even when they belong to a non-Jew, because of the precept not to be cruel to animals, lest the owner smite them to force them to draw more than their strength permits.

> It is forbidden to tie the legs of a beast or of a bird in a manner which will cause them pain.

2. "You shall not muzzle the ox when he threshes out the corn." (Deuteronomy 25:4)

At the time of threshing, when the ox is surrounded by the food that he enjoys so much, he should not be prevented from satisfying his appetite. Rabbi Samson Raphael Hirsch states that this prohibition gives the animal that helps you harvest the fruits of the earth a right to these fruits while working; no means may be used to prevent him from eating.[11] He cites the *Shulchan Aruch*[12] as indicating that one may prevent an animal from eating when the fruits might harm him.[13] Rashi, citing *Baba Kamma* 54b in support, contends that this law also applies to other animals, including birds.[14]

Professor C. H. Cornill contrasts the humanitarianism of this law with a modern European grape harvest, in which "one of the richest Italian real estate owners fastened iron muzzles to the miserable, fever-stricken workmen, so that it might not occur to these poor peasants working for starvation wages under the glowing sun of Southern Italy to satiate their burning thirst and their gnawing hunger with a few of the millions of grapes of the owner."[15] Because of this and similar legislation, William Lecky, the distinguished British historian, argues that "tenderness to animals is one of the most beautiful features in the [Hebrew Scriptures]."[16]

3. "You shall not plow with an ox and an ass together." (Deuteronomy 22:10)

Such an act would cause the weaker animal great pain in trying to keep up with the stronger. The stronger would also suffer by being deprived of his usual routine, by having to act contrary to his instinctive nature. The Talmud extends this law to apply to any case where there are two animals involved, one strong and one weak, and to other activities such as driving carts or wagons.[17]

> You may not allow one task to be done together by animals of two species. You may not allow them to carry the smallest thing together, even if it be only a seed....You may not sit in a wagon drawn by animals of differing species.[18]

Rabbi Hirsch concludes that one should not unite animals of different species and different capabilities for any activities.[19] The *Sefer Hachinuch*, a classic work on the 613 *mitzvot* (commandments) of the Torah, indicates: "This involves the biblical prohibition against causing suffering to animals, since it is known that there are species of animals and birds which develop anxiety if they dwell together with those that are not of their species—even more so if one works them together."[20]

4. A person should not eat before first providing for his or her animals.[21]

This is based on Deuteronomy 11:15: "And I will give grass in your fields for your cattle, and you shall eat and be satisfied." God provides food for the cattle before people, and we are to imitate God. According to Rabbi Eliezer ha-Kapar, a Talmudic sage, no one should buy a domestic animal, wild beast, or bird unless he or she is able to feed the animal properly.[22] The duty to feed an animal first is so great that a person must interrupt the performance of a rabbinic commandment if one is not sure animals have been properly fed.[23]

5. Animals, as well as people, must be allowed to rest on the Sabbath day.

The *Kiddush* (sanctification over wine or grape juice) that is recited on Sabbath mornings includes the following verse from the Ten Commandments:

Remember the Sabbath day, to keep it holy. Six days shall you labor, and do all your work; but the seventh day is a Sabbath unto the Lord, your God; in it you shall not do any manner of work, you, nor your son, nor your daughter, nor your man-servant, nor your maid-servant, nor your cattle, nor the stranger that is within your gates. (Exodus 20:8–10)

Similar statements occur in Exodus 23:12 and Deuteronomy 5:12–14. Based on these Torah statements, Rashi states that animals must be free to roam on the Sabbath day and graze freely and enjoy the beauties of nature.[24] The fact that animals are mentioned within the Ten Commandments expresses the importance placed on compassion for animals in Judaism. Rabbi J. H. Hertz, in commenting on Exodus 20:10, writes: "It is one of the glories of Judaism that thousands of years [ago] it so fully recognized our duties to animals."[25]

In a similar manner, animals are to be provided for during the Sabbatical year. The produce that grows freely during that period is to be enjoyed by animals of the field as well as by the poor. (Leviticus 25:6–7)

6. It is forbidden to sacrifice a newborn ox, sheep, or goat until it has had at least seven days of warmth and nourishment from its mother. (Leviticus 22:27)

This precept shows the desire of the Torah to spare the feelings of living creatures and to instill a spirit of compassion in people. Rabbi Elie Munk, a 20th-century biblical commentator, writes concerning the above precept: "For the sages of the *Midrash*, this waiting period is symptomatic of the Divine compassion for the mother; it would be cruel to tear away her young so soon after birth."[26] A *midrash* (a rabbinic commentary, expressed in parables and stories, that brings out a deeper meaning of a Torah verse) on the above *mitzvah* states:

> "The righteous person knows the soul of his animal" (Proverbs 12:10) is referring to the Holy One (God), Blessed be He, as it is written in the Torah: "When a bull, sheep, or goat is born, he shall remain under his mother for seven days...".[27]

7. "And whether it be ox or ewe, you shall not kill the animal and her young both in one day." (Leviticus 22:28)

This law prohibits a practice performed in some ancient cults of sacrificing an animal and her young together. Maimonides comments on this verse as follows:

> It is prohibited to kill an animal with her young on the same day, in order that people should be restrained and prevented from killing the two together in such a manner that the young is slain in the sight of the mother, for the pain of animals under such circumstances is very great. There is no difference in this case between the pain of people and the pain of other living beings, since the love and the tenderness of the mother for her young ones

is not produced by reasoning but by feeling, and this faculty exists not only in people but in most living things.[28]

8. We are forbidden to take the mother bird and her young together.

"The mother bird must be sent away before her young are taken." (Deuteronomy 22:6–7). For showing compassion to the mother bird, the Torah promises us a long life. Maimonides comments that when the mother bird is sent away she does not see the taking of her young ones, and thus does not feel any pain at that time.[29] Furthermore, in most cases, the commandment will result in the entire nest being left untouched, because the young or the eggs, which people are allowed to take, are generally unfit for human food, because eggs with blood or veins developing are not kosher.[30] Maimonides also observes that if we are commanded not to cause grief to animals and to birds, we must be even more careful not to cause grief to people.[31]

However, in their commentaries on the above Torah verse, Nachmanides and Rabbi Bachya Ben Asher (a 13th-century sage) connect the above law and the prohibition against slaughtering an animal along with its young to the preservation of species.[32] Thus, it may be that these prohibitions are intended to remind us of the limits on our power over other creatures, and of our need to respect and preserve the manifold species which God created.

9. We should not boil a kid in the milk of his mother. (Exodus 23:19, 34:26; Deuteronomy 14:21)

Commenting on Exodus 23:19, Rashi notes that the repetition of this prohibition in three different biblical passages implies a three-fold ban: (1) milk and meat must not be eaten together; (2) they must not be cooked together; and (3) it is forbidden to benefit from food containing a mixture of milk and meat.

Some Torah authorities, including Maimonides, see the above law as a rejection of an ancient pagan practice. However, Abraham Ibn Ezra, a 12th-century sage, writes that, although the ultimate reason for this prohibition is beyond human understanding, it may be because "it is an act of a cruel heart to cook a kid in his mother's milk."[33] That is, it is insensitive and cruel to take milk, a substance that the Creator made to nurture life, and to use it in a way connected to the destruction of that life. Rashbam (1080–1174) also considered this practice as denoting gross insensitivity and cruelty.[34]

10. Animals should not be allowed to suffer discomfort from a heavy burden.

"If you see the ass of him who hates you fallen due to its burden, you shall surely not pass him by; you shall surely unload it with him." (Exodus 23:5) According to the sages, this commandment mandates both a humane approach toward the animal and a charitable approach toward an enemy. Indeed, they teach that the greatest hero is a person who turns an enemy into a friend.[35] The Talmud connects the above precept to the prohibition of causing pain to animals, since the animal is clearly suffering from the burden. It is, therefore, a *mitzvah* to relieve the suffering of the animal.[36]

11. We must be vigilant concerning the well-being of a lost animal.

"You shall not see your brother's ox or his sheep driven away and hide yourself from them; you shall surely bring them back unto your brother" (Deuteronomy 22:1). In addition, the animal must be cared for until the owner's return.

12. We are to "walk in God's ways." (Deuteronomy 28:9)

In his explanation of the precept "to walk in God's ways," Rabbi Hirsch amplifies the ancient teachings of the sages:

As God is merciful, so you also be merciful. As He loves and cares for all His creatures because they are His creatures and His children and are related to Him, because He is their Father, so you also love all His creatures as your brethren. Let their joys be your joys, and their sorrows yours. Love them and with every power which God gives you, work for their welfare and benefit, because they are the children of your God, because they are your brothers and sisters.[37]

Another 19th-century authority, Rabbi Moshe Sofer (known as the Hatam Sofer), regards obligations toward animals as predicated upon emulation of Divine conduct. Thus, he cites the verse "His tender mercies are over all His creatures" (Psalms 145:9) as imposing an obligation upon human beings to show compassion toward animals.[38]

13. Throughout the ages, the rabbis strongly disapproved of hunting as a sport.[39]

A Jew is permitted to capture fish, animals, or fowl only for purposes of human food or what is considered another essential human need. But to destroy an animal for "sport" constitutes wanton destruction and is to be condemned. Based on the statement "not to stand in the way of sinners" (Psalms 1:1), the Talmud prohibits association with hunters.[40] A query was addressed to Rabbi Yechezkel Landau (1713–1793) by a man wishing to know if he could hunt in his large estate, which included forests and fields. His response in the classic *Nodah b'Yehudah* is as follows:

> In the Torah the sport of hunting is imputed only to fierce characters like Nimrod and Esau, never to any of the patriarchs and their descendants....I cannot comprehend how a Jew could even dream of killing animals merely for the pleasure of hunting.... When the act of killing is prompted by that of sport, it is downright cruelty.[41]

14. *Shechitah* (Jewish ritual slaughter).

Although the consumption of meat is permitted as a concession to people's weakness and people came to think about it as necessary for proper nutrition, the Torah restricts this indulgence in various ways—especially through the complex laws of *shechitah* (ritual slaughter).[42] Aside from their spiritual effects and meanings, the laws of *shechitah* provide the most humane method of slaughtering animals. The knife to be used is regularly examined to ensure that it is perfectly smooth, without a notch that might tear the flesh. The cut severs the arteries to the head of the animal, thus instantly stopping blood circulation to the head and minimizing the pain.

The slaughterer, the *shochet*, must meet stringent scholarly and moral standards. He is obligated to examine the animal for any possible disease and to slaughter the animal according to Jewish law. The *shochet* is required to be a learned, observant person who demonstrates a complete knowledge of the laws of *shechitah*. Also, he must recite a blessing prior to slaughter, an act that shows reverence for life. Thus the laws of *shechitah* may serve as a reminder that meat-eating is a concession. Question 6 in Chapter 7 will consider *shechitah* further.

15. On Yom Kippur, the most sacred day of the Jewish year, when Jews fast, confess their sins, and pray for life and good health from God in the coming year, it is forbidden to wear leather shoes. One reason is that it is not proper to plead for compassion when one has not shown compassion toward other living creatures.[43]

Rabbi Moses Isserles (c.1528–1572), known as the Rema, states: "How can a man put on shoes, a piece of clothing for which it is necessary to kill a living thing, on Yom Kippur, which is a day of grace and compassion, when it is written 'His tender mercies are over all His works' " (Psalms 145:9).[44] Jews are required to recite a special benediction, "Blessed are you, Lord our God, King of the Universe, who has kept us in life, and has preserved us and enabled us to reach this season," when putting on a piece of clothing for the first time. However, an exception is made for furs and leather shoes because an animal had to be killed in making them.[45]

The Code of Jewish Law has a similar statement:

It is customary to say to one who puts on a new garment: "May you wear it out and acquire a new one." But we do not express this wish to one who puts on new shoes or a new garment made of fur or leather...because a garment like this requires the killing of a living creature, and it is written: "And His mercy is upon all His works" (Psalms 145:9).[46]

16. Although the Torah contains no explicit general prohibition against cruelty to animals, there are so many commandments mandating humane treatment for them that the Talmudic rabbis explicitly declared this prohibition to be a biblical law.[47]

Hence, various rabbinic Sabbath laws could be relaxed to relieve the suffering of an animal. For such purposes, one has permission to capture domestic animals,[48] take care of their wounds when they are fresh and painful,[49] race them around as a remedy for overeating,[50] place them in water to cool them following an attack of congestion,[51] and assist them to free themselves from a pit or a body of water into which they have fallen.[52] In view of the paramount importance of the Sabbath in Judaism (indeed, the Zohar equates its observance to fulfillment of all of the Torah's commandments in their entirety) and the many restrictions on labor on this day, the above considerations indicate the importance that Judaism places on compassion to animals.

Rabbi Hirsch eloquently summarizes the Jewish view on treatment of animals:

> Here you are faced with God's teaching, which obliges you not only to refrain from inflicting unnecessary pain on any animal, but to help and, when you can, to lessen the pain whenever you see an animal suffering, even through no fault of yours.[53]

Examples of Kindness to Animals by Biblical Heroes

Many biblical leaders of Israel were trained for their tasks by being shepherds of flocks. As the *midrash* quoted at the beginning of this chapter states, God tested Moses through his shepherding. The greatest Jewish teacher, leader, and prophet was found worthy, not because of abilities as a speaker, statesman, politician, or warrior, but because of his compassion for animals!

God deemed David worthy of leading the Jewish people because he, like Moses, tended his sheep with devotion, bestowing upon them the care each one needed. David used to prevent the larger sheep from going out before the smaller ones. The smaller ones were then able to graze upon the tender grass. Next he permitted the old sheep to feed on the ordinary grass, and finally the young, mature sheep consumed the tougher grass.[54]

Rebecca was judged suitable to be Isaac's wife because of the kindness she showed to animals. Eliezer, the patriarch Abraham's servant, asked Rebecca for water for himself. She not only gave him water, but also eagerly provided water for his ten thirsty camels. Rebecca's concern for camels was evidence of a tender heart and compassion for all God's creatures. It convinced Eliezer that Rebecca would make a suitable wife for Isaac (Genesis 24:11–20).

The patriarch Jacob also demonstrated concern for animals. After their reconciliation, his brother Esau said to him, "Let us take our journey and let us go, and I will go before you." But Jacob, concerned about his children and flocks, replied: "My lord knows that the children are tender, and that the flocks and the herds giving suck are a care to me; and if my workers overdrive them one day, all the flocks will die. Let my lord, I pray you, pass over before his servant and I will journey on gently, according to the pace of the cattle that are before me and according to the pace of the children, until I come unto my lord, unto Seir" (Genesis 33:12–14).

Consistent with the fact that concern for the well-being of animals is the test for a righteous individual, Jacob instructed his son Joseph to determine "whether it is well with your brethren and well with the flock" (Genesis 37:14). In the wilderness, the Israelites sought water for both themselves and their cattle (Numbers 20:4).

The Torah states: "But Jacob journeyed to *Sukkot* and built himself a house, and for his livestock he made shelters; he therefore named the place *Sukkot* (booths)" (Genesis 33:17). The Ohr HaChayim, in his comment on the above verse, suggested the name *Sukkot* commemorated the shelters that Jacob built for his animals, for this may have been the first time that anyone had taken the trouble to spare animals from the distress of sun and cold.

Noah was called a *tzaddik* (righteous person) because of his extraordinary care of the animals on the ark.[55] He was careful to feed each species its appropriate food at the proper time. Indeed, the *midrash* tells us that Noah did not sleep due to his continuous concern for the welfare of the animals.[56] The Torah explicitly designates only one other personality,

Joseph, as a *tzaddik*. In times of crisis, they both provided food for humans and animals.

Stories from the Jewish Tradition Related to Compassion for Animals

Rabbi Judah the Prince was sitting and studying the Torah in front of the Babylonian Synagogue in Sepphoris. A calf being taken to the slaughterhouse came to him as if pleading, "Save me!" Rabbi Judah said to it, "What can I do for you? For this you were created." As a punishment for his insensitivity, he suffered from a toothache for thirteen years.

One day, a creeping thing [a weasel] ran past Rabbi Judah's daughter who was about to kill him. He said to her, "My daughter, let it be, for it is written, 'and God's tender mercies are over all his works' (Psalms 145:9)." Because Rabbi Judah prevented an act of cruelty and unkindness to an animal, his health was restored to him and his toothache went away.[57]

Evidently, even a person as important as Rabbi Judah the Prince, redactor of the *Mishnah*, could forget to treat animals properly; and even such an important person is not forgiven by God until he performs an act to show that he properly understands the need to treat animals compassionately.

Someone once asked the eminent Rav Sherira Gaon: "If Rabbi Judah was punished because he handed a calf over to the slaughterer, and was once again rewarded because he protected an animal from death, should we learn from this not to slaughter any animal and not to kill harmful animals?"[58] The Gaon's answer: "Animals that may harm people, such as snakes, lions, wolves, must be killed [if posing a danger]; on the other hand, animals that do us no harm and are not needed for food or medicine should not be killed....To save a calf that we need for nourishment is not required of us."[59]

Now that we know that we do not need meat for nourishment and that, as a matter of fact, the consumption of flesh products harms our health, what a tremendously powerful argument for vegetarianism this story is!

The Maharshah (1555–1631) notes that Rabbi Judah was punished because it was a calf, rather than a mature animal that had at least tasted life's joys, that was being led to slaughter.[60] This implies that if animals have had a sufficient chance to experience life's pleasures, it would be permissible to slaughter them for food. However, today this concept also provides a strong argument for vegetarianism for, as discussed in the next section, modern day farmed animals lack "life's pleasures" as they are raised from birth in closed confined spaces and denied fresh air, sunlight, exercise, and emotional fulfillment.

The following stories also illustrate Jewish teachings related to compassion to animals:

Rabbi Israel Salanter, one of the most distinguished Orthodox rabbis of the nineteenth century, failed to appear one Yom Kippur eve to chant the sacred *Kol Nidre* prayer. His congregation became concerned, for it was inconceivable that their saintly rabbi would be late or absent on this very holy day. They sent out a search party to look for him. After much time, their rabbi was found in the barn of a Christian neighbor. On his way to the synagogue, Rabbi Salanter had come upon one of his neighbor's calves, lost and tangled in the brush. Seeing that the animal was in distress, he freed him and led him home through many fields and over many hills. His act of mercy represented the rabbi's prayers on that Yom Kippur evening.[61]

Rabbi Zusya of Hanipol, a Chassidic master, once was on a journey to collect money to ransom prisoners. He came to an inn and in one room found a large cage with many types of birds. He saw that the birds wanted to fly out of the cage and be free again. He burned with pity for them and said to himself, "Here you are, Zusya, walking your feet off to ransom prisoners. But what greater ransoming of prisoners can there be than to free these birds from their prison?" He then opened the cage, and the birds flew out into freedom.

When the innkeeper saw the empty cage, he was very angry and asked the people in the house who had released the birds. They answered that there was a man loitering around who appeared to be a fool and that he must have done it. The innkeeper shouted at Zusya: "You fool! How could you rob me of my birds and make worthless the good money I paid for them?" Zusya replied: "Have you read these words in the Psalms: 'His tender mercies are over all His work'?" Then the innkeeper beat Zusya and then threw him out of the house. And Zusya went his way serenely.[62]

Rabbi Abramtzi was a man full of compassion—his compassion was for all living things. He would not walk on the grass of the field lest he trample it down. He was very careful not to tread on grasshoppers or crawling insects. If a dog came to the door of his house, he would instruct the members of his household to feed the animal. In winter he would scatter crumbs of bread and seed on the window sills. When sparrows and other birds arrived and began to pick at the food, he could not remove his gaze from them and his face would light up with joy like that of a little child. He looked after his horses far better than his coachmen did. When traveling and the coach had to ascend an incline, he would climb down in order to lighten the load and, more often than not, he would push the cart from behind.

On summer days he would compel his coachman to stop on the way and turn aside to a field in order that the horses should rest and partake of the grass. The rabbi loved these rest periods in the forest. While the horses were grazing, he would sit under a tree and read a book. At times he would pray in the field or the forest. This gave him great pleasure, for he used to say, "The field and the forest are the most beautiful and finest of the Houses of the Lord."

It happened once that the rabbi was on the road on a Friday. It would take another three hours to reach home. Due to the rain, the road was very muddy. The wagon could only proceed with difficulty. The mud gripped the wheels and slowed down its progress. It was midday and they had not even completed half the journey. The horses were tired and worn out. They had no energy to proceed further.

The rabbi told the driver to stop and give fodder to the horses, so that they could regain their strength. This was done. Afterwards the journey was continued, but the going was heavy and the wagon sunk up to the hubs of the wheels in the mud. It was with the greatest difficulty that the horses maintained their balance on the swampy ground. The vapor of sweat enveloped their skin. Their knees trembled and at any moment they would have to rest. The coachman scolded and urged them on. He then raised his whip on the unfortunate creatures. The rabbi grabbed him by the elbow and cried out: "This is cruelty to animals, cruelty to animals." The coachman answered in fury: "What do you want me to do? Do you want us to celebrate the Sabbath here?"

"What of it?" replied the rabbi. "It is better that we celebrate the Sabbath here than cause the death of these animals by suffering. Are they not the creatures of the Lord? See how exhausted they are. They have not the energy to take one more step forward."

"But what of the Sabbath? How can Jews observe the Sabbath in the forest?" asked the coachman.

"My friend, it does not matter. The Sabbath Queen will come to us here also, for her glory fills the whole world, and particularly in those places where Jews yearn for her. The Lord shall do what is good in His eyes. He will look after us, supply us with our wants and guard us against all evil."[63]

As the following dialogue indicates, the African King Kazia was astounded when he observed the cruel and unjust way in which Alexander of Macedonia judged disputes, and wondered why Macedonia was still blessed with God's beneficence:

King: Does the rain fall in your country?

Alexander: Yes.

King: Does the sun shine in your country?

Alexander: Yes.

King: Perhaps there are small cattle in your country?

Alexander: Yes.

King: Cursed be the man [who would render such evil judgments]. It is only because of the merit of the small cattle that the sun shines upon you and the rain falls upon you. For the sake of the small cattle you are saved![64]

The *midrash* concluded: "Hence it is written, 'People and animals You preserved, Oh Lord' (Psalms 36:7), as if to say, 'You preserve people, Oh Lord, because of the merit of the animals.' "[65] This suggests that God provides rain and sun, the essentials of a healthy environment, even when people are evil and do not deserve it, because of God's concern for animals.

Treatment of Animals Today

As we have seen, the Jewish tradition stresses compassion for animals and commands that we strive to avoid causing them pain (*tsa'ar ba'alei chayim*). Unfortunately, the conditions under which animals are raised for food today are quite different from any the Torah would endorse.

Chickens are raised for slaughter in long, windowless, crowded sheds, where they never see sunlight, breathe fresh air, or get any exercise.[66] When the tiny chicks arrive, there is plenty of room, but they have progressively less room as they grow, and just prior to slaughter they have about a half a square foot per chicken, barely enough to move. The lives of "broiler" chickens are marked by mutilation, overcrowding, and stress, and they are generally slaughtered when only about seven or eight weeks old; by contrast, a normal chicken's lifespan is eight to ten years.

There is tremendous cruelty in the forced feeding of ducks and geese to produce pâté de foie gras.[67] *Foie gras* literally means fat liver. The liver of a goose or duck is fattened by having pounds of grain forced down its gullet. The owner generally holds the neck of the goose between his legs, pouring the corn with one hand and rubbing it down the neck with the other. When this process ceases to be effective, the owner uses a wooden plunger to compact it still further. The bird suffers unimaginable pain, and as the liver grows to an enormous size, sclerosis of the liver develops. Finally, after twenty-five days of such agony, when completely stupefied with pain and unable to move, the bird is killed and the gigantic liver, considered a delicacy, is removed. Currently, machines are used to force-feed birds to make the process more "efficient," with greater resultant agony.

In response to my request for his views on the production and consumption of *foie gras*, Rabbi David Rosen, a contemporary Israeli Orthodox rabbi and former Chief Rabbi of Ireland, sent me the following response:

> It should be obvious that pâté de foie gras is produced in a manner that is in complete contravention of the Torah's prohibition of causing *tsa'ar ba'alei chayim*—pain to animals (see Maimonides, *Yad Chazakah, Hilchot Rozeah*, Ch. 13, M. 8). Rabbi Yechezkel Landau, the Noda Bi-Yehuda, clarifies that causing any cruelty to an animal while alive is a desecration of this prohibition (Noda Bi-Yehuda, *Yoreh Deah*, Response No. 10) and that if food can be obtained in a manner that does not involve additional pain and one chooses to obtain such through causing pain to an animal, one desecrates a Torah prohibition. Pâté de foie gras is obtained through the willful desecration of a Torah prohibition and any truly God-revering Jew will not partake of such a product which is an offense against the Creator and His Torah.

Unfortunately, Israel is one of the world's major exporters of pâté de foie gras.[68]

The raising of calves to produce veal generally involves great cruelty. After being allowed to nurse for only one or two days, the owners take the calf from his mother, with no consideration of his need for motherly nourishment, affection, and physical contact. They lock the calf in a small slotted stall without enough space to move around, stretch, or even lie down. To obtain the pale, tender veal desired by consumers, the owners purposely keep the calf anemic by giving him a special high-calorie, iron-free diet. The calf craves iron so much that he licks the iron fittings on his stall and his own urine if he can; he is tied to the stall so he can't turn his head. The stall is kept very warm and the calf is deprived of water, so he will be forced to drink more of his high-calorie liquid diet. The very unnatural conditions of the veal calf—the lack of exercise, sunlight, fresh air, proper food and water, and any emotional stimulation—make for a very sick, anemic animal. Antibiotics and drugs are used to keep the calf disease free. The calf leaves his dark stall only to be taken to slaughter; sometimes he drops dead from the stress and exertion of going to slaughter.

Rabbi Moshe Feinstein (d. 1985), perhaps the most influential Orthodox Jewish *halachic* authority in the United States in this generation, ruled in 1982 that it is forbidden for Jews to raise calves for veal under current intensive livestock agricultural conditions, since this violates the prohibition of *tsa'ar ba'alei chayim*. In a *responsum*, he explained that the production of veal is not a legitimate necessity that justifies such suffering.[69] In a two-part article in the *Jewish Press*[70], Rabbi Aryeh Spero discusses *kashrut* problems related to current methods of raising veal calves. Basing his position on Rabbi Feinstein's *responsum*, he points out that animals who are too weak or sick to walk by their own strength are not suitable for ritual slaughter. He indicates that the horrible conditions under which calves are raised should result in only thirty percent of calves meeting kosher requirements, and that there should be concern with any packing-house yielding consistently higher percentages.

The transportation of animals to slaughterhouses by rail or truck involves additional cruelties.[71] They are jammed into a confined area for many hours, sometimes days, where they suffer from lack of food, water, exercise, and ventilation. They are often exposed to extreme heat, cold, and humidity and are generally not fed for the last twenty-four to forty-eight hours prior to slaughter.

There is also much cruelty in the raising of animals to produce eggs and milk. The next few paragraphs give just a small sampling of this treatment, described in much more detail in *Diet For a New America* by John Robbins,

Old McDonald's Factory Farm by C. David Coats, and other books (see Bibliography).

Layer hens are extremely crowded, with four or five hens generally squeezed into a twelve-by-eighteen-inch cage. Crowding is so bad that a chicken cannot stretch even one wing. The results of these very unnatural conditions are pecking and cannibalism. To avoid this, the lighting is kept very dim and the chickens are "debeaked." Debeaking is a very painful and often debilitating procedure that involves cutting off part of the beak with a hot knife while the hen's head is held by hand or in a vise. This is industry's answer to the fact that birds are often driven to crazed pecking, which harms and sometimes kills their fellow cellmates, thus reducing the producers' profits.[72]

Ruth Harrison describes the results of her observations of current methods of raising chickens for eggs in her landmark book, *Animal Machines*. She found that the chickens seemed to have lost their minds; their eyes gleamed through the bars, they viciously pecked at any hand within reach, and they pulled feathers out of other chickens' backs looking for flesh and blood to eat.[73]

Since they have no value to the egg industry, male chicks are discarded shortly after birth and disposed of by "chick-pullers." Each day in the United States workers stuff over half a million chicks into plastic bags, where they crush and suffocate them. Alternately, they grind them up while still alive to use them as fertilizer or feed them to other livestock.[74]

Today's modern milk factories raise cows for maximum milk production at a minimum cost. They artificially inseminate each cow annually and then take her calves away from her almost immediately so that she constantly produces milk for human consumption (her calf goes into a veal crate and is slaughtered four months later). The cow lives with an unnaturally enlarged and sensitive udder, and she is likely to be kept inside a stall nearly her whole life and milked up to three times a day. While the dairy industry would like people to believe that its cows are contented, today's factory-bred cows have to be fed tranquilizers to calm their nerves. As soon as they are milked-out after a few years, they are slaughtered to produce hamburgers.[75]

The following two selections summarize the inhumane treatment of animals raised for food:

How far have we the right to take our domination of the animal world? Have we the right to rob them of all pleasures in life simply to make more money more quickly out of their carcasses? Have we the right to treat living creatures solely as food-converting machines? At what point do we acknowledge cruelty?[76]

Every year millions of animals are born and bred for the sole purpose of satisfying those who like the taste of meat. Their lives vary in length from a few weeks to a few years; most live a fraction of the time they would in more natural conditions. They die in slaughterhouses where, if the tranquilizers have their effect, they know only a few moments of the awful fear of death before they are stunned, and their throats cut. This is what all meat-eaters actively support, for there would be no batteries, no sweat-boxes, no need to castrate male animals or artificially inseminate females, no cattle markets and no slaughterhouses if there was no one insensitive enough to buy their products. It is simply impossible to farm animals for food without imprisoning, mutilating, and eventually slaughtering them, and no one can ignore this price that has to be paid for the pleasure of eating meat.[77]

Ruth Harrison eloquently summarizes how animals are raised today:

To some extent...farm animals have always been exploited by man in that he rears them specifically for food. But until recently they were individuals, allowed their birthright of green fields, sunlight, and fresh air; they were allowed to forage, to exercise, to watch the world go by, in fact to live. Even at its worst...the animal had some enjoyment in life before it died. Today the exploitation has been taken to a degree which involves not only the elimination of all enjoyment, the frustration of all natural instincts, but its replacement with acute discomfort, boredom, and the actual denial of health. It has been taken to a degree where the animal is not allowed to live before it dies.[78]

The conditions under which animals are raised today are completely contrary to the Jewish ideals of compassion and avoiding *tsa'ar ba'alei chayim*. Instead of animals being free to graze on the Sabbath day to enjoy the beauties of creation, they are confined for all of their lives to darkened, crowded stalls and cages without air, natural light, or the room in which to exercise. Whereas the Torah mandates that animals should be able to eat the products of the harvest as they thresh in the fields, today animals are fed chemical fatteners and other additives in their food, based on computer programs. Whereas Judaism indicates consideration for animals by prohibiting the yoking of a strong and weak animal together, veal calves spend their entire lives standing on slats, their necks chained to the sides, without sunlight, fresh air, or exercise.

Rabbi Hirsch indicates how great our concern for animals must be:

There are probably no creatures that require more the protective Divine word against the presumption of man than the animals, which like man have sensations and instincts, but whose body and powers are nevertheless subservient to man. In relation to them man so easily forgets that injured animal muscle twitches just like human muscle, that the maltreated nerves of an animal sicken like human nerves, that the animal being is just as sensitive to cuts, blows, and beating as man. Thus man becomes the torturer of the animal soul.[79]

Rabbi Aryeh Carmell, a Torah scholar living in Jerusalem, states: "It seems doubtful from all that has been said whether the Torah would sanction factory farming, which treats animals as machines, with apparent insensitivity to their natural needs and instincts. This is a matter for decision by *halachic* authorities."[80] Rabbi David Rosen uses even stronger language: "The current treatment of animals in the livestock trade definitely renders the consumption of meat as halachically unacceptable as the product of illegitimate means."[81] He indicates that he is referring not only to the production of veal and goose liver, the "most obvious and outrageous" examples of animal mistreatment, but also to common practices in the livestock trade, such as massive drug dosing and hormonal treatment.[82]

Hence, in view of the horrible conditions under which most animals are raised today, Jews who eat meat raised under such conditions seem to be supporting a system contrary to basic Jewish principles and obligations.

3: JUDAISM, VEGETARIANISM, AND HEALTH

You may not rob yourself of your life nor cause your body the slightest injury....Only if the body is healthy is it an efficient instrument for the spirit's activity....Therefore you should avoid everything which might possibly impair your health....And the law asks you to be even more circumspect in avoiding danger to life and limb than in the avoidance of other transgressions.—Rabbi Samson Raphael Hirsch[1]

HEALTH CARE ISSUES ARE CLEARLY AMONG THE MOST critical facing many countries today. National health care costs in the United States have been soaring, increasing from six percent of the United States gross national product in 1970 to about fifteen percent in 2000. Efforts to reduce medical expenditures have caused major changes in the U.S. health care system, with treatment decisions often made for economic rather than medical reasons. Over forty-three million Americans lack adequate health insurance. Costs of prescription drugs have soared. In spite of billions of dollars spent on medical research, degenerative diseases still afflict many people.

Most doctors today focus on the treatment of diseases rather than on their prevention. Medical schools primarily teach that prescription drugs are the most powerful tools doctors have for treating disease. Diet and other lifestyle changes are almost never emphasized as preventive tools. Once a doctor enters medical practice the drug message is reinforced: drug companies give out free samples; virtually all the advertisements in medical journals are for prescription drugs; the bulk of medical literature relates to the use of drugs and drug comparisons. Hence, the most common response to many diseases today is to prescribe medications first and perhaps recommend lifestyle changes as an afterthought.

Judaism's historical approach is fundamentally different from the approaches of most physicians today.[2] While treating sick people is certainly a Torah obligation, Judaism puts a priority on the *prevention* of disease.

The foundation for the Jewish stress on preventive medicine can be found in the verse in the Torah in which God is described as the *rofeh* (healer) of the Israelites:

And God said: "If you will diligently hearken to the voice of the Lord your God, and will do that which is right in His sight, and will give ear to His commandments, and keep all His statutes, I will put none of the diseases upon you which I put on the Egyptians; for I, the Lord, am your healer." (Exodus 15:26)

Rashi interprets this verse:

I, the Lord, am your healer, and I teach you the Torah and the commandments in order that you may be saved from these diseases—like a physician who says to a person: "Do not eat this thing lest it bring you into danger from this illness."

What are the implications of this Torah approach for modern medicine? Just as God's healing role in this Torah verse above is to prevent illness, so, too, a physician must emulate the Divine role by emphasizing the prevention of illness. For we are obligated to "follow in God's ways" (Deuteronomy 11:22).[3]

The following anecdote about Maimonides is instructive: During the period when Maimonides served as the royal physician to the Sultan of Egypt, the Sultan never became ill. One day the Sultan asked Maimonides, possibly in jest, "How do I know that you are an expert physician, since during the period that you have been here, I have never been ill, and you have not had the opportunity to test your skills?" Maimonides replied, "In truth, the great and faithful physician is the Holy One, Blessed be He, as it is written, 'I, the Lord, am your healer.' And this Great and Faithful Physician was able to promise His people that because He is their Physician, He will be able to protect them from all the illnesses that were inflicted on Egypt." Maimonides concluded, "Therefore, we learn that the ability of a physician to prevent illness is a greater proof of his skill than his ability to cure someone who is already ill."[4]

The Torah imposes another moral obligation which might impel physicians to practice preventive medicine: "Do not stand idly by the blood of your neighbor" (Leviticus 19:16). One must not remain passive if another person is in danger. For example, the sages indicate, if someone sees a person drowning or being attacked by robbers, he or she should do everything possible (short of seriously endangering oneself) to rescue the person.[5] Based on this verse, the Chafetz Chaim taught in his classic work *Shemirat HaLashon* that one must not withhold information that can save another from death or any type of injury. The following Talmudic teaching reinforces this principle: "Those who have the capacity to eliminate a wrong and do not do so bear the responsibility for its consequences."[6] Accordingly, it would seem that the Jewish approach is that physicians should emphasize preventive medicine, advising their patients about the dangers of smoking and animal-based diets and the benefits of positive lifestyle choices.

The Torah does not place the entire responsibility for maintaining good health on physicians. In fact, the Talmudic sages place the major responsibility on the individual. To take care of one's health is a *mitzvah*, and the sages find this mandate in the words, "take heed to yourself and take care of your lives," (Deuteronomy 4:9) and, "be extremely protective of your lives." (Deuteronomy 4:15).

Judaism regards the preservation of physical well-being as a crucial religious commandment. Jews must take care of their health and do nothing that might unnecessarily endanger themselves. Life is regarded as a very great value and we are obligated to protect it.

A vital Jewish principle is *pikuach nefesh*, the duty to preserve a human life. The Talmudic sages applied the principle—"You shall therefore keep my statutes and ordinances, which if a man do he shall live by them" (Leviticus 18:5)—to all the laws of the Torah. Hence, Jews are commanded to be more cautious about matters concerning danger to health and life than about ritual matters.[7] If it might save a life, one is obligated to violate the Sabbath, eat forbidden foods, and even eat on Yom

Kippur.[8] The only laws that may not be violated to preserve a life are those prohibiting murder, idolatry, and sexual immorality.[9]

Maimonides summarizes the importance that Judaism places on the preservation of health:

> Since maintaining a healthy and sound body is among the ways of God—for one cannot understand or have any knowledge of the Creator if he is ill—therefore one must avoid that which harms the body and accustom oneself to that which is helpful and helps the body become stronger.[10]

Rabbi Hirsch writes passionately about the importance of preserving health in his classic book, *Horeb*: "Limiting our arrogance toward our own body, God's word calls to us: 'Do not commit suicide!' 'Do not injure yourself!' 'Do not ruin yourself!' 'Do not weaken yourself!' 'Preserve yourself!' "[11]

Although their primary purpose may be spiritual purification, many Torah commandments promote proper hygiene and good health. Hygienic living and prevention of disease are religious mandates designed for the preservation and well-being of the community. For example, to keep the Israelites' camps clean, latrines were established outside their bounds, and soldiers were equipped with spades with which they were to dig holes and bury their excrement (Deuteronomy 23: 13–15). Lepers and others who might spread serious diseases were excluded from the camp for specific quarantine periods (Leviticus 15:1–15; Numbers 5:1–4).

The rabbis also emphasized the importance of public measures to protect health. The Talmud states that no tannery, grave, or carcass may be placed close to a human dwelling,[12] and stresses that streets and market areas are to be kept clean.[13] The sages declare it forbidden for a scholar to reside in a city that does not contain a public bath.[14]

The rabbis regard the human body as a sanctuary.[15] They give much advice on types of food conducive to good health[16] and stress the importance of regular nutritious meals.[17] They mandate that one must wash one's face, hands, and feet daily in honor of one's Creator,[18] as well as wash one's hands on specific occasions, including after urination and/or defecation.[19] It is an especially important *mitzvah* to ritually wash hands before eating a meal.[20]

The seriousness with which the rabbis regard proper individual hygiene for the preservation of health is illustrated by this anecdote from the life of the sage Hillel:

> Once when Hillel was leaving his disciples, they said to him: "Master, where are you going?" He replied: "To do a pious deed." They asked: "What may that be?" He replied: "To take a bath." They asked: "Is that a pious deed?" He replied: "Yes. If, in the Roman theaters and circuses, the images of the king must be kept clean by the man to whom they have been entrusted, how much more is it a duty of man to care for the body, since man has been created in the Divine image and likeness."[21]

The Torah, Talmud, and codes of Jewish Law stress the avoidance of danger through the positive commandment of making a parapet (guard rail) for one's roof so that no one will fall from the roof (Deuteronomy 22:8). Rabbi J. H. Hertz, in his commentary on this commandment, states that failure to protect human life renders one guilty in God's eyes of the spilling of blood.[22] The Talmudic sages extend this prohibition to cover all cases where negligence endangers life, such as placing a broken ladder against a wall or keeping a dangerous dog.[23]

In his classic legal code, the *Mishneh Torah*, Maimonides describes a variety of prohibitions, all based on the necessity to do everything possible to preserve human life:

> It makes no difference whether it be one's roof or anything else that is dangerous and might possibly be a stumbling block to someone and cause his death—for example, if one has a well or a pit, with or without water, in his yard, the owner is obliged to build an enclosing wall ten hand breadths high, or else to put a cover over it lest someone fall into it and be killed. Similarly, regarding

any obstacle which is dangerous to life, there is a positive commandment to remove it and to beware of it, and to be particularly careful in this matter, for Scripture says, "Take heed unto yourself and take care of your life" (Deuteronomy 4:9). If one does not remove dangerous obstacles but allows them to remain, he disregards a positive commandment and transgresses the prohibition: "Bring not blood" (Deuteronomy 22:8).

Many things are forbidden by the Sages because they are dangerous to life. If one disregards any of these and says, "If I want to put myself in danger, what concern is it of others?" or "I am not particular about such things," he must be prevented from such behavior.

The following are prohibited acts: One may not put his mouth to a flowing pipe of water and drink from it, or drink at night from rivers or ponds, lest he swallow a leech while unable to see. Nor may one drink water that has been left uncovered, lest he drink from it after a snake or other poisonous reptile has drunk from it, and die.[24]

Maimonides' statements clearly indicate that Judaism absolutely prohibits the placing of one's health or life in possible danger. He disallows the popular rationalization, "What concern is it to others if I endanger myself?"

Similar prohibitions against endangering one's life appear in the *Shulchan Aruch* of Rabbi Joseph Caro (1488–1575) and other Codes of Jewish Law.[25] In *Choshen Mishpat* 427, Rabbi Caro devotes an entire chapter to "the positive commandment to remove any object or obstacle which constitutes a danger to life." In his commentary on Caro's *Shulchan Aruch*, Rabbi Moses Isserles (the Rema) concludes:

One should avoid all things that might lead to danger because one is obligated to be stricter about danger to life than about a prohibition. Therefore, the Sages prohibited walking in a place of danger such as near a leaning wall [for fear of collapse], or alone at night [for fear of robbers]. They also prohibited drinking water from rivers at night...because these things may lead to danger...and one who is concerned with his health [literally: watches his soul] avoids them. And it is prohibited to rely on a miracle or to put one's life in danger by any of the aforementioned or the like.[26]

The Talmud relates that Rabbi Huna would personally inspect all the walls of his town of Sura before the onset of the winter storms. Any walls that he found unsafe, he would order torn down. If the owner could not afford to rebuild the wall, Rabbi Huna would pay for it from his own funds.[27]

Life is considered so sacred in Judaism that the tradition asserts that "if a person saves one life, it is as if he [or she] saved an entire world."[28] The preservation of human life is so important that it takes precedence over acts of reverence for a dead person, even if that person is a leader or great hero: "For a one-day-old child [who is dangerously ill], the Sabbath may be profaned; for David, King of Israel, once he is dead, the Sabbath must not be profaned."[29] Also, one must sooner rescue from flames any living infant than the dead body of one's own parent.[30] As will be discussed in detail in Chapter 5, the Jewish sages prohibit the unnecessary destruction of anything of value. This prohibition is extended to include the intentional destruction of any part of one's own body by Rabbi Israel Lipshutz, (d. 1782), author of the mishnaic commentary *Tifereth Yisrael*.[31]

People rationalize and justify continuing dangerous habits, such as smoking. But Jewish tradition rejects all such defenses in the name of *pikuach nefesh*, the requirement to preserve human life.[32] If it can be clearly and convincingly shown that consuming is dangerous to people's health, it would be prohibited by Jewish law. As the following sections demonstrate, there are strong indications that this is indeed the case.

Results When People Have Lived Under Vegetarian Diets
During World War I, Denmark was cut off from its meat supply because of a blockade by the Allied forces. To avoid acute food shortages, the

government sought the aid of Denmark's vegetarian society for advice about nutritious alternate foods. Dr. Mikkel Hindhede writes about the results in the *Journal of the American Medical Association.* He points out that only the wealthy could afford to buy meat, and most of the population ate bran, bread, barley, porridge, potatoes, greens, milk, and some butter.[33] This primarily vegetarian diet led to better health and reduced mortality rates (by seventeen percent) for the Danish people during the first year of the new diet.[34]

Similarly in Norway when food rationing was instituted during World War II and the consumption of meat was sharply cut, health improved. With this primarily vegetarian diet, the Norwegian death rate dropped from thirty-one per 10,000 people in 1938 to about twenty per 10,000 people in 1944 (a thirty-six percent decrease).[35] After the war, when the prewar diets resumed, the mortality rate rose sharply, reaching twenty-six per 10,000 people in 1946.[36]

Unlike the short wartime experiences of the Danes and Norwegians, the Seventh Day Adventist churches have followed a vegetarian diet for over 100 years. Many Adventists also abstain from smoking, alcohol, coffee, tea, spices, hot condiments, and highly refined foods. A study of their health shows that colonic, rectal, and intestinal cancer are fifty to seventy percent lower than in the general population.[37] In another study, Seventh Day Adventist women, about half of whom were vegetarian, had lower blood pressure and forty percent less endometrial cancer than women in the general population.[38] An Australian study found the blood pressures of Seventh Day Adventist vegetarians between thirty and seventy-nine years of age to be "significantly less" than the levels found in non-vegetarian control groups.[39] The study concluded that dietary factors, probably intake of animal protein, animal fat, or other dietary components associated with them, were likely responsible for the differences in blood pressure readings.[40]

After studying the mainly vegetarian diet of the Hunzas of Kashmir, noted for their longevity, Major General Sir Robert McCarrison, once physician to the king of England, wrote: "I never saw a case of asthenic dyspepsia, of gastric or duodenal ulcer, of appendicitis, or mucus colitis or cancer."[41] Dr. Paul Dudley White, the famous heart specialist, visited the Hunzas in 1964. His studies showed that the ninety and 110-year-old men tested showed no evidence of heart disease and that there was a correlation between their diet and lifestyles and the low incidence of heart disease.[42]

The Bible contains an interesting case of people eating only vegetarian foods. The Book of Daniel tells how Daniel and his three companions were captives in the court of Nebuchadnezzar, king of Babylon. They refused to defile themselves with the king's meat and wine, which were not kosher. The king's servant was fearful that their health would suffer and the king would blame him. But Daniel said: "For ten days, give us pulse (peas, beans, and lentils) to eat and water to drink. Then look at our countenances, and the countenance of those children that eat of the portion of the king's meat; and as you observe (the differences), deal with your servants." The king's servant consented to wait the period and "at the end of the ten days their countenances appeared fairer and fatter in flesh than all the children who did eat the portion of the king's meat." The king's servant then took away from the others their meat and wine and fed them also pulse and water (Daniel 1:8–16).

Connections Between Diet and Health

Comprehensive discussions of health issues and their relation to diet may be found in *The Power of Your Plate* by Neal D. Barnard, M.D., *McDougall's Medicine: A Challenging Second Opinion* by John McDougall, M.D., and *MegaHealth* by Marc Sorensen, Ed.D. Graphs and charts connecting nutrition to health and illness can be found in the *The Scientific Basis of Vegetarianism* by William Harris, M.D. These books provide many primary sources from established medical journals. The Physicians Committee For Responsible Medicine (PCRM) has documented information about the relations between diet and disease. The tremendously important message documented in these sources is that vegetarian diets can help prevent, and in some cases reverse, a wide variety of degenerative diseases and medical problems that have been strongly linked to the consumption of animal products, including: arthritis; asthma; breast cancer; colon cancer; constipation; diabetes; diverticulosis;

gallstones; heart disease; hemorrhoids; hypertension; hypoglycemia; impotence; kidney disease; obesity; osteoporosis; peptic ulcers; prostate cancer; salmonellosis; and strokes. Readers are urged to consult the sources mentioned above and other sources in the annotated Bibliography for more information on health issues. Additional information on nutrition and health appears later in some of the questions and answers in Chapter 8.

Because of the abundance of documented evidence in these books and other sources, and because of space limitations, this book does not focus on dietary connections to each disease. Rather it focuses on issues not generally discussed, including:

1. The position on nutrition and health of the American Dietetic Association;

2. The Cornell/China/Oxford Study, perhaps the largest epidemiological study in history;

3. Studies led by Dean Ornish, M.D. that show that heart disease may be reversed without surgery or medical drugs;

4. A book by a veteran breast cancer surgeon who believes many scientific studies show that the risk of contracting breast cancer (and, by implication, other diseases) can be sharply reduced;

5. The negative health effects of the overuse of antibiotics in medicine and in animal feed.

Position of The American Dietetic Association: Vegetarian Diets

The following information from the "Position of the American Dietetic Association: Vegetarian Diets" (*Journal of the American Dietetic Association* (ADA), November, 1997, Volume 97, Number 11) indicates that a well planned vegetarian diet is not only nutritionally adequate, but can reduce the risk of many diseases. A summary of the position follows:

Scientific data suggest positive relationships between a vegetarian diet and reduced risk for several chronic degenerative diseases and conditions, including obesity, coronary artery disease, hypertension, diabetes mellitus, and some types of cancer. Vegetarian diets, like all diets, need to be planned appropriately to be nutritionally adequate.

It is the position of the American Dietetic Association (ADA) that appropriately planned vegetarian diets are healthful, are nutritionally adequate, and provide health benefits in the prevention and treatment of certain diseases.

Among the many other positive statements the ADA 1997 position paper makes about connections between plant-based diets and health are the following (they cite appropriate peer-reviewed scientific articles in each case):

1. Studies indicate that vegetarians often have lower morbidity and mortality rates from several chronic degenerative diseases than do non-vegetarians. Although non-dietary factors, including physical activity and abstinence from smoking and alcohol, may play a role, diet is clearly a contributing factor.

2. Vegetarian diets offer disease protection benefits because of their lower saturated fat, cholesterol, and animal protein content and often higher concentration of folate (which reduces serum homocysteine levels), antioxidants such as vitamins C and E, carotenoids, and phytochemicals.

3. Not only is mortality from coronary artery disease lower in vegetarians than in non-vegetarians, but vegetarian diets have also been successful as part of comprehensive health programs to reverse severe coronary artery disease.

4. Vegetarians tend to have a lower incidence of hypertension than non-vegetarians.

5. Type 2 diabetes mellitus is much less likely to be a cause of death in vegetarians than non-vegetarians.

6. Incidence of lung and colorectal cancer is lower in vegetarians than in non-vegetarians. Reduced colorectal cancer risk is associated with increased consumption of fiber, vegetables, and fruit.

7. Plant sources of protein alone can provide adequate amounts of essential amino acids if a variety of plant foods are consumed and energy needs are met.

Recent Major Health Studies

There have been two major health studies that have the potential to radically affect medical practice. They dramatically show how dietary changes and other lifestyle changes can prevent and in some cases reverse diseases.

A major ongoing health study is the "Cornell/China/Oxford Study," a collaborative effort between Cornell University, represented by T. Colin Campbell, Ph.D., the Chinese Academy of Preventive Medicine, the Chinese Academy of Medical Sciences, and Oxford University, England, as well as scientists from the United States, Britain, France, and other countries. It is an epidemiological study that has looked at the eating habits and diseases of 6,500 people in 65 Chinese provinces. The summary below is based on material in *The China Project: Keys to Better Health, Discovered in Our Living Laboratory*, by T. Colin Campbell, Ph.D. and Christine Cox (see the Bibliography).

The China Project differs from other scientific studies in several important ways:

1. It utilizes the most comprehensive database on the multiple causes of disease ever compiled; the Chinese government provided background data on eighty million Chinese people.

2. It examines relationships between health and diet in a holistic way, by considering ways in which complete diets and other lifestyle patterns affect health. By contrast, most contemporary studies focus on relationships between single nutrients or foods and single diseases.

3. China provided a "natural (living) laboratory" for the study of nutrition and disease that is unmatched anywhere else in the world; while people in most of the world's countries frequently change their places of residence, and eat foods from many different regions of the world, most Chinese live their entire lives in one area, and eat the same kinds of locally grown food throughout their lives. Yet, diets (and disease rates) vary sharply from one area to another.

The China Project has received much critical acclaim. Jane Brody, nutrition editor of the *New York Times*, has called it "the grand prix" of epidemiology, and has hailed its "tantalizing findings" from "the most comprehensive large study ever undertaken of the relationship between diet and the risk of developing disease." The *East West Journal* has called the study "one of the most rigorous and conclusive [studies] in the history of health research," one that has "unprecedented authority."

Here are some of the "tantalizing findings" that can (and should) have a global impact:

1. The Chinese diet, composed primarily of rice and other grains, vegetables, and legumes, such as soy products, is far healthier than the standard American diet. While Americans get an average of thirty-seven percent of their calories from fat, Chinese get an average of 14.5 percent, with a range of about six percent to twenty-four percent. The Chinese get only ten percent of their protein from animal sources, while Americans get seventy percent. One result of the healthier Chinese diets is that the range of cholesterol levels in China vary from seventy mg to 170 mg, while in the United States, the average cholesterol level is over 200.

2. In China, regions in which people eat the most animal products have the highest rates of heart disease, cancer, and other degenerative diseases. In many cases, the differences are extremely large; for example, in one part of China where people eat more meat, the rate of esophageal cancer for men is 435 times greater than the rate for men in another region, and twenty times as many women in one county with high meat consumption suffer from breast cancer as women in another county where meat consumption is much lower.

3. Degenerative diseases are associated with high levels of blood cholesterol and urea nitrogen (what is left over after the metabolism of protein in the body), and both of these factors increase as people eat more meat, dairy products, and eggs.

4. The more a diet is composed of foods of plant origin, the better. Even small increases in the amount of animal products (meat, eggs, and dairy products) consumed result in significant increases in chronic degenerative diseases.

5. Because cholesterol levels in the United States are almost double those in China, heart disease deaths among American men occur seventeen times more often, per thousand men, than for Chinese men.

Also, Chinese at the lower end of the cholesterol range have significantly less cancer and heart disease than those at the upper end.

6. Deaths from breast cancer are linkd to five factors associated with diets high in animal-based foods: high intakes of dietary fat, high levels of blood cholesterol, high amounts of estrogen, high levels of blood testosterone, and early age at first menstruation. The Chinese's plant-based diets give them benefits in each of these areas. For example, Chinese girls reach menstruation when they are fifteen to nineteen years of age, significantly later than the ten to fourteen years of age for most American girls.

7. Chinese eat very few dairy products, and low levels of calcium-rich foods; yet they get far less osteoporosis than Westerners. For example, hip fractures per thousand people in China are only one-fifth of what they are in the West. (As will be discussed in more detail in Chapter 8, the reason is that excessive animal protein causes calcium to be excreted from the body.)

8. While the Chinese eat an average of almost 300 calories per day more than Westerners do, they are generally thinner. Dr. Campbell believes that in a very low-fat diet, a higher percentage of calories may be burned up rather than stored as fat.

9. The amount of animal protein in the diet correlates well with overall cancer rates, Hence, dietary protein may be a bigger health problem than dietary fat. Thus a shift from red meat to fish and chicken is generally not helpful since, while dietary fat is reduced, dietary animal protein is not.

* * * * *

A second major study that can have a major impact if its lessons are heeded is the "Lifestyle Heart Trial," conducted by Dean Ornish, M.D. of the Preventive Medicine Research Institute in Sausalito, California and his medical colleagues. The objective was to study if changes in diet, exercise, and stress levels can unblock clogged arteries and save lives, without the use of expensive surgical techniques or drugs. Dr. Ornish spells out the philosophy, science, and diet behind his approach in *Dr. Dean Ornish's Program for Reversing Heart Disease* (see Bibliography).

Ornish's initial study involved forty-eight patients with severe heart disease. He randomly divided them into two groups: twenty-eight received his experimental regimen, and the other twenty were put into a control group, so that they could serve as a basis of comparison. The experimental group was put on a strict diet including only plant-based foods, supplemented by egg whites and one cup daily of nonfat milk or yogurt. Their dietary fat content was a very low ten percent of calories, and their cholesterol intake was only five mg per day. To control stress, they did stretching exercises, meditated, and performed other relaxation techniques. In addition, they walked for at least half an hour three times a week, and met as a support group twice weekly.

After one year, most of the experimental group indicated a complete or nearly complete disappearance of chest pains. Arterial clogging was significantly reversed for eighty-two percent of the patients. In one case, the change was especially dramatic. Werner Hebenstreit, a seventy-five-year-old retired businessman who reported that before starting the program he could barely cross the street without chest pains, was able to hike for six hours in the Grand Tetons at 8,000 feet by the end of the program. Other patients also experienced significant improvements.

What makes the results even more spectacular is a comparison with the findings for members of the control group. They received standard medical care, generally following the recommendations of the American Heart Association and/or their doctors: up to thirty percent fat in their diets; dietary cholesterol limited to 300 mg per day; no red meat, but chicken without the skin and fish were permitted; a moderate amount of exercise, but no set stress reduction activities. None of these patients got better; in almost all cases, their arterial blockages worsened significantly, and they reported an increase in chest pains. Evidently, the standard recommendations of the medical establishment were not sufficient, at least with regard to reversing heart disease.

Although Dr. Ornish initially found it difficult to find funding for his study because of the medical establishment's skepticism about reversing heart disease without surgery or drugs, there are several indications of the increasing acceptance of his approach:

1. In 1990, Ornish's initial findings were published in the *Lancet*, a highly respected British medical journal, and later results were published in the *Journal of the American Medical Association* in 1995.

2. In a break from previous policies of medical insurers, which only reimbursed patients who underwent surgery or drug-related therapies, at least forty insurance companies now reimburse patients who receive the Ornish treatment. The insurers found that, of the patients motivated enough to try the Ornish approach, ninety percent stuck with it, and, of those, almost eighty percent avoided bypass surgery or angioplasty. Since these surgical approaches are much more expensive than Ornish's approach, insurance companies are saving about five dollars for every dollar invested.

3. At least eight hospitals throughout the United States, including Beth Israel in New York City, now provide outpatient treatment using the Ornish approach.

4. There have been many television programs and news reports about the success of the program.

Since more Americans die from heart and blood vessel diseases annually than any other cause of death, and more money is spent in the United States on the treatment of heart disease than on any other illness, Ornish's results have the potential to revolutionize health care.

Taken together, Ornish's study and the China Project, along with many other recent scientific studies, clearly show that a shift to plant-based diets can have enormous health benefits and can sharply reduce today's huge health care expenditures. It can only be hoped that increasing numbers of people will become aware of the "tantalizing findings" from these studies and change their dietary habits accordingly. The health of billions of people and, ultimately, the entire planet is at stake.

Can Breast Cancer Be Prevented?

An analysis of many additional significant health studies is found in a very important book, *Save Yourself From Breast Cancer: Life Choices That*

Can Help You Reduce the Odds, by Robert M. Kradjian, M.D. (see the Bibliography). Dr. Kradjian, a breast cancer surgeon for thirty years, knows cancer as an expert and his conclusions are very important. After analyzing a wide variety of scientific studies, Kradjian has concluded that the main cause of breast cancer is animal-based diets. He contests the medical establishment's position that breast cancer is "all in the genes" and he demonstrates that prevention, not early detection, is the best defense against the disease.

Among the studies that Dr. Kradjian investigated are:

1. Human population studies (epidemiology). His dramatic findings show that, without exception, countries with high fat contents in the diet have high rates of breast cancer and vice versa. As he points out, "this information alone should be enough to cause a thoughtful woman to markedly reduce her dietary fat intake." The differences in cancer rates are also great—as much as twenty-five times greater for countries where high-fat diets are the norm, compared to countries where fat consumption is low.

2. Migration studies. Eleven migration studies have all shown that when people move from an area of low consumption of animal products, where the breast cancer rate is low (such as Japan), to an area where the consumption of animal products is higher, their breast cancer rate rises substantially and soon approaches that of the host country's population. These studies demonstrate that genetics is not the key factor in causing breast cancer.

3. Time trend studies. The average fat content in the Japanese diet increased from seven-and-a-half percent of total calories in 1950 to twenty-eight percent in 1994, and it has continued to rise. This has resulted in a major increase in the breast cancer rate, a fifty-eight percent increase between 1975 and 1985 alone. There are similar findings in other countries where meat consumption has been increasing.

4. Wartime studies. Consistent with the studies mentioned above, there were dramatic decreases in breast cancer rates in several countries during both World Wars I and II when wartime conditions resulted in large decreases in the consumption of animal products.

Based on these studies and other considerations and analyses, Dr. Kradjian concludes that the evidence that breast cancer is a dietary disease is "clear, convincing, and compelling." He asserts that the remedy required is simple: "a switch from the traditional high-fat/low-fiber diet to a low-fat/high fiber diet."

Since breast cancer is feared so much by women, and increasing numbers of women are being afflicted by this disease, and since the China study discussed above and other studies show similar results for other chronic degenerative diseases, it is essential that Dr. Kradjian's recommendation of a shift toward plant-based diets be widely heeded.

Threats Due to Increased Antibiotic Resistance[43]

Over half the antibiotics produced in the U.S. are routinely fed to animals in their feed.[44] It would be impossible to maintain healthy animals under the cramped conditions of "factory farming" without these drugs. Further, for reasons not fully understood, the antibiotics also seem to act as "growth promoters," leading to heavier animals and thus more weight for the market, providing even greater incentive to administer drugs.

Unfortunately, this practice places enormous "selective pressure" on the bacteria that inhabit these animals to develop resistance to the antibiotics in the feed. Genes which neutralize the effects of antibiotics arise as a result of this selective pressure (i.e., in the presence of antibiotics, only those organisms that have the capability of neutralizing the antibiotics will survive). These resistant genes are easily transferred from one bacterium to another, and they may protect germs that cause human disease from antibiotic treatment.

There has already been a tremendous increase in antibiotic resistance in common food poisoning bacteria like salmonella,[45] but the problem is even worse than simply the antibiotic-resistant bacteria in the food animals themselves. Bacteria also have the capability of rapidly transferring and spreading the antibiotic-resistant character to other bacterial species, including those which cause other diseases. Therefore, diseases that are not even related to food consumption may become resistant to antibiotics, and hence a much greater threat. For example, staphylococcus bacteria have been isolated in recent years that are resistant to every known commercially available antibiotic.[46] If this organism gets into one's blood stream, you will very likely die.

As a result, there is a scientific consensus that the extensive use of antibiotics to produce meat and other animal products, along with their over-use in medicine, has increased resistance among bacteria and jeopardized human health by causing diseases that are difficult or impossible to cure. For example, in 1997, the World Health Organization called for a ban on the routine use of antibiotics in livestock feed.[47] In 1998, the journal *Science* called the meat industry "the driving force behind the development of antibiotic resistance in certain species of bacteria that cause human disease,"[48] and, later that year, the Centers for Disease Control blamed the use of antibiotics in livestock feed for the emergence of salmonella bacteria resistant to five different antibiotics.[49] As Joshua Lederberg, M.D., a Nobel Laureate, has said: "We're running out of bullets for dealing with a number of these infections. Patients are dying because we no longer, in many cases, have antibiotics that work."[50]

The widespread use of antibiotics in animal feed is thus a global threat to human health for every individual on earth. People need prescriptions for these drugs, yet the animal industry uses them casually. This irresponsible misuse of antibiotics is unilaterally disarming our species from a last line of defense, and devastating epidemics may well be the legacy of the hunger for inexpensive meat.

Conclusion

Since medical and statistical evidence demonstrates that the eating of animal products is hazardous to health and can lead to fatal diseases, it is significant that Orthodox Rabbi Alfred Cohen concludes his comprehensive article, "Vegetarianism From a Jewish Perspective," with this statement:

Following the many precedents prescribed in the Code of Jewish Law, we would have little difficulty in arriving at the conclusion that, if indeed eating meat is injurious to one's health, it is not only permissible, but possibly even mandatory that we reduce our ingestion of an unhealthful product to the minimal level.[51]

Rabbi David Rosen, former Chief Rabbi of Ireland, is more emphatic: "As it is halachically prohibited to harm oneself and as healthy, nutritious vegetarian alternatives are easily available, meat consumption has become halachically unjustifiable."[52]

In view of all of the material in this chapter and many well-documented books, it would seem that the numerous *halachic* rules prohibiting dangerous activities should be extended to include a mandate reducing the ingestion of meat to a minimal level, and there should be a recommendation that those who continue to eat small amounts of kosher meat, possibly as an interim step, should only use organically raised meat from animals not raised under cruel "factory farm" conditions. Such an extension by leading rabbinic authorities of our time, with proper publicity, would save many lives and improve the health and life expectancy of the Jewish people and many others.

4: JUDAISM, VEGETARIANISM, AND FEEDING THE HUNGRY

If one takes seriously the moral, spiritual, and humanitarian values of biblical, prophetic, and rabbinic Judaism, the inescapable issue of conscience that must be faced is: How can anyone justify not becoming involved in trying to help save the lives of starving millions of human beings throughout the world—whose plight constitutes the most agonizing moral and humanitarian problem in the latter half of the 20th century? (Rabbi Marc H. Tannenbaum, former National Interreligious Affairs Director of the American Jewish Committee)[1]

ON YOM KIPPUR, THE HOLIEST DAY OF THE JEWISH YEAR, while fasting and praying for a good year, Jews hear the words of the Prophet Isaiah that fasting and prayers are not sufficient; they must work to end oppression and provide food for needy people:

Is not this the fast that I have chosen? To loose the chains of wickedness, to undo the bonds of oppression, and to let the oppressed go free....Is it not to share your bread with the hungry? (Isaiah 58:6–7)

Helping the hungry is fundamental in Judaism. The Talmud states: "Providing charity for poor and hungry people weighs as heavily as all the other commandments of the Torah combined."[2]

A *midrash* teaches:

God says to Israel, "My children, whenever you give sustenance to the poor, I impute it to you as though you gave sustenance to Me...." Does then God eat and drink? No, but whenever you give food to the poor, God accounts it to you as if you gave food to Him.[3]

On Passover we are reminded not to forget the poor. Besides providing *ma'ot chittim* (charity for purchasing holiday necessities) for the needy before Passover, we specifically reach out to them at the *seder*:

> This is the bread of affliction which our ancestors ate in the land of Egypt. Let all who are hungry come and eat. Let all who are in need come and celebrate the Passover.[4]

We are even admonished to feed our enemies, if they are in need:

> If your enemy is hungry, give him bread to eat.
> If your enemy is thirsty, give him water to drink.
> (Proverbs 25:21)

This is consistent with the Jewish teaching that the greatest hero is a person who converts an enemy into a friend (*Avot de Rabbi Nathan*, Ch. 23).

It is a basic Jewish belief that God provides enough for all. In the traditional daily prayers, it is said "He opens His hand and provides sustenance to all living things" (Psalms 145:16). Jews are obligated to give thanks to God for providing enough food for us and for all of humanity. In the *Birkat Hamazon* (grace after meals), Jews thank God "who feeds the whole world with goodness, grace, loving kindness, and mercy."

The blessing is correct. God has provided enough for all. The bounties of nature, if properly distributed and properly consumed, would sustain all people. Millions of people are hungry today, not because of insufficient agricultural capacity, but because of unjust social systems and wasteful methods of food production, especially the feeding of tremendous amounts of grains to animals to fatten them for slaughter to feed meat-eaters.

World Hunger Today

World hunger statistics are staggering. Nearly a billion people, roughly one out of five people in the developing (poorer) countries, are chronically hungry.[5] The UN Food and Agricultural Organization (FAO) estimates that twenty-one percent of India's population is chronically undernourished, but the situation may be far worse, since recent on-the-ground surveys indicate that forty-nine percent of adults and fifty-three percent of children in India are underweight—a proxy measurement for hunger.[6] Hunger is found in the industrial world as well: the U.S. Department of Agriculture estimated that in 1998 some ten percent of U.S. households were hungry, on the edge of being hungry, or concerned about being hungry.[7]

Malnutrition particularly victimizes children. Worldwide, over twelve million children under the age of five (about 34,000 per day) die annually from diseases caused or complicated by malnutrition.[8] Almost eight million children die annually before their first birthday, largely due to malnutrition.[9] Malnourishment also brings listlessness and reduced capacity for learning and other activities, which perpetuates the legacy of poverty.

Jeremy Rifkin summarizes well the anomaly of rich people dieting while poor people are starving:

> While millions of Americans anguish over excess pounds, spending time, money, and emotional energy on slimming down, children in other lands are wasting away, their physical growth irreversibly stunted, their bodies racked by parasitic and opportunistic diseases, their brain growth diminished by lack of nutrients in their meager diets.[10]

The extensive hunger and malnutrition make rebellion and violence more likely in many parts of the world. Professor Georg Borgstrom, internationally known expert on food science, fears that "the rich world is on a direct collision course with the poor of the world....We cannot survive behind our Maginot line of missiles and bombs."[11] Hence the outlook for global stability is very poor, unless the problem of global hunger is solved soon. Professor Robert Heilbroner, a noted economist, has predicted that, in times of severe famine, some countries may be be sorely tempted to resort to nuclear blackmail.[12]

One important reason why many are starving today is that tremendous quantities of grain are used to fatten animals for slaughter, grain that could be feeding hungry people. Animal-centered diets are very wasteful of grain, land, water, fuel, and fertilizer. Half of U.S. farm acreage is used to produce feed crops for livestock. An animal-centered diet requires about seventeen times the land area per person than would be required for a purely vegetarian diet. Animal agriculture also requires huge inputs of chemical fertilizer and pesticides, irrigation water, and fuel—commodities becoming scarce worldwide.[13]

Research at the Institute for Food and Development in California shows that the world produces enough grain alone to provide every person with sufficient protein and about 3,000 calories a day, about the average American's caloric intake.[14] The 3,000-calorie estimate does not include fruits, vegetables, nuts, root crops, and non-grain-fed meat produced by the world's people. Grains are increasingly being fed to livestock in the developing world as well, although the majority of people there can't afford to eat meat. Much of the best land in poorer countries is used to graze livestock, mostly for export. In Central America, two-thirds of the agriculturally productive land is used for livestock production, for the wealthy or for export.[15]

Prospects for the reduction of hunger are not good. In his book, *Tough Choices: Facing the Challenge of Food Scarcity* (New York: W. W. Norton, 1996), Lester R. Brown, President of the Worldwatch Institute, argues that a combination of rapidly increasing world population and affluence, environmental strains, climate changes, and significant decreases in clean water, arable land, fish catches, and land productivity threaten the world's food security.

The Worldwatch Institute believes that providing enough food for the world's rapidly increasing population will be a critical issue facing the world for many decades. Among the significant points that Lester Brown and the Worldwatch Institute make about threats to the world's future food security are the following (updated, based on the year 2000 World Population Sheet of the Population Reference Bureau):

1. Rapid Population Growth

The world's population is currently increasing by almost eighty million people per year. At this rate the world's population increases by approximately the United States every three years. While most of the children are born in less developed countries, this rapid growth in population has major impacts on land, water, pollution, and other factors related to the food supply. Another indication of the potential severity of the problem is that, while it took all of the world's history to reach the 1999 population of about six billion people, this number is projected to double in about fifty years, with major implications for increased consumption of food and other resources.

2. Increasing Affluence

There has been a sharp increase in affluence in many countries, especially in Asia, and this has increased the demand for animal products and thus for grain to feed livestock. China is a significant example: it was a net exporter of eight million tons of grain in 1994, but became a net importer of sixteen million tons of grain in 1995, due to the increased affluence of many of China's 1.3 billion people. While China, with over twenty-one percent of the world's people, was basically self-sufficient with regard to grain in 1990, it is estimated that it will need to import 215 million tons of grain by 2030, an amount greater than all grain exported by all countries today. Yet, on December 22, 1999, the World Bank approved a $93.5 million loan to build 130 feedlots and five meat processing centers to help China greatly expand its meat production.[16]

3. Water Scarcity

Depletion of aquifers due to increased demand for water and diversion of irrigation waters to expanding cities are decreasing the water available for irrigation in many countries. Water tables are falling in key food-producing areas, including the southern Great Plains of the United States, much of northern China, and several states in India.

4. Decreasing Arable Land

The world's grainland per person has been decreasing more rapidly due to the combined effects of rapid population growth and the loss of agricultural land to meet the growing needs of industry and transportation.

5. Climate Changes

There is increasing concern about the effects of global warming, especially of increasingly severe heat waves on agriculture. The droughts and severe storms that are increasingly accompanying global warming are another great threat to future food security.

6. Decreasing Fish Catches

While the seafood catch per person doubled from 1950 to 1989, it has decreased seven percent from 1989 to 1995, and is projected to continue decreasing as rapid population growth continues. The U.N.'s Food and Agriculture Organization (FAO) indicated that all fifteen oceanic fisheries are being fished at or beyond their capacities, and thirteen of them are in a state of decline.

7. Decreasing Land Productivity

As farmers are forced to use less productive land, and as the agricultural benefits of increased fertilization and irrigation decrease, the productivity of cropland is decreasing. While grain yield per hectare more than doubled from 1950 to 1990, it has increased far more slowly since 1990, in spite of increasing agricultural inputs.

The net result of these interacting factors, according to the Worldwatch Institute, is that, while the past was dominated by food surpluses, with competition among exporters for access to markets, the future probably will be dominated by food scarcity, with increasing competition among importers for access to markets.

Jewish Responses to Hunger
1. Involvement

Judaism teaches involvement and concern with the plight of fellow human beings. Every life is sacred, and we are obligated to do what we can to help others. The Torah states, "You shall not stand idly by the blood of your brother" (Leviticus 19:16). We speak out justifiably against the silence of the world when six million Jews and five million other people were murdered in the Holocaust. Can we be silent when millions die agonizing deaths because of lack of food? Can we acquiesce to the apathy of the world at the fate of starving people?

Elie Wiesel has pointed out that there can be no analogies to the Holocaust, but that it can be used as a reference. In that context, we can consider the over seven million infants who die each year due to malnutrition. Victims of hunger are not being singled out because of their religion, race, or nationality, as were the Nazis' victims, but they too die while the world goes about its business, grumbling about "high" taxes and personal inconveniences, indifferent to the plight of starving millions.

The Hebrew prophets berated those who were content and comfortable while others were in great distress:

Tremble you women who are at ease,
Shudder you complacent ones;
Strip and make yourselves bare,
Gird sackcloth upon your loins. (Isaiah 32:11)

Woe to those who are at ease in Zion...
Woe to those who lie upon beds of ivory
And stretch themselves upon their couches...
Who drink wine from bowls
And anoint themselves with the finest oils
But are not grieved at the ruin of Joseph. (Amos 6:1,4,6)

Like other people, Jews have frequently experienced hunger. Because of famines, Abraham was forced to go to Egypt (Genesis 12:10), Isaac went to the land of Abimelech, king of the Philistines, in Gerar (Genesis 26:1), the children of Jacob went to Egypt to buy grain (Genesis 42:1–3), and Naomi and her family fled Israel and went to Moab (Ruth 1:1–2). There were also famines in the reigns of King David (2 Samuel 21:1) and King Ahab (1 Kings 18:1–2). Jews know the sorrow of great hunger. The Prophet Jeremiah describes the time of Jerusalem's destruction: "Happier were the victims of the sword than the victims of hunger, who pined away, stricken by want of the yield of the field" (Lamentations 4:9).

Based on Jewish values and Jewish history, we must identify with the starving people of the world. We must be involved by speaking out and acting. Some traditional Jewish ways to help needy people are to pursue justice, practice charity, show compassion, share resources, and simplify lifestyles.

2. Pursuing Justice

The pursuit of a just society is one of the most fundamental concepts of Judaism. The statement in Deuteronomy (16:20), "Justice, justice shall you pursue," is a cornerstone of the Torah's humane legislation and of the prophets' demand for social righteousness. Words are seldom repeated in the Torah. When they are, it is generally to add emphasis. Since we are told to pursue justice, we are not to wait for the right opportunity, the right time and place, but instead to be alert for opportunities to practice justice. Proverbs 21:3 asserts: "To do righteousness and justice is preferred by God above sacrifice." The psalmist writes: "Give justice to the weak and the fatherless; maintain the right of the afflicted and the destitute" (Psalms 82:3–4). The prophet Amos warns the people that without the practice of justice, God is repelled by their worship:

> Take away from Me the noise of your songs;
> And let Me not hear the melody of your psalteries.
> But let justice well up as waters,
> And righteousness as a mighty stream. (Amos 5:23, 24)

Isaiah states:

> The Lord of Hosts shall be exalted in justice,
> The Holy God shows Himself holy in righteousness. (Isaiah 5:16)

The prophets constantly stress the importance of furthering justice:

> Learn to do well—seek justice, relieve the oppressed, judge the fatherless, plead for the widow....Zion shall be redeemed with justice, and they that return to her with righteousness.
> (Isaiah 1:17, 27)

To practice justice is considered among the highest demands of prophetic religion:

> It has been told you, O man, what is good,
> And what the Lord requires of you:
> Only to do justly, love mercy
> And walk humbly with your God. (Micah 6:8)

The practice of justice is even part of the symbolic betrothal between the Jewish people and God:

> And I will betroth you unto Me forever; And, I will betroth you unto Me in righteousness, justice, loving kindness, and compassion. And I will betroth you unto Me in faithfulness. And you shall know the Lord. (Hosea 2:21–22)

Justice is such an important concept in Judaism that the patriarch Abraham even pleads with God to practice justice: "That be far from You to do after this manner, to slay the righteous with the wicked...shall not the Judge of all the earth do justly?" (Genesis 18:25)

Rabbi Emanuel Rackman points out that Judaism teaches a special kind of justice, an "empathic justice," which

> ...seeks to make people identify themselves with each other—with each other's needs, with each other's hopes and aspirations, with each other's defeats and frustrations. Because Jews have known the distress of slaves and the loneliness of strangers, we are to project ourselves into their souls and make their plight our own.[17]

He notes that in thirty-six places in the Torah we are commanded not to mistreat the stranger in our midst.[18] In Jewish numerology, the number thirty-six is associated with righteousness, and the Talmud states that there are never less than thirty-six *tzaddikim* (righteous individuals) in the world.[19]

3. Giving Charity (*Tzedakah*)

Judaism places great stress on the giving of charity to help the poor and hungry. The Hebrew word for charity (*tzedakah*) literally means justice. In the Jewish tradition, *tzedakah* is not an act of condescension from one person to another who is in need. It is the fulfillment of a *mitzvah* (commandment) toward a fellow human being, who has equal status before God. Although Jewish tradition recognizes that the sharing of our resources is also an act of love—as the Torah states, "Love your neighbor as yourself" (Leviticus 19:18)—it emphasizes that this act of sharing is an act of justice. This is to teach that we are obligated to assist people in need. They too are human beings created in the Divine image; they too have a place and a purpose within God's creation.

In the Jewish tradition, failure to give charity is equivalent to idolatry.[20] This may be because a selfish person forgets the One Who created us all, and, in becoming preoccupied with personal material needs, makes himself or herself into an idol. So important is the giving of charity by Jews that Maimonides could say: "Never have I seen or heard of a Jewish community that did not have a charity fund."[21]

Charity was considered so important that it took priority even over the building of the Holy Temple. King Solomon was prohibited from using the silver and gold that David, his father, had accumulated for the building of the Temple, because that wealth should have been used to feed the poor during the three years of famine in King David's reign (I Kings 7:51).

Judaism urges lending to needy people, to help them become economically self-sufficient:

> And if your brother becomes impoverished, and his means fail in your proximity; then you shall strengthen him....Take no interest of him or increase....You shall not give him your money upon interest....(Leviticus 25:35–37)

Every third year of the sabbatical cycle, the needy were to be recipients of the tithe for the poor (one-tenth of one's income) (Deuteronomy 14:28;

26:12). The general Jewish view about aiding the poor is indicated in the following Torah verse :

> If there be among you a needy man, one of your brethren, within any of your gates, in your land which the Lord your God gives you, you shall not harden your heart, nor shut your hand from your needy brother; but you shall surely open your hand unto him, and shall surely lend him sufficient for his need. (Deuteronomy 15: 7–8)

According to Maimonides, the highest form of *tzedakah* is to prevent a person from becoming poor by providing a loan, a gift, or a job to enable him to adequately support himself.[22] Consistent with this concept is the following Talmudic teaching: "It is better to lend to a poor person than to give him alms, and best of all is to provide him with capital for business."[23]

4. Reducing Poverty

Judaism places emphasis on charity because of the great difficulties that poor people face: "If all afflictions in the world were assembled on one side of the scale and poverty on the other, poverty would outweigh them all."[24] Judaism believes that poverty is destructive to the human personality and negatively shapes a person's life experiences: "The ruin of the poor is their poverty" (Proverbs 10:15). "Where there is no sustenance, there is no learning."[25] "The world is darkened for him who has to look to others for sustenance."[26] "The sufferings of poverty cause a person to disregard his own sense [of right] and that of his Maker."[27] Judaism generally does not encourage an ascetic life. Insufficiency of basic necessities does not ease the path toward holiness.[28]

Many Torah laws are designed to aid the poor: the corners of the field are to be left uncut for the poor to pick (Leviticus 19:9); the gleanings of the wheat harvest and fallen fruit are to be left for the needy (Leviticus 19:10); during the sabbatical year, the land is to be left fallow so that the poor (as well as animals) may eat of whatever grows freely (Leviticus 25:2–7). Failure to treat the poor properly is a desecration of God's name:

"The person who mocks the poor blasphemes his Maker" (Proverbs 17:5). The patriarch Abraham always went out of his way to aid the poor. He set up inns on the highways so that the poor and the wayfarer would have access to food and drink when in need.[29]

God sides with the poor and oppressed. He intervenes in Egypt on behalf of poor, wretched slaves. His prophets constantly castigate those who oppress the needy. Two proverbs reinforce this message: "He who oppresses a poor man insults his Maker" (Proverbs 14:31). "He who is kind to the poor lends to the Lord" (Proverbs 19:17). Hence, helping a needy person is like providing a loan to the Creator of the universe.

5. Applying Compassion

Closely related to the Jewish values of justice and charity is the importance Judaism places on compassion. The entire Torah is designed to teach us to be compassionate: "The purpose of the laws of the Torah is to promote compassion, loving kindness, and peace in the world."[30] The Talmud teaches that "Jews are compassionate children of compassionate parents, and one who shows no pity for fellow creatures is not of the seed of Abraham, our father."[31] The rabbis consider Jews to be distinguished by three characteristics: compassion, modesty, and benevolence.[32] As indicated previously, we are to feel empathy for strangers, "for we were strangers in the land of Egypt" (Deuteronomy 10:19). The Birkat Hamazon (grace after meals) speaks of God feeding the whole world with compassion.

While in Egypt, Joseph had two sons during the seven good years of abundant food, but no children during the seven years of famine. The great Torah commentator Rashi interpreted this to mean that while some people are starving, others who have enough should engage in acts of self-denial to show compassion and sympathy.[33] We are not only to have concern and compassion for Jews, but for all who are in need. "Have we not all one Father? Has not one God created us? Why, then, do we deal treacherously with one another, profaning the covenant of our ancestors?" (Malachi 2:10) As indicated previously, we are to help even our enemies when they lack sufficient food or water (Proverbs 25:21).

Rabbi Samson Raphael Hirsch writes eloquently of the importance of compassion:

> Do not suppress this compassion, this sympathy, especially with the sufferings of your fellow man. It is the warning voice of duty, which points out to you your brother in every sufferer, and your own sufferings in his, and awakens the love which tells you that you belong to him and his sufferings with all the powers that you have. Do not suppress it!...See in it the admonition of God that you are to have no joy so long as a brother suffers by your side.[34]

6. Sharing

Compassion for the poor and hungry is not enough. A fundamental Jewish principle is that those who have much should share with others who are less fortunate. The Talmudic sage Hillel stresses that we must not be concerned only with our own welfare: "If I am not for myself, who will be for me? But if I am for myself alone, what am I?"[35] The *Haggadah*, which is read at the Passover *seder*, exhorts the sharing of food. We are to reach out to all who are hungry and in need. The act of prolonging one's meal, on the chance that a poor person may come so that one may give him food, is so meritorious that the table of the person who does this is compared to the altar of the ancient Temple.[36] Judaism's great emphasis on sharing is also illustrated in the following Chassidic tale:

> The story is told of a great rabbi who is given the privilege of seeing the realms of Heaven and Hell before his death. He was taken first to Hell, where he was confronted with a huge banquet room in the middle of which was a large elegant table covered with a magnificent tablecloth and crystal. The table was covered from one end to the other with the most delicious foods that the eyes have ever seen or the mouth tasted. And all around the table, people were sitting looking at the food...and wailing.
>
> It was such a wail that the rabbi had never heard such a sad sound in his entire life and he asked, "With a luxurious table and

the most delicious food, why do these people wail so bitterly?" As he entered the room, he saw the reason for their distress. For although each was confronted with this incredible sight before him, no one was able to eat the food. Each person's arms were splinted so that the elbows could not bend. They could touch the food but could not eat it. The anguish this caused was the reason for the great wail and despair that the rabbi saw and heard.

He was next shown Heaven, and to his surprise he was confronted by the identical scene witnessed in Hell: the large banquet room, elegant table, lavish settings, and sumptuous foods. And, in addition, once again everyone's arms were splinted so the elbows could not bend. Here, however, there was no wailing, but rather joy greater than he had ever experienced in his life. For whereas here too the people could not put the food into their own mouths, each picked up the food and fed it to another. They were thus able to enjoy, not only the beautiful scene, the wonderful smells, and the delicious foods, but the joy of sharing and helping one another.[37]

Rabbi Jay Marcus of the Young Israel of Staten Island comments on the fact that *karpas* (eating of greens) and *yahatz* (breaking of the middle matzah for later use as the dessert) are next to each other in the Passover *seder* service.[38] He suggests that those who can live on simple things like greens (vegetables, etc.) will more readily divide their possessions and share with others.

To help share God's abundant harvests with the poor, the Torah instructs farmers:

- If less than three ears of corn are dropped during the harvest, they must not be gleaned, but are to be left for the poor (*Leket*) [Leviticus 19:9–10].
- A sheaf forgotten by the farmer cannot be retrieved but has to be left for the poor (*Shik'khah*) [Deuteronomy 24:19–21].
- A corner of the field always has to be left unharvested; it is the property of the poor (*Pe'ah*) [Leviticus 19:9–10].

- Every third year a part of the tithe of the harvest has to be set aside for the poor (Ma'aser Ani).
- On the eve of every holy day, mat'not Yad, a special gift to the poor, has to be put aside.

Vegetarianism is consistent with this Jewish concept of sharing. As Jay Dinshah, late long-time president of the American Vegan Society, said:

> After all, vegetarianism is, more than anything else, the very essence and the very expression of altruistic *sharing*...the sharing of the One Life...the sharing of the natural resources of the Earth...the sharing of love, kindness, compassion, and beauty in this life.[39]

The Jewish group Mazon attempts to help Jews share their joyous occasions with hungry people. It urges people to contribute three percent of the money spent for weddings, bar mitzvahs, and other celebrations to the group, which then funnels the money to organizations working to reduce hunger.

7. Simplifying Lifestyles

While millions starve, it is imperative that those who have much simplify their lives, so they can share more with others. A group of outstanding religious leaders, including several Jewish representatives from the United States and Israel, met in Bellagio, Italy, in May 1975 to consider "The Energy/Food Crisis: A Challenge to Peace, a Call to Faith." They agreed on a statement that includes this assertion:

> The deepest and strongest expression of any religion is the "styles of life" that characterize its believers. It is urgent that religious communities and individuals scrutinize their life style and turn from habits of waste, over consumption, and thoughtless acceptance of the standards propagated by advertisements and social pressures. The cry from millions for food brought us together

from many faiths. God...calls us to respond to the cry for food. And we hear it as a cry not only for aid but also for justice.[40]

Simpler lifestyles, with less wasteful diets, can be an important first step toward justice for the hungry of the world. Simpler diets do not imply a lack of joy or a lack of fellowship. As Proverbs 15:17 states: "Better a dinner of herbs with love than a fattened ox with hatred."

During the Middle Ages, local Jewish councils sometimes established "sumptuary laws" for the community. People were forbidden to spend more than a specified amount of money at weddings and other occasions. These laws were designed so that the poor should not be embarrassed at not being able to match the expenditures of the wealthy, and so that a financial strain was not placed on the community as a whole. Perhaps the spirit of such laws should be invoked today. (Actually, several Chassidic communities currently have such regulations.) Can we continue to consume flesh that requires so much grain to be fed to animals at a time when millions of people are starving? Is it time for officiating rabbis to suggest guidelines to reduce waste and ostentation at weddings, bar mitzvahs, and other occasions?

Realities of Animal-Based Agriculture

Can a shift to a vegetarian diet make a difference with regard to world hunger? Consider these statistics:

1. Today, over seventy percent of the grain produced in the United States and over one-third of the world's grain production is fed to animals destined for slaughter.[41]

2. It takes about nine pounds of grain to produce one pound of feedlot beef.[42]

3. While the average Asian consumes between 300 and 400 pounds of grain a year, the average middle-class American consumes over 2,000 pounds, mostly by eating meat from grain-fed animals.[43]

4. While fifty-six million acres of U.S. land are producing hay for livestock, only four million acres of U.S. land are producing vegetables for human consumption.[44]

5. While 2.5 acres of land growing potatoes can feed twenty-two people, and one hectare growing rice can feed nine people, that same area producing beef can only feed one person.[45]

6. If Americans reduced their beef consumption by ten percent, it would free up ten million tons of grain, enough to feed all of the world's people who annually die of hunger and related diseases.[46]

7. U.S. livestock consume over six and a half times as much grain as the U.S. human population does. According to the Council for Agricultural Science and Technology, an Iowa-based non-profit research group, the grain fed to animals to produce meat, milk, and eggs could feed five times the number of people that it presently does if it were consumed directly by humans.[47]

8. Feeding grain to livestock wastes ninety percent of the protein, almost 100 percent of the carbohydrates, and 100 percent of the fiber. While grains are a rich source of fiber, animal products have no fiber at all.[48]

Additional facts related to the wastefulness of animal-centered diets are discussed in Chapter 5, and can be also be found in many of the vegetarian books in the Bibliography, especially *Diet for a Small Planet* by Frances Moore Lappé, *Beyond Beef* by Jeremy Rifkin, *Diet for a New America* by John Robbins, and *A Vegetarian Sourcebook* by Keith Akers.

These facts indicate that the food being fed to animals in the affluent nations could, if properly distributed, end both hunger and malnutrition throughout the world. A switch from animal-centered diets would free up land and other resources, which could then be used to grow nutritious crops for people. It would also be necessary to promote policies that would enable people in the underdeveloped countries to use their resources and skills to become food self-reliant.

With so much hunger in the world, explicit Jewish mandates to feed the hungry, help the poor, share resources, practice charity, show compassion, and pursue justice, plus the trials and tribulations of Jewish history, point to vegetarianism as the diet most consistent with Jewish teachings related to helping hungry people.

5: JUDAISM, VEGETARIANISM, AND ECOLOGY

THERE ARE MANY FUNDAMENTAL TORAH PRINCIPLES that express and make concrete the biblical concept: "The earth is the Lord's and the fullness thereof" (Psalms 24:1).

1. People are to be co-workers with God in helping to preserve and improve the world.

The Talmudic sages assert that the role of humanity is to enhance the world as "co-partners of God in the work of creation."[1] There is a *midrash* that beautifully expresses the idea that God needs people to help tend the world:

In the hour when the Holy one, blessed be He,
  created the first human being,
He took him and let him pass before all the trees of
  the Garden of Eden and said to him:
"See my works, how fine and excellent they are!
Now all that I have created, for you have I created them.
Think upon this and do not corrupt and desolate My World,
For if you corrupt it, there is no one to set it right after you."[2]

The Psalmist also expresses the idea that God, the Creator, treats every person as a partner in the work of creation:

When I look at Your heavens, the work of Your hands,
The moon and work which you have established,
What is man that You are mindful of him, and the son of
  man that You do care for him?
Yet You have made him little less than God, and do crown

79

him with glory and honor.
You have given him dominion over the works of Your hands;
You have put all things under his feet....(Psalms 8:4–7)

The Talmudic sages indicate great concern about preserving the environment and preventing pollution. They state: "It is forbidden to live in a town which has no garden or greenery."[3] Threshing floors were to be placed far enough from a town so that the town would not be polluted by chaff carried by winds.[4] Tanneries are to be kept at least fifty cubits (a cubit is about half a meter) from a town and are to be placed only on the east side of a town, so that odors and pollution would not be carried toward the town by the prevailing winds from the west.[5]

2. Everything belongs to God. We are to be stewards of the earth, to see that its produce is available for all God's children.

There seems to be a contradiction between two verses in the Psalms: "The earth is the Lord's" (Psalms 24:1) and "The heavens are the heavens of God, but the earth He has given to human beings" (Psalms 115:16). The apparent discrepancy is cleared up in the following way: Before a person says a *bracha* (a blessing), before he acknowledges God's ownership of the land and its products, then "the earth is the Lord's"; after a person has said a *bracha*, acknowledging God's ownership and that we are stewards to see that God's works are properly used and shared, then "the earth He has given to human beings."[6]

Property is a sacred trust given by God; it must be used to fulfill God's purposes. No person has absolute or exclusive control over his or her possessions. The concept that people have custodial care of the earth, as opposed to ownership, is illustrated by the following ancient Jewish story:

Two men were fighting over a piece of land. Each claimed ownership and bolstered his claim with apparent proof. To resolve their differences, they agreed to put the case before the rabbi. The rabbi listened but could come to no decision because both seemed to be right. Finally he said, "Since I cannot decide to whom this land belongs, let us ask the land." He put his ear to the ground and, after a moment, straightened up. "Gentlemen, the land says it belongs to neither of you, but that you belong to it."[7]

As indicated previously, even the produce of the field does not belong solely to the person who farms the land. The poor are entitled to a portion:

And when you reap the harvest of your land, you shall not wholly reap the corner of your field, neither shall you gather the gleaning of your harvest. And you shall not glean your vineyard, neither shall you gather the fallen fruit of your vineyard; you shall leave them for the poor and for the stranger; I am the Lord, your God. (Leviticus 19:9–10)

These portions set aside for the poor were not voluntary contributions based on kindness. They were, in essence, a regular divine assessment. Because God is the real owner of the land, He claims a share of His own gifts for the poor.

As a reminder that "the earth is the Lord's," the land must be permitted to rest and lie fallow every seven years (the Sabbatical Year):

And six years you shall sow your land, and gather in the increase thereof, but the seventh year you shall let it rest and lay fallow, that the poor of your people may eat; and what they leave, the animals of the field shall eat. In like manner you shall deal with your vineyard, and with your olive yard. (Exodus 23:10–11)

The Sabbatical Year also has ecological benefits. The land was given a chance to rest and renew its fertility.

Judaism asserts that there is one God who created the entire earth as a unit, in ecological balance, and that everything is connected to everything else. This idea is expressed beautifully in Psalm 104:

...You [God] are the One Who sends forth springs into

brooks, that they may run between mountains,
To give drink to every animal of the fields; the creatures
    of the forest quench their thirst.
Beside them dwell the fowl of the heavens;...
You water the mountains from Your upper chambers,...
You cause the grass to spring up for the cattle,
    and herb, for the service of humans, to bring forth
    bread from the earth....
How manifold are your works, O Lord! In wisdom You have
    made them all; the earth is full of Your property....

3. We are not to waste or unnecessarily destroy anything of value.
This prohibition, called *bal tashchit*, is based on the following Torah
statement:

> When you besiege a city a long time, in making war against it to
> take it, you shall not destroy (*lo tashchit*) the trees thereof by
> wielding an ax against them; for you may eat of them but you shall
> not cut them down; for is the tree of the field man, that it should
> be besieged by you? Only the trees of which you know that they
> are not trees for food, them you may destroy and cut down, that
> you may build bulwarks against the city that makes war with you,
> until it fall. (Deuteronomy 20:19–20)

This prohibition against destroying fruit-bearing trees in time of warfare
was extended by the sages. It is forbidden to cut down even a barren tree
or to waste anything if no useful purpose is accomplished.[8] The Talmud
makes a general prohibition against waste: "Whoever breaks vessels or
tears garments, or destroys a building, or clogs up a fountain, or destroys
food violates the prohibition of *bal tashchit*."[9] In summary, *bal tashchit*
prohibits the destruction, complete or incomplete, direct or indirect, of all
objects of potential benefit to people. The seriousness with which the
rabbis consider the violation of *bal tashchit* is illustrated by the following
Talmudic statements:

The sage Rabbi Hanina attributed the early death of his son to the fact that the boy had chopped down a fig tree.[10]

Jews should be taught when very young that it is a sin to waste even small amounts of food.[11]

Rav Zutra taught: "One who covers an oil lamp or uncovers a naptha lamp transgresses the prohibition of bal tashchit [because it causes the fuel to burn more wastefully]."[12]

Rabbi Hirsch says that bal tashchit is the first and most general call of God: We are to "regard things as God's property and use them with a sense of responsibility for wise human purposes. Destroy nothing! Waste nothing!"[13] He states that destruction includes using more things (or things of greater value) than is necessary to obtain one's aim.[14] The following midrash is related to this concept:

Two men entered a shop. One ate coarse bread and vegetables, while the other ate fine bread, fat meat, and drank old wine. The one who ate fine food suffered harm, while the one who had coarse food escaped harm. Observe how simply animals live and how healthy they are as a result.[15]

Ecology in Jewish History and Prayers

Much of early Jewish history is closely related to the natural environment. The Patriarchs and their descendants were shepherds. Their work led them into many types of natural settings, including mountains, prairies, wilderness, and deserts. They developed a love and appreciation of natural wonders and beauty. According to Charles W. Eliot, "No race has ever surpassed the Jewish descriptions of either the beauties or the terrors of the nature which environs man."[16] The greatest prophet, Moses, while a shepherd, learned many things about nature that were useful in leading the Israelites in the desert. The Ten Commandments and the Torah were revealed to the Jews at Mount Sinai, in a natural setting. The forty years of wandering in the wilderness trained Israel in the appreciation of natural beauty.

Jews have often pictured God through His handiwork in nature. Abraham, the father of the Jewish people, when marveling at the heavenly bodies, intuited that there must be a Creator of these wonders. The prophet Isaiah exclaims:

Lift up your eyes on high,
And see: Who has created these?
He that brings out their host by numbers,
He calls them all by name;
By the greatness of His might, for He is strong in power,
Not one fails. (Isaiah 40:26)

Many Jewish prayers extol God for His wondrous creations. In the morning, religious Jews say the following prayer to thank God for the new day:

Blessed are You, O Lord our God, King of the universe.
Who forms light and creates darkness,
Who makes peace and creates all things.
Who in mercy gives light to the earth
And to them who dwell thereon,
And in Your goodness renews the creation
Every day continually.
How manifold are Your works, O Lord!
In wisdom You have made them all;
The earth is full of Your possessions....
Be blessed, O Lord our God,
For the excellency of Your handiwork,
And for the bright luminaries
Which You have made:
They shall glorify You forever.

At the Sabbath morning services, the following prayer is recited: "The heavens declare the glory of God, and the firmament shows His handiwork" (Psalms 19:2).

The sensitivity of the Torah to environmental cleanliness is illustrated by the following law, which commands disposal of sewage, even in wartime, by burial in the ground, not by dumping into rivers or littering the countryside:

> You shall have a place outside the camp, when you shall go forth abroad. And you shall have a spade among your weapons; and it shall be when you sit down outside, you shall dig therewith, and shall turn back and cover that which comes from you. (Deuteronomy 23:13–14)

The preservation of the land of Israel has been a central theme in Judaism. The three pilgrimage festivals (*Pesach*, *Shavuot*, and *Sukkot*) are agricultural as well as spiritual celebrations. Jews pray for dew and rain in their proper time so that there will be abundant harvests in Israel. Jewish tradition prohibits abuse of natural resources and the environment.

Ecological Problems Related to Current Livestock Agriculture

Unfortunately, the wisdom of *bal tashchit* is seldom applied today. Our society is based on waste, on buying, using, and throwing away. Advertisements constantly try to make us feel guilty if we do not have the newest gadgets and the latest styles of clothing. Every national holiday in the United States has become an orgy of consumption.

Our animal-centered diets are extremely wasteful:

1. As stated in the previous chapter, the average person in the United States eats over five times as much grain (mostly in the form of animal products) as a person in an undeveloped country, it takes about nine pounds of grain and soybeans to produce one pound of feedlot beef for our plates, and over seventy percent of the grain grown in the United States is fed to farm animals. Perhaps the modern counterpart of destroying fruit-

bearing trees is taking grain which could feed starving people and feeding it to animals.

2. About 800 million acres (forty percent of U.S. land area) is devoted to livestock grazing, and an additional sixty million acres is used to grow grain for feeding livestock.[17] As indicated in the last chapter, land growing potatoes, rice, and other vegetables can support about twenty times as many people as land producing grain-fed beef.

3. The standard diet of a person in the United States requires 4,200 gallons of water per day (for animals' drinking water, irrigation of crops, processing, washing, cooking, etc.).[18] A person on a vegan diet requires only 300 gallons a day.[19]

4. Animal agriculture is the major consumer of water in the U.S. According to Norman Myers, author of *Gaia: An Atlas of Planet Management*, irrigation, primarily to grow crops for animals, uses over eighty percent of U.S. water.[20] Almost ninety percent of the fresh water consumed annually in the U.S. goes to agriculture, according to agronomist David Pimentel.[21] The production of only one pound of edible beef in a semi-arid area such as California requires as much as 5,200 gallons of water, as contrasted with only twenty-five gallons or less to produce an edible pound of tomatoes, lettuce, potatoes, or wheat.[22] *Newsweek* reported in 1988 that "the water that goes into a 1,000 pound steer would float a (Naval) destroyer."[23]

5. A non-vegetarian diet wastes much energy. In the United States, an average of ten calories of fuel energy are required for every calorie of food energy obtained; in many other countries, they consume twenty or more calories of food energy per calorie of fuel energy.[24] To produce one pound of steak (500 calories of food energy) requires 20,000 calories of fossil fuels, most of which is expended for feed crops.[25] It requires seventy-eight calories of fossil fuel for each calorie of protein obtained from feedlot-produced beef, but only two calories of fossil fuel to produce a calorie of protein from soybeans.[26] Grains and beans require only two to five percent as much fossil fuel as beef.[27] The energy needed to produce a pound of grain-fed beef is equivalent to one gallon of gasoline.[28]

6. According to a comprehensive study sponsored by the U.S. departments of Interior and Commerce, the value of raw materials consumed to produce food from livestock is greater than the value of all oil, gas, and coal produced in this country.[29] One third of the value of all raw materials consumed in the U.S. for all purposes is consumed in livestock foods.[30] As these facts indicate, a vegetarian diet is far less wasteful than an animal-centered diet and is therefore much more consistent with the principle of *bal tashchit*.

Modern agricultural methods related to meat production are a prime cause of the environmental crises facing the United States and much of the world today.

1. The tremendous quantity of grains grown to feed animals requires extensive use of chemical fertilizer and pesticides. Air and water pollution is caused by the production and use of these products. Various constituents of fertilizer, particularly nitrogen, are washed into surface waters. High levels of nitrates in drinking water have caused illnesses for people as well as animals. According to Norman Myers' *Gaia*, fertilizers and pesticides are responsible for over half of U. S. water pollution.[31]

2. Mountains of manure produced by cattle raised in feedlots wash into and pollute streams, rivers, and underground water sources. U.S. livestock produce an astounding 1.4 billion tons of wet manure per year (this amount works out to 89,000 pounds per second!), or about 130 times that of the U.S. human population.[32] Food geographer Georg Borgstrom estimates that American livestock contribute five times more organic waste to water pollution than do people, and twice as much as does industry.[33]

3. According to mathematician Robin Hur, nearly six billion of the seven billion tons of eroded soil in the United States is directly due to cattle and feedlot production.[34] David Pimentel has indicated that about ninety percent of U.S. cropland is losing soil at a rate at least thirteen times faster than the sustainable rate.[35] William Brune, a former Iowa State conservation official, has warned that two bushels of topsoil are being lost for every bushel of corn harvested in Iowa's sloping soils.[36] Lower yields are

occurring in many areas due to erosion and the reduction in fertility that it causes.[37]

4. Grazing animals have destroyed large areas of land throughout the world. Overgrazing has been a prime cause of erosion in various parts of the world throughout history. Over sixty percent of all U.S. range lands are overgrazed, with billions of tons of soil lost every year.[38] Cattle production is a prime contributor to all the causes of desertification: overgrazing of livestock, over-cultivation of land, improper irrigation techniques, deforestation, and prevention of reforestation.

5. The huge amounts of grain grown to feed animals require increasing amounts of pesticides. The amount of these synthetic poisons has increased by 400 percent since 1962 when Rachel Carson wrote *Silent Spring*, the book that so eloquently sounded the alarm about the dangers of pesticides to our health, to rivers, and wildlife.[39] Also, in a "circle of poison," pesticides banned or heavily restricted in the U.S. are legally exported to poor countries where they are sometimes used on foods imported into the U.S. Due to the increased biological accumulation of pesticides in the body fat of animals through movement up the food chain, people eating meat and other animal products ingest large amounts of pesticides.

6. In the U.S., more plant species have been eliminated due to overgrazing by livestock than through any other cause.[40]

7. Demand for meat in wealthy countries leads to environmental damage in poor countries. Largely to lower by a few pennies the price of a fast-food hamburger exported to the U.S., the earth's tropical rain forests are being bulldozed at a rate of a football field per second.[41] Each imported quarter-pound fast-food hamburger patty requires the destruction of fifty-five square feet of tropical forest for grazing.[42] Half of the rain forests are already gone forever and, at current rates of destruction, the rest will be gone by the middle of the next century. What makes this especially serious is that half of the world's species of plants and animals reside in tropical rain forests, some of which might hold secrets for cures of some of today's deadly diseases, such as cancer and AIDS; others might prove to be good sources of food. Also, the destruction of the rain forests is altering climate

and reducing rainfall, with potentially devastating effects on the world's agriculture.

8. Current livestock agriculture and the consumption of meat contribute significantly to the four major chemical compounds associated with potential global warming: carbon dioxide, methane, nitrous oxides, and chlorofluorocarbons. The burning of tropical forests to create pastureland and land to grow feed crops releases tons of carbon dioxide into the atmosphere, while eliminating trees which formerly were absorbing carbon dioxide. Also, the highly mechanized agricultural sector uses a significant amount of fossil fuel for energy and to produce pesticides, chemical fertilizer, and other agricultural resources. This also contributes to carbon dioxide emissions. Cattle emit methane as part of their digestive processes, as do termites who feast on the charred remains of trees. The large amounts of petrochemical fertilizers used to produce feed crops for grain-fed animals create significant amounts of nitrous oxides. Also, the increased refrigeration necessary to prevent animal products from spoiling adds chlorofluorocarbons to the atmosphere.

Global climate change is arguably the most critical problem the world will face in the coming decades. It threatens the destruction of our civilization and the survival of humanity. There is a growing scientific consensus that we are already experiencing the effects of global warming, and that human actions are playing a significant role.[43] Global average temperatures have increased about one degree Fahrenheit since 1900. The warmest decade in recorded history is the 1990s. The ten warmest years on record have all occurred since 1983, with seven of them since 1990. In 1998, global temperatures were the warmest in recorded history. A recent report indicated that average temperatures could increase anywhere from two to ten degrees Fahrenheit in the 21st century.

Researchers were uncertain until recently whether human activities contributed to the warming, or whether it reflected natural variations in the earth's climate. However, in the fall of 1995, scientists with the Intergovernmental Panel on Climate Change, the authoritative international group charged with studying this issue, concluded that the observed global temperature increase during the last century "is unlikely to be entirely natural in origin" and that "the balance of evidence suggests that there is a discernible human influence on human climate." These conclusions are in the panel's Second Assessment Report, a document that received contributions and peer review from over 2,500 of the world's leading climate scientists, economists, and risk analysis experts.

The main cause of this global warming has been the increase in atmospheric concentrations of heat trapping gases, including carbon dioxide, methane, nitrous oxides, and chlorofluorocarbons. These gases act as a "greenhouse" trapping heat radiated out from the earth. While a certain amount of these gases is natural and necessary to retain the right amount of the sun's energy to support life on earth, current excessive amounts cause more heat to be trapped, and this raises the earth's temperature. A world map that showed eighty-nine "Global Warming Early Warning Signs" was produced in 1999 by seven environmental groups, including the "Union of Concerned Scientists" (www.climatehotmap.org). The groups conclude that "the earth is heating up." They group the "early warning signs" into ten categories:

1. Heat waves and periods of unusually warm weather (frequent and severe heat waves lead to increases in heat related illness and death, especially in urban areas, and among the ill, the poor, the elderly, and the young).

2. Spreading disease (warmer temperatures allow disease-transmitting mosquitoes to extend their ranges).

3. Earlier spring arrival (this may disrupt animal migrations, alter competitive balances among species, and cause additional unforeseen problems).

4. Plant and animal range shifts and population declines (this can hasten extinctions).

5. Sea level rise and coastal flooding; global sea level has risen four to ten inches in the past 100 years and may rise an additional half a foot to three feet during the next 100 years, causing major losses of coastal areas.

6. Coral reef bleaching; reefs in thirty-two countries experienced major bleaching in 1997–98, and continued bleaching due to warmer sea temperatures and other factors is likely. Since these are the richest

environmental communities on earth (except for some tropical rain forest areas), this can have a major negative impact on aquatic life.

7. Glaciers melting (over the past 150 years, the majority of monitored mountain glaciers have been shrinking and many at low altitudes are disappearing. Continued shrinkage could disrupt an important source of water).

8. Arctic and Antarctic warming (as parts of Canada, Alaska, Siberia, and Antarctica have been experiencing warming well above the global average for the past few decades, melting permafrost requires the reconstruction of buildings, roads, and airports, and is increasing soil erosion and the frequency of landslides).

9. Downpours, heavy snowfalls, and flooding (heavy rainfall and other types of storms have been more frequent recently and this has substantially increased storm damage. It is significant that U.S. insurance companies have become major advocates of efforts to reduce global warming because of major payments they have had to make due to recent severe storms and flooding).

10. Droughts and fires (as temperatures increase, droughts have become more frequent and severe in many areas). In the summer of 2000, forest fires burned out of control for weeks throughout the western U.S. and destroyed six million acres.

When we consider all of the above negative environmental and climate-change effects, and then add the very harmful effects of animal-based diets and agriculture related to human health and global hunger, we can safely say that animal-centered diets and the livestock agriculture needed to sustain them pose tremendous threats to global survival. It is not surprising that the Union of Concerned Scientists ranks the consumption of meat and poultry as the second most harmful consumer activity (surpassed only by the use of cars and trucks).[44] Clearly, a shift toward vegetarianism is imperative to move our precious but imperiled planet away from its present catastrophic path. While an increased concern about global warming and other environmental threats is very welcome, the many connections between Western animal-centered diets and these threats are generally overlooked.

Jeremy Rifkin eloquently summarizes the very negative effects of animal-based agriculture:

> The ever-increasing cattle population is wreaking havoc on the earth's ecosystems, destroying habitats on six continents. Cattle raising is a primary factor in the destruction of the world's remaining tropical rain forests. Millions of acres of ancient forests in Central and South America are being felled and cleared to make room for pastureland to graze cattle. Cattle herding is responsible for much of the spreading desertification in the sub-Sahara of Africa and the western rangeland of the United States and Australia. The overgrazing of semiarid and arid lands has left parched and barren deserts on four continents. Organic runoffs from feedlots is now a major source of organic pollution in our nation's ground water. Cattle are also a major cause of global warming....The devastating environmental, economic, and human toll of maintaining a worldwide cattle complex is little discussed in public policy circles....Yet, cattle production and beef consumption now rank among the gravest threats to the future well-being of the earth and its human population.[45]

The Vegetarian Imperative

When God created the world, He was able to say it was very good (Genesis 1:31). Everything was in harmony as God had planned: the waters were clean, the air was pure. But what must God think about the world today? What must God think when the rain He provides to nourish our crops is often acidic due to the many chemicals emitted into the air by industries; when the ozone layer is being rapidly depleted; when the abundance of species of plants and animals are becoming extinct at so rapid a rate that we are not even able to catalog them; when the fertile soil is rapidly being depleted and eroded; when the climatic conditions He designed to meet our needs are threatened by global warming?

Today's environmental threats can be compared in many ways to the biblical ten plagues, which appear in the Torah portions read in the weeks immediately preceding the ecological holiday of *Tu B'Shvot*. However, today's plagues are even more devastating:

1. We can easily enumerate ten modern "plagues," including threats to our land, water, and air; pesticides and other chemical pollutants; resource scarcities; threats to our climate; etc.

2. The Egyptians were subjected to one plague at a time, while the modern plagues are threatening us all at once.

3. The Jews in Goshen were spared most of the biblical plagues, while every person on earth is imperiled by the modern plagues.

4. Instead of an ancient Pharoah's heart being hardened, our hearts today have been hardened by the greed, materialism, and waste that are at the root of current environmental threats.

5. God brought the biblical plagues to free the Israelites, while today we must apply God's teachings in order to save ourselves and our endangered planet.

In 1993, over 1,670 scientists, including 104 Nobel laureates—a majority of the living recipients of the prize in the sciences—signed a "World Scientists' Warning To Humanity."[46] Their introduction stated:

Human beings and the natural world are on a collision course. Human activities inflict harsh and often irreversible damage on the environment and on critical resources. If not checked, many of our current practices put at serious risk the future that we wish for human society and the plant and animal kingdoms, and may so alter the living world that it will be unable to sustain life in the manner that we know. Fundamental changes are urgent if we are to avoid the collision our present course will bring about.

The scientists' analysis discussed threats to the atmosphere, water resources, oceans, soil, living species, and forests. Their warning:

We the undersigned, senior members of the world's scientific community, hereby warn all humanity of what lies ahead. A great change in our stewardship of the earth and the life on it is required, if vast human misery is to be avoided and our global home on this planet is not to be irretrievably mutilated.

Vegetarianism is an essential component of the changes necessary to reduce global environmental threats. A shift to plant-based diets would greatly simplify agricultural practices and would put far less stress on the environment. Land presently used to grow feed crops could be used to grow food for hungry people and could even be permitted to lay fallow periodically, thus enabling it to restore its fertility. Far fewer chemical fertilizers and pesticides would be necessary. There would be far less demand for scarce water, fuel, and other resources. Giant feedlots, which result in much animal manure washing into streams and rivers, could be converted to more ecologically sound uses. It would no longer be necessary to destroy tropical forests and other habitats in order to create grazing land and to grow feed crops for livestock.

The aims of vegetarians and ecologists are similar: simplify our life styles, have regard for the earth and all forms of life, and thereby apply the knowledge that "the earth is the Lord's." In view of the many negative effects that animal-based agriculture has on the earth's environment, resources, and climate, it is becoming increasingly clear that a shift toward a vegetarian diet is a planetary imperative.

6: JUDAISM, VEGETARIANISM, AND PEACE

Seek peace and pursue it. (Psalms 34:15)

OUR AGE IS CONTINUOUSLY THREATENED BY VIOLENCE, war, and the potential for war. The application of Jewish teachings related to peace and vegetarianism can help to reduce these threats, since Judaism mandates a special obligation to work for peace. The tradition does not command that people merely love peace or merely seek peace but that they actively pursue peace. The Midrash states that there are many commandments that require a certain time and place for their performance, but with regard to peace, we are to "seek peace and pursue it" (Psalms 34:15); we are to seek it in our own place and pursue it everywhere else.[1] The famous Talmudic sage, Hillel, states: "Be of the disciples of Aaron, loving peace and pursuing peace."[2] On the special duty of Jews to work for peace, the sages comment: "Said the Holy One, blessed be He: 'The whole Torah is peace and to whom do I give it? To the nation which loves peace!' "[3] The Midrash uses lavish words of praise to indicate the significance of peace:

> Great is peace, for God's name is peace....Great is peace, for it encompasses all blessings....Great is peace, for even in times of war, peace must be sought....Great is peace, seeing that when the Messiah is to come, He will commence with peace, as it is said, "How beautiful upon the mountains are the feet of the messenger of good tidings, who announces peace" (Isaiah 52:7).[4]

The whole Torah was given for the sake of peace, and it is said, "all her paths are peace" (Proverbs 3:17).[5] The important Jewish prayers, such as the *Amidah* (*Sh'moneh Esrei*), the *kaddish*, the Priestly Blessing, and *Birkat Hamazon*, all conclude with a prayer for peace. In spite of Judaism's adamant opposition to idolatry, peace is so important that the rabbis taught that If Israel should worship idols, but she be at peace, God had no power, in effect, over her.[6]

The Jewish tradition does not mandate absolute pacifism, or peace at any price. The Israelites often went forth to battle and not always in defensive wars. But they always upheld the ideal of universal peace, and yearned for the day when there would be no more bloodshed or violence:

> And they shall beat their swords into plowshares,
> And their spears into pruning hooks;
> Nation shall not lift up sword against nation,
> Neither shall they learn war any more. (Isaiah 2:4);

> But they shall sit every man under his vine and under his fig tree;
> And none shall make them afraid;
> For the mouth of the Lord of hosts has spoken. (Micah 4:3–4)

Judaism teaches that violence and war result directly from injustice:

> The sword comes into the world because of justice delayed, because of justice perverted, and because of those who render wrong decisions (in matters of Torah law).[7]

The Hebrew word for war, *milchama*, is directly derived from the word *locham*, which means both "to feed" as well as "to wage war."[8] The Hebrew word for bread, *lechem*, comes from the same root. This led the sages to suggest that lack of bread and the search for sufficient food tempt people to make war. The seeds of war are often found in the inability of a nation to provide adequate food for its people. Hence, feeding tremendous amounts of grain to animals destined for slaughter, instead of feeding hungry people, can increase the potential for war.

Links Between Animal-Centered Diets and Violence Among People
1. Jewish Views

Many Jewish sages felt that the biblical laws related to kindness to animals were meant to condition people to treat fellow human beings kindly. Several medieval Jewish philosophers including Rabbi Don Isaac Abarbanel (1437–1509) and Rabbi Joseph Albo consider vegetarianism to be a moral ideal because it avoids the cruelty associated with meat consumption.[9] Commenting on the biblical prohibition against taking a mother bird with her young, Nachmanides states: "The motivating purpose is to teach us the quality of compassion and not to become cruel; for cruelty expands in a man's soul, as is well known with respect to butchers."[10] Maimonides indicates that the general obligation with regard to *tsa'ar ba'alei chayim* "is set down with a view to protecting us that we not acquire moral habits of cruelty and learn to inflict pain gratuitously, but that we should be kind and merciful."[11]

The *Sefer Ha-chinuch* connects the muzzling of an ox treading corn to the negative treatment of human laborers:

> When a man becomes accustomed to have pity even upon animals who were created to serve us, and he gives them a portion of their labors, his soul will likewise grow accustomed to be kind to human beings.[12]

Rabbis Moses Luzzato (1707–1747), Abraham Ibn Ezra, and Don Isaac Abarbanel all taught that boiling a kid in its mother's milk is a barbaric practice that could lead people to cruel acts.[13]

Rabbi Samson Raphael Hirsch stresses that vegetables are the preferable food to help make the human body an instrument of the soul and to implement its aims of holiness and moral freedom.[14] He says that every food which makes the body too active in a carnal direction makes people more indifferent and less sensitive to the loftier impulses of the moral life.[15] He adds: "The boy who, in crude joy, finds delight in the convulsions of an injured beetle or the anxiety of a suffering animal will soon also be dumb toward human pain."[16] Many serial killers and other violent criminals were cruel to animals when they were children. Albert Einstein stated: "The vegetarian manner of living, by its purely physical effect on the human temperament, would most beneficially influence the lot of mankind."[17]

The prophet Isaiah (66:3) says, "He who kills an ox is as if he slew a person." In its original context, this refers to insincere sacrifice. However, there are several ways of interpreting this verse from a vegetarian point of view—beyond the obvious one that it is wrong to kill an animal or a person unnecessarily:

1. By eating animals, we are consuming the grain that fattened the animal; this grain could have been used to save human lives.

2. In poor countries, the ox helps farmers to plow the earth and grow food. Hence the killing of an ox leads to less production of food and hence more starvation.

3. When a person is ready to kill an animal for his pleasure or profit, he may be more likely to kill another human being.

2. Non-Jewish Views

Many people relate the cruelty involved in slaughtering animals for food to cruelty to people and eventually to war. G. S. Arundale, late president of the Theosophical Society, discussed the relationship between the treatment of animals and war:

> Whenever I see a meat- and fish-laden dining table, I know that I am looking upon one of the seeds of war and hatred—a seed that develops into an ugly weed of atrocity....When people ask me, "Is there likely to be a future war?" I answer, "Yes, until the animals are treated as our younger brothers."[18]

The relationship between the consumption of meat and war is dramatized by the following dialogue from Plato's *Republic*:

> ...and there will be animals of many other kinds, if people eat them?

Certainly.

And living in this way we shall have much greater need of physicians than before?

Much greater.

And the country which was enough to support the original inhabitants will be too small now, and not enough?

Quite true.

Then a slice of our neighbors' land will be wanted by us for pasture and tillage, and they will want a slice of ours, if, like ourselves, they exceed the limit of necessity, and give themselves up to the unlimited accumulation of wealth?

That, Socrates, will be inevitable.

And so, we shall go to war, Glaucon. Shall we not?

Most certainly, he replied.[19]

As the following poem, "Song of Peace," indicates, the vegetarian writer George Bernard Shaw felt that the killing of animals today logically leads to the killing of men on the battlefield tomorrow:

We are the living graves of murdered beasts,
Slaughtered to satisfy our appetites,
We never pause to wonder at our feasts,
If animals like men, can possibly have rights.
We pray on Sundays that we may have light,
To guide our foot-steps on the paths we tread,
We're sick of war, we do not want to fight,
The thought of it now fills our heart with dread,
And yet we gorge ourselves upon the dead.
Like carrion crows, we live and feed on meat,
Regardless of the suffering and pain
We cause by doing so. If thus we treat
Defenseless animals, for sport or gain,
How can we hope in this world to attain
The *peace* we say we are so anxious for?

We pray for it, o'er hecatombs of slain,
To God, while outraging the moral law,
Thus cruelty begets its offspring—War.[20]

U Nu, former prime minister of Burma, stated:

World peace, or any other kind of peace, depends greatly on the attitude of the mind. Vegetarianism can bring about the right mental attitude for peace. In this world of lusts and hatred, greed and anger, force and violence, vegetarianism holds forth a way of life which, if practiced universally, can lead to a better, juster, and more peaceful community of nations.[21]

Conclusion

In view of the enormous waste of grain and other resources related to livestock agriculture, the following statement by former Senator Mark Hatfield of Oregon is relevant:

Hunger and famine will do more to destabilize this world; [they are] more explosive than all atomic weaponry possessed by the big powers. Desperate people do desperate things....Nuclear fission is now in the hands of even the developing countries in many of which hunger and famine are most serious.[22]

Richard J. Barnet, a former director of the Washington-based Institute for Policy Studies and author of *The Lean Years*, an analysis of resource scarcities, believes that the anger and despair of hungry people could lead to acts of terrorism and economic class wars.[23] Jeremy Rifkin writes:

Feeding grain to cattle and other livestock while people starve has triggered bitter political struggles in developing countries and political strife between northern industrial nations and the poor nations of the southern hemisphere.[24]

Just as scarcity of food can lead to war, so can scarcity of sources of energy. A major current threat to peace is the affluent countries' need to obtain sufficient oil to keep their economies running smoothly. Since much of the world's oil is produced in the Persian Gulf area, in 1990, after Iraq invaded Kuwait and threatened Saudi Arabia, and hence Western oil supplies, the U.S. led a broad coalition against Iraq.

Animal-centered diets contribute to potential energy shortages. Producing food for factory-bred animals rather than directly for people requires far more irrigation, fertilizer, pesticides, mechanization, refrigeration, and processing, all of which consume considerable energy. It takes more than eight times as much fossil fuel energy to produce animal protein than for the production of a comparable amount of plant protein.[25] Several other examples of the large amounts of energy required for producing food with intensive animal-based agriculture were given in the previous chapter.

Judaism emphasizes the pursuit of justice and harmonious relations between nations to reduce violence and the prospects for war. The prophet Isaiah declares:

And the work of righteousness shall be peace; And the
effect of righteousness quietness and confidence forever.
(Isaiah 32:17)

There are many causes for war and violence, and it would be simplistic to suggest that a shift toward vegetarianism, by itself, would eliminate all conflicts. However, by adopting a diet that shows concern and loving kindness for the hungry people of the world as well as for abused, innocent animals, and by working for righteousness through more equitable sharing of God's abundant harvests, we can play a significant role in helping to move the world toward that day when "nations shall not learn war any more."

7: QUESTIONS & ANSWERS: JEWISH ISSUES

I keep six honest serving men,
They taught me all I knew;
Their names are what, and why, and when,
And where, and how, and who.
(Rudyard Kipling)

1 DON'T JEWS HAVE TO EAT MEAT TO HONOR THE
Sabbath and to rejoice on Jewish holidays?
Rabbi Yehuda Ben Batheira, the Talmudic sage, states that the
obligation to eat meat for rejoicing only applied at the time when the Holy
Temple was in existence.[1] He adds that after the destruction of the Temple
one can rejoice with wine. Based on this, Rabbi Yishmael states, "From the
day the Holy Temple was destroyed, it would have been right to have
imposed upon ourselves a law prohibiting the eating of flesh."[2] The reason
that the rabbis did not make such a law was that they felt that most Jews
were not ready to accept such a prohibition.[3]

Other sources who maintain that it is no longer necessary to eat meat
on festivals are Ritva, *Kiddushin 36* and *Teshuvot Rashbash*, No. 176.[4] In a
scholarly article in *The Journal of Halacha and Contemporary Society* (Fall
1981), Rabbi Alfred Cohen, the publication's editor, concludes: "If a
person is more comfortable not eating meat, there would be no obligation
for him to do so on the Sabbath" and "we may clearly infer that eating
meat, even on a Festival, is not mandated by the *Halacha* [Jewish law]."[5] He
also points out that "the *Shulchan Aruch*, which is the foundation for
normative law for Jews today, does not insist upon the necessity to eat meat
as *simchat Yom Tov* (making the holiday joyful)."[6]

In a *responsum* (an answer to a question based on Jewish law) Rabbi
Moshe Halevi Steinberg of Kiryat Yam, Israel, argues: "One whose soul
rebels against eating living things can without any doubt fulfill the
commandment of enhancing the Sabbath and rejoicing on festivals by
eating vegetarian foods....Each person should delight in the Sabbath

according to his own sensibility, enjoyment, and outlook."[7] In the same *responsum*, Rabbi Steinberg points out that there is no barrier or impediment to converting a non-Jew who is a vegetarian, since vegetarianism in no sense contradicts Jewish law.

Can sensitive, compassionate people enhance a joyous occasion by eating meat if they are aware that, for their eating pleasure, animals are cruelly treated, huge amounts of grain are fed to animals while millions of people starve, the environment is negatively affected, and their own health is being harmed?

All of the above is reinforced by the fact that there are chief rabbis, including Rabbi Shear Yashuv Cohen, Ashkenazi Chief Rabbi of Haifa, and Rabbi David Rosen, former Chief Rabbi of Ireland, who are strict vegetarians, including on Shabbat and *Yom Tov*. The late Rabbi Shlomo Goren, former Ashkenazi Chief Rabbi of Israel, was also a strict vegetarian.

2. If Jews don't eat meat, won't they be deprived of the opportunity to do many *mitzvot* (commandments)? If God did not want meat to be eaten, why are there so many laws concerning the slaughter, preparation, and consumption of meat?

As indicated previously, Rav Kook indicates that God provided many laws and regulations related to the consumption of meat as a reprimand, as a reminder that animals' lives are being destroyed, and in the hope that this would eventually lead people back to vegetarianism in the messianic period.[8] He and others maintain that vegetarianism is the ideal Jewish diet and that God permitted the eating of meat as a temporary concession, with many associated regulations, designed to keep alive a sense of reverence for life.

There are other cases where laws have been provided to regulate actions that God would prefer people not do. For example, God wishes people to live at peace, but he provides commandments related to waging war because he knows that human beings quarrel and seek victories over others. Similarly, the laws in the Torah related to taking a beautiful captive woman in wartime are a concession to human weakness. We cannot conclude from this that we are therefore obligated to make war or take captive women. In the same way, the laws related to meat consumption do not mean that we must eat meat. By not eating meat, Jews are acting consistently with many *mitzvot*, such as showing compassion to animals, preserving health, not wasting, feeding the hungry, and preserving the environment. Also, by not eating meat, a Jew cannot violate many possible prohibitions of the Torah, such as mixing meat and milk, eating nonkosher animals, and eating blood or fat.

It should be noted that the laws of *kashrut* involve not only the technical details of preparing foods, but also the blessings to be recited before and after eating. None of these blessings would cease with vegetarian diets, since the blessing for meat is the same as that for many other foods, such as soup and juice. Also, vegetarianism would not affect "food-orientated" *mitzvot*, such as *kiddush, Birkat Hamazon* (blessing after meals), or Passover *seder* observances.

3. Judaism considers it sinful not to take advantage of the pleasurable things that God has put on the earth. As He put animals on the earth, is it not a transgression to refrain from eating meat?

Can eating meat be pleasurable to a religious person when he or she knows that as a result animals are being cruelly treated, his or her health is endangered, the environment is polluted, and grain is wasted? There are many other ways to gain pleasure without harming living creatures. The prohibition against abstaining from pleasurable things only applies when there is no plausible basis for the abstention. Vegetarians abstain because eating meat is injurious to health, because their soul rebels against eating a living creature, and/or because they wish to have a diet that minimizes threats to the environment and that best shares resources with hungry people.

There are other cases in Judaism where actions that some people consider pleasurable are forbidden or discouraged, such as the use of tobacco, drinking liquor to excess, sexual relations out of wedlock, and recreational hunting.

4. Weren't people given dominion over animals? Didn't God put them here for our use?

Dominion does not mean that we have the right to conquer and exploit animals. Immediately after God gave people dominion over animals (Genesis 1:26), He prohibited their use for food (Genesis 1:29). Dominion means guardianship or stewardship—being co-workers with God in taking care of and improving the world.[9]

The Talmud interprets "dominion" as the privilege of using animals for labor only.[10] It is extremely doubtful that the concept of dominion permits factory-farming style breeding animals and treating them as machines designed solely to meet our needs. Rav Kook asserts that dominion does not imply the rule of a tyrannical ruler who cruelly governs in order to satisfy personal desires.[11] Rav Kook also indicates that he cannot believe that such a repulsive form of servitude could be forever sealed in the world of God whose "tender mercies are over all His work." (Psalms 145:9)[12]

Rabbi Hirsch stresses that people have not been given the right or the power to have everything subservient to them. In commenting on Genesis 1:26, he states: "The earth and its creatures may have other relationships of which we are ignorant, in which they serve their own purpose."[13] Hence, people, according to Judaism, do not have an unlimited right to use and abuse animals and other parts of nature.

Commenting on Genesis 1:26, Rashi notes: "If a person is found worthy, he has dominion over the animals. If he is not found worthy, he becomes subservient before them, and the animals rule over him."

5. If God wanted us to have vegetarian diets and not harm animals, why were the Temple sacrificial services established?

During the time of Moses, it was the general practice among all nations to worship by means of sacrifices.[14] There were many associated idolatrous practices. The great Jewish philosopher Maimonides writes that God did not command the Israelites to give up and discontinue all these manners of service, because "to obey such a commandment would have been contrary to the nature of man, who generally cleaves to that to which he is accustomed."[15] For this reason, God allowed Jews to make sacrifices, but

"He transferred to His service that which had [previously] served as a worship of created beings and of imaginary and unreal things."[16] The elements of idolatry were removed. Maimonides concludes:

> By this divine plan it was effected that the traces of idolatry were blotted out, and the truly great principle of our faith, the existence and unity of God, was established. This result was thus obtained without confusing the minds of the people by the abolition of a service they were accustomed to and which was familiar to them.[17]

The philosopher Abarbanel reinforces Maimonides' argument. He cites a *midrash* that indicated that the Jews had become accustomed to sacrifices in Egypt. To wean them from these idolatrous practices, God tolerated the sacrifices but commanded that they be offered in one central sanctuary:[18]

> Thereupon the Holy One, blessed be He, said "Let them at all times offer their sacrifices before Me in the Tabernacle, and they will be weaned from idolatry, and thus be saved."[19]

Rabbi J. H. Hertz, former Chief Rabbi of Great Britain, has written that if Moses had not instituted sacrifices, which were admitted by all to have been the universal expression of religious homage, his mission would have failed, and Judaism would have disappeared.[20] After the destruction of the Temple, Rabbi Yochanan Ben Zakkai has indicated that prayer and good deeds should take the place of Temple sacrifices.

Rashi argues that God did not require the Israelites to bring certain sacrifices; it was their decision to do so.[21] He based this on a statement by Isaiah in the *Haftorah* (portion from the Prophets) that is read on the Sabbath when the section in Leviticus which discusses sacrifices is read: "I have not burdened you with a meal-offering, nor wearied you with frankincense." (Isaiah 43:23)

Biblical commentator Rabbi David Kimchi (1160–1235) also suggests that certain sacrifices were never mandatory, but voluntary.[22] He ascertained this from the words of Jeremiah:

> For I spoke not unto your fathers, nor commanded them on the day that I brought them out of the land of Egypt, concerning burnt-offerings or sacrifices; but this thing I commanded them, saying, "Obey my voice, and I will be your God, and you shall be my people; and walk in all the ways that I have commanded you, that it may be well unto you. (Jeremiah 7:22–23)

Kimchi noted that nowhere in the Ten Commandments is there any reference to sacrifice. Even when sacrifices are first mentioned (Leviticus 1:2) the expression used is "when any man of you brings an offering." The first Hebrew word ki, literally "if," implies that it was a voluntary act.[23]

While Jewish teachers including Maimonides believe that with the Third Holy Temple animal sacrifices will be reestablished, other Jewish scholars such as Rav Kook argue that animal sacrifices will not be reinstated in messianic times, even with the reestablishment of the Temple.[24] They base this on a midrash that states that during the messianic period human conduct will have advanced to such high standards that there will no longer be a need for animal sacrifices to atone for sins and, thus, all offerings will cease except the Thanksgiving offering, which will continue forever.[25] The abolition of animal sacrifices is consistent with Rav Kook's view, based on the prophecy of Isaiah (11:6–9), that people and animals will be vegetarian at that time, and "none shall hurt nor destroy on all My holy mountain."

Sacrifices, especially animal sacrifices, were not the primary concern of God. As a matter of fact, they could be an abomination to God if not carried out together with deeds of loving kindness and justice. Consider these words of the prophets, the spokespeople of God:

> I desire mercy, not sacrifice. (Hosea 6:6)

"To what purpose is the multitude of your sacrifices unto Me?" says the Lord. "I am full of the burnt offerings of rams, and the fat of fed beasts; and I delight not in the blood of bullocks, or of lambs or of he-goats...bring no more vain oblations....Your new moon and your appointed feasts my soul hates;...and when you spread forth your hands, I will hide my eyes from you; yes, when you make many prayers, I will not hear; your hands are full of blood." (Isaiah 1:11–16)

I hate, I despise your feasts, and I will take no delight in your solemn assemblies. Though you offer me burnt offerings and your meal offerings, I will not accept them; neither will I regard the peace-offerings of your fat beasts. Take you away from me the noise of your song; and let Me not hear the melody of your psalteries. But let justice well up as waters, and righteousness as a mighty stream. (Amos 5:21–4)

Deeds of compassion and kindness toward all creation are of greater significance to God than sacrifices: "To do charity and justice is more acceptable to the Lord than sacrifice" (Proverbs 21:3).

Perhaps a different type of sacrifice is required of us today:

When Rabbi Shesheth kept a fast for Yom Kippur, he concluded with these words: "Sovereign of the Universe, You know full well that in the time of the Temple when a man sinned he used to bring a sacrifice, and though all that was offered of it was fat and blood, atonement was made for him. Now I have kept a fast and my fat and blood have diminished. May it be Your will to account my fat and blood which have been diminished as if I have offered them before you on the altar, and favor me."[26]

6. Don't the laws of *shechitah* provide for a humane slaughter of animals so that we need not be concerned with violations of *tsa'ar ba'alei chayim*?

It is true that *shechitah* has been found in scientific tests conducted in the United States and other countries to be a relatively painless method of slaughter.[27] But can we consider only the final minutes of an animal's life? What about the tremendous pain and cruelty involved in the entire process of raising and transporting animals and forcing them into the slaughterhouse to be robbed of their lives? When the consumption of meat is not necessary and is even harmful to people's health, can any method of slaughter be considered humane? Is this not a contradiction in terms?

Some animal rights advocates have been critical of *shechitah* because of the practice of shackling and hoisting, a very painful process in which the animal is raised off the ground by its hind leg prior to slaughter. It is important to recognize that shackling and hoisting is not a part of *shechitah*. It was instituted by the U.S. Department of Agriculture in 1906 in order to avoid the blood of diseased animals contaminating other animals when they were cast upon the floor.[28]

Fortunately, an alternative, more humane method that is acceptable to Jewish law has been developed and put into practice in many slaughterhouses, especially for large animals. Holding pens have been produced that meet the requirements of ritual slaughter and also Department of Agriculture requirements, while avoiding the use of shackling and hoisting. These pens have been endorsed by the Jewish Joint Advisory Committee on *shechitah*, the Rabbinical Council of America, and prominent Orthodox rabbis.[29]

Several animal rights groups have pushed for legislation banning shackling and hoisting. Unfortunately, some anti-Semitic groups have used the issue to try to attack *shechitah*, and this has caused some Jews to see any criticism of *shechitah* as anti-Semitic. The Jewish community must work to extend the use of humane alternatives to shackling and hoisting. However, the improvement of living conditions imposed by factory-farming methods is no less important, and this is everyone's responsibility. Of course, as indicated earlier, the best way to be consistent with Jewish teachings concerning animals is to be vegetarian so no animals need be mistreated and killed for one's diet.

7. Doesn't vegetarianism place greater priority on animal rights than on the many problems related to human welfare?

Vegetarian diets are not beneficial only to animals. As previously discussed, they also improve human health, help hungry people through better sharing of food and other resources, put less stress on endangered ecosystems, conserve valuable resources, and reduce the potential for war and violence. In view of the many global threats related to today's livestock agriculture, working to promote vegetarianism may be the most important action that one can take for global survival. Also, a concern for animal suffering hardly excludes concern for human suffering. There is no limit to human moral concern.

8. Doesn't vegetarianism elevate animals to a level equal to that of people, an idea inconsistent with Judaism?

While some vegetarians equate human and animal life, the vast majority of vegetarians do not. Concern for animals and a refusal to treat them brutally and slaughter them for food that is not necessary for proper nutrition (indeed, is harmful to human health) does not mean that vegetarians regard animals as equal to people. Also, many people are vegetarians for reasons other than animal rights, such as preservation of health, reduction of ecological threats, and help for hungry people.

As the British philosopher Jeremy Bentham (1748–1832) put it, our behavior toward animals should not be based on whether they can reason or talk, but whether they can suffer.[30] And, as noted earlier, the great Jewish philosopher Maimonides felt that animals are like people in fleeing from pain and death. Also, as English author Brigid Brophy (1929–1995) indicated: "We are the species uniquely capable of imagination, rationality, and moral choice—and this is precisely why we are under the obligation to recognize and respect the rights of animals."[31]

While Judaism does not assert the moral equivalence of the species, this does not negate the ethical mandates to treat animals with empathy and good will. Rabbi Hirsch expresses the case for sympathy toward all creatures powerfully:

Compassion is the feeling of empathy which the pain of one being awakens in another; and the higher and more human the beings are, the more keenly attuned they are to re-echo the note of suffering, which, like a voice from heaven, penetrates the heart, bringing all creatures a proof of their kinship in the universal God. And as for human beings, whose function it is to show respect and love for God's universe and all its creatures, his heart has been created so tender that it feels with the whole organic world... mourning even for fading flowers; so that, if nothing else, the very nature of his heart must teach him that he is required above everything to feel himself the brother of all beings, and to recognize the claim of all beings to his love and his beneficence.[32]

9. Won't a movement by Jews toward vegetarianism mean less emphasis on *kashrut* (kosher laws) and eventually a disregard of these laws?

Quite the contrary. One of the purposes of the laws of *kashrut* is reverence for life. Another purpose is to avoid pagan practices, which often involved much cruelty to animals and people. These concepts are consistent with vegetarian ideals.

In many ways, becoming a vegetarian makes it easier and cheaper to observe the laws of kashrut. This might attract many new adherents to keeping kosher and eventually to other important Jewish values. As a vegetarian, one need not be concerned with separate dishes, mixing *milchigs* (Yiddish for dairy products) with *fleischigs* (Yiddish for meat products), waiting three or six hours after eating meat before being allowed to eat dairy products, storing four sets of dishes and utensils (two for regular use and two for Passover use), and many other concerns that are imposed upon the non-vegetarian who wishes to strictly observe *kashrut*. In addition, a vegetarian is in no danger of eating blood or fat, which are prohibited, or the flesh of a nonkosher animal. It should be noted that being a vegetarian does not automatically guarantee that one will maintain the laws of *kashrut* as, for example, certain baked goods and cheeses may not be kosher. Also, checking vegetables and grains for insect infestation is an important *kashrut* concern. When in doubt, a trusted rabbinic authority should be consulted.

A growing problem in the American Jewish scene today is the possible unreliability of *kashrut* supervision.[33] As diligent as supervising agencies attempt to be, there is always the chance of an error. A single issue of the *Jewish Press* (a New York-based weekly newspaper) listed eighty-four food establishments that paid fines related to violations of the kosher laws.[34] Some observant Jews avoid all possible problems by not eating meat.

Some people reject *kashrut* because of the high costs involved. Since a person can obtain proper nourishment at far lower costs with a vegetarian diet, this may prevent the loss of many *kashrut* observers.

In a personal letter to the author, Rabbi Robert Gordis, late Professor of Bible at the Jewish Theological Seminary, wrote that he believed that vegetarianism, the logical consequence of Jewish teaching, would be a way of protecting *kashrut*. He stated, "Vegetarianism offers an ideal mode for preserving the religious and ethical values which kashrut was designed to concretize in human life."

There are several examples in Jewish history when a change to vegetarianism enabled Jews to adhere to *kashrut*. As indicated in the Book of Daniel, Daniel and his companions avoiding eating nonkosher food by adopting a vegetarian diet (Daniel 1:8–16). The historian Josephus relates that some Jews on trial in Rome ate only figs and nuts to avoid eating flesh that had been used in idol worship.[35] Some of the Maccabees, during the struggles against the Syrian Greeks, escaped to the mountains and lived on plant foods to avoid "being polluted like the rest," through eating nonkosher foods.[36]

10. Isn't a movement toward vegetarianism a movement away from Jewish traditions with regard to diet? Isn't there a danger that once some traditions are changed, others may readily follow, and little will be left of Judaism as we have known it?

A move toward vegetarianism is actually a return to Jewish traditions, to taking Jewish values seriously. A movement toward vegetarianism can help revitalize Judaism. It can show that Jewish values can be applied to help solve current world problems related to hunger, waste, and pollution. Hence, rather than a movement away from Jewish traditions, it would have the opposite effect.

11. Weren't the Jewish sages aware of the evils related to eating meat? If so, why does so much of Talmudic literature discuss laws and customs related to the consumption of meat? Are you suggesting that Judaism has been morally wrong in not advocating vegetarianism?

Conditions today differ greatly from those in biblical times and throughout most of Jewish history. Only recently has strong medical evidence linked animal-centered diets to many types of disease. Modern intensive livestock agriculture results in conditions quite different from those that prevailed previously. To produce meat today, animals are treated very cruelly, they are fed tremendous amounts of grain (and chemicals) while millions of people starve, and pollution and misuse of resources result. When it was felt that eating meat was necessary for health and the many problems related to modern intensive livestock agriculture did not exist, the sages were not morally wrong in not advocating vegetarianism. Also, people did not eat meat so frequently then.

12. By putting vegetarian values ahead of Jewish teachings, aren't vegetarians, in effect, creating a new religion, with values contrary to Jewish teachings?

Most Jewish vegetarians do not place so-called "vegetarian values" above Torah principles. They are saying that Jewish mandates to treat animals with compassion, guard our health, share with hungry people, protect the environment, conserve resources, and seek peace make vegetarianism the ideal diet for Jews today, especially in view of the many problems related to modern methods of raising animals on factory farms. Rather than rejecting Torah values, Jewish vegetarians are challenging the Jewish community to apply Torah values to their diets in a daily meaningful way. They are respectfully challenging Jews to live up to Judaism's splendid teachings. They are arguing that vegetarianism is a fulfillment of Judaism, not a deviation.

13. Aren't vegetarians trying to be more righteous than God, since God gave permission to eat meat?

There is no obligation to eat meat today. As discussed before, God's first dietary law (Genesis 1:29) was strictly vegetarian and, according to Rav Kook and others, God's permission to people to eat meat was a reluctant concession, and the messianic period will again be vegetarian.

Jewish vegetarians believe their diet is most consistent with God's desires that we protect our health, be kind to animals, provide for hungry people, protect the environment, and conserve resources. Rather than being more righteous than God, they are urging people to live up to God's highest ideals, as expressed in the Torah and the Jewish tradition.

This viewpoint is conceded by Rabbi Alfred Cohen: "If a person tends toward vegetarianism because he sees it as a lifestyle consonant with the way the Almighty really wanted the world to be, there can be no denying that he has a valid point of view."[37]

14. How can you advocate making changes in Judaism?

What is really advocated is a return to Jewish values of showing compassion, sharing, helping the needy, preserving the environment, conserving resources, and seeking peace. Also, throughout Jewish history rabbinic enactments consistent with Jewish values and teachings have been applied to meet changing conditions.

Global threats today—pollution, hunger, resource scarcity, violence—are so great that a new thinking or rethinking about values and new methods is necessary. Albert Einstein's statement—"The unleashed power of the atom has changed everything except our ways of thinking; hence we drift toward unparalleled catastrophe"[38]—has a parallel in the effects of our diets today.

Jewish vegetarians are not advocating changes in the Torah, but want the Torah to fully address present world conditions, as it has in the past. Global survival today requires the application of Torah values to our diets, as well as other aspects of our lives.

15. Wasn't Genesis 1:29 (the first dietary law) overridden by later biblical commandments and teachings?

While God's original intention was that people be vegetarians, God later gave permission for meat to be eaten as a reluctant concession to people's weakness. Many biblical commentators look at vegetarianism as the ideal diet, and modern science has verified that our body structure and digestive system are most consistent with this type of diet.

In the *responsum* previously referred to, Rabbi Moshe Halevi Steinberg expressed his belief that the fact that meat was initially forbidden and later permitted indicates that each person is thereby given a free hand to either be a vegetarian as was the first human, or to eat meat, as Noah did.

The question is, on what basis should that choice be made? Should it be on the basis of convenience, habit, and conformity, or on considerations of basic Jewish values and teachings?

Rabbi Alfred Cohen writes: "The Torah does not establish the eating of meat as a desirable activity, only as something which is not forbidden to do."[39] As a matter of fact, the less meat eaten, the better; one who eats meat too often is considered a "glutton," though he or she is within the technical limits of the Torah.

Perhaps the rabbinic approach recommending the consumption of meat on the Sabbath was for the benefit of the poor, who depended on charity to appease their hunger.[40] Hence, the needy would be provided with what was then considered nutritious food, at least once a week.

16. While vegetarians are not violating *Halacha* (Jewish law) by not eating meat, isn't their failure to eat meat at least on *Yom Tov* (holidays) and the Sabbath in violation of the spirit of Jewish law?

This question is based on the fact that many Jewish sages felt that one could only experience joy on holidays by eating meat. Maimonides, for example, states that "There is no joy except with meat and wine."[41]

Once again we must recognize the tremendous changes that have occurred in livestock agriculture and our medical knowledge. Health problems from the consumption of meat have become far worse since the time of Maimonides. In the time of our sages, animals were not raised under horrible conditions on factory farms, nor were they fed or injected with hormones, antibiotics, and ground-up parts of other animals. Modern problems related to the production of meat such as widespread hunger, ecological threats, and resource scarcities were not as prevalent. Since we now are, or should be, aware of these modern problems, it is vegetarian diets that are most consistent with the spirit of Jewish tradition and values.

It should be noted that while in the days of the Talmudic sages vegetarians were generally ascetics who rejected life's joys, today vegetarianism is viewed as life-sustaining and life-enhancing.

It is also important to note that (1) the above quote from Maimonides fails to include the previously mentioned Talmudic qualifier in *Pesachim* 109a that the obligation to eat meat to rejoice on holidays only directly applied "in the time when the Temple was standing," and (2) that earlier in the same quote, Maimonides indicates that people rejoice in different ways: sweets and nuts for children and new clothing for women.

Also, as mentioned before, there have been a number of chief rabbis who were strict vegetarians, and ate no flesh products at all (see Chapter 11).

17. Because the majority of Jews will probably continue to eat meat, isn't it better that they do so without being aware of the Jewish principles such as *bal tashchit,* **(the mandate not to waste resources),** *tsa'ar ba'alei chayim* **(the mandate to avoid causing unnecessary suffering to animals), and** *pikuach nefesh* **(the mandate to protect human life) that are being violated? Shouldn't a Jewish vegetarian abstain from meat quietly and not try to convert others to his or her type of diet?**
This is a common attitude that the author has found. Many people feel that if there are benefits to vegetarianism, and if some people want to have such a diet, fine, but they should keep it to themselves and not try to convert others.

The question really becomes one of how seriously we take Jewish values. Are we to ignore Torah mandates to preserve our health, show compassion for animals, conserve resources, help feed hungry people, and preserve the earth, which animal-centered diets directly or indirectly violate? Is it proper that people be kept uninformed about the many contraventions of Torah values so that they can continue their eating habits with a clear conscience?

The following powerful Talmudic teaching shows the importance of speaking out when improper actions occur:[42]

> Whoever is able to protest against the transgressions of his own family and does not do so is punished for the transgressions of his family. Whoever is able to protest against the transgressions of the people of his community and does not do so is punished for the transgressions of his community. Whoever is able to protest against the transgressions of the entire world and does not do so is punished for the transgressions of the entire world.[43]

The Talmud also relates a story of how apparently righteous individuals were punished along with the wicked because "they had the power to protest but they did not."[44] Related to these principles are the following teachings of the Jewish sages:

> If a man of learning participates in public affairs and serves as judge or arbiter, he gives stability to the land. But if he sits in his home and says to himself, "What have the affairs of society to do with me?...Why should I trouble myself with the people's voice of protest? Let my soul dwell in peace!" If he does this, he overthrows the world.[45]

> If the community is in trouble, a man must not say, "I will go to my house, and eat and drink, and peace shall be with you...." But a man must share in the trouble of his community, even as Moses did. He who shares in its troubles is worthy to see its consolation.[46]

18. Since Rav Kook indicates that a vegetarian period will come in a later era, after people have advanced to a higher ethical level much progress has been made in meeting *human* needs, shouldn't we refrain from promoting vegetarianism now?

Many of the problems related to modern intensive livestock agriculture have become far worse since Rav Kook died in 1935. One can only wonder what his view would be today if he were aware of the diseases, soaring medical costs, increasing environmental threats, widespread hunger, cruel treatment of animals, and other negative effects of animal-centered diets.

As discussed previously, advocating vegetarianism is not in opposition to trying to help people. Vegetarianism is one of the most important ways we can improve the lot of the world's population and of our imperiled planet, as well as show that the Torah's message speaks to today's many threats. Also, a shift to vegetarianism often empowers people to see other issues more clearly and act more effectively.

19. How would a Jewish vegetarian celebrate *Pesach* (Passover)?

Today there is no need to cook or eat meat on Passover. The eating of the Paschal lamb is no longer required now that the Temple is not standing. One is obligated to commemorate this act, not to participate in it. (Indeed, a Paschal sacrifice today is prohibited by Jewish law.) The late Dayan Feldman stated that mushrooms, which have a fleshy appearance, may be used on the *seder* plate to commemorate the Paschal lamb. Rabbi Huna, a Talmudic sage, stated that a beet can be used for the same purpose.[47] In a personal note to the author, Rabbi David Rosen pointed out that the objects on the *seder* plate are symbolic, and hence there is no sin in improvising. He suggested that vegans use a beet to represent the Paschal offering (instead of a shank bone), and a mushroom to represent the Festive offering (instead of an egg).[48]

The proper celebration of Passover requires the absence of leaven and the use of unleavened bread, which we are commanded to eat "throughout your generations." There are many vegetarian recipes that are appropriate for *seders* and other Passover meals, a number of which can be found in several books listed in the Bibliography.

Because Passover is the celebration of our redemption from slavery, we should also consider freeing ourselves from the slavery of harmful eating habits. As our homes are freed from leaven, perhaps we should also free our bodies from harmful foods. Because Passover is a time of regeneration, physical as well as spiritual, maximum use should be made of raw fruits and vegetables, which have cleansing properties.

There are other Passover themes related to vegetarian ideas. The call at the *seder* for "all who are hungry to come and eat" can be a reminder that our diets can be a factor in reducing global hunger. The Passover theme of freedom may be extended to the horrible conditions of "slavery" under which animals are raised today.

The *Haggadah for the Liberated Lamb* (see Bibliography) has many ideas and suggestions connecting Passover themes to compassion for animals that can be used to supplement traditional Haggadahs. Low-fat vegetarian Passover recipes can be found on the Internet at the Vegetarian Resource Group's and Vegsource's websites (see Appendix).

20. In Jewish literature, it is stated that with the advent of the Messiah a banquet will be given by God for the righteous in which the flesh of the giant fish Leviathan will be served.[49] Isn't this inconsistent with the idea that the messianic period will be vegetarian?
These legends concerning the Leviathan are interpreted as allegories by most Jewish scholars.[50] According to Maimonides, the banquet is an allusion to the spiritual enjoyment of the intellect.[51] Abarbanel and others consider the descriptions of the Leviathan to be allusions to the destruction of the powers that are hostile to the Jews.[52]

21. Some people believe that vegetarians should aspire to become vegans (those who don't use milk, eggs, leather, or any product from an animal). How can an Orthodox Jew be a vegan since he would not be able to use *tefillin*, a *shofar* (ram's horn), a *Sefer Torah*, and other ritual items that are made from animals?
If a person became a vegetarian but not a vegan, he or she would still do much good for animals, the environment, hungry people, and the preservation of his or her health. If a person embraces veganism except in cases where specific *mitzvot* require the use of some animal product, even more good will be done.

It is important to emphasize that, for *hiddur* (enhancement of) *mitzvah*, it is preferable for the religious items mentioned above to be made from animals that were raised compassionately and died natural deaths.[53]

The number of animals slaughtered for Jewish ritual purposes is minute compared to the billions killed annually for food. The fact that there would still be some animals slaughtered to meet Jewish ritual needs shouldn't stop us from doing all we can to end the horrible abuses of factory farming. Also, most problems related to animal-centered diets—poor human health, waste of food and other resources, and ecological threats—would not occur if animals were slaughtered solely to meet Jewish ritual needs. Our emphasis should be on doing a minimum amount of harm to other people, the environment, and animals.

22. During the messianic period, when the Temple in Jerusalem is rebuilt, won't the sacrificial services be restored and won't people have to eat meat?

As indicated previously, Rav Kook and others believed that in the messianic period, human conduct will have improved to such a degree that animal sacrifices will not be necessary to atone for sins. There will only be non-animal sacrifices to express thanks to God. As mentioned before, Maimonides believed that the sacrifices were only a concession to human weakness to begin with, and, had we not fallen back into idolatry and built the Golden Calf, we might not have had sacrifices at all. So we must ask ourselves: If the messianic era represents a return to the pristine holiness of Sinai before the Golden Calf was built, why would we need to restore the sacrifices?

While most Jewish scholars assume that all Jews ate meat during the time that the Temple stood, it is significant that some (*Tosafot, Yoma* 3a, and Rabbeinu Nissim, *Sukkah* 42b)[54] assert that even during the Temple period it was not an absolute requirement to eat meat. Rabbeinu Nissim characterizes the "requirement" to eat the meat of festival offerings as *mitzvah min ha-muvchar*, that is, the optimal way of fulfilling the *mitzvah* of rejoicing on the festival, but not an absolute requirement.[55]

Rabbi Moshe Halevi Steinberg, in the *responsum* previously mentioned, points out that vegetarianism for health reasons did not conflict with *Halacha* even in Temple times.[56] He writes that one could be a vegetarian the whole year, and by eating a *kazayit* (olive-size portion which, due to its size, would not damage one's health) of meat, the person would fulfill the *mitzvah* of eating the meat of sacrifices. Even a *Kohen* (priest) could be vegetarian except when his turn came to eat of the sacrifices, during his period of duty (about two weeks), when he, too, could eat just a *kazayit*. According to the *Hatam Sofer*, since many *Kohanim* could join together to eat the required amount, the vegetarian *Kohen* could eat even less than a *kazayit*.[57] Rabbi Steinberg notes that, among the things listed as disqualifying a *Kohen* from service in the Temple, vegetarianism is not included, since the vegetarian could arrange the problem of the eating of the sacrifices in one of the ways listed above. However, Rabbi Steinberg adds, a *Kohen* who became a vegetarian because his soul recoiled against eating meat would not have been allowed to serve in the sanctuary since, if he forced himself to swallow a *kazayit* of meat, it would not fulfill the *halachic* definition of "eating."

23. How can an Orthodox Jewish vegetarian sincerely recite synagogue prayers for the restoration of the Temple sacrificial services?

The following response is based on an essay by Rabbi David Rosen.[58] He reminds us that (1) Maimonides believed that the sacrifices were a concession to the times, (2) Rav Kook felt that the messianic period in which the Temple would be rebuilt would be a vegetarian period, and (3) the Temple service can be maintained without animal sacrifices, as is indicated by the rabbinic teaching that in the future all sacrifices will be abolished, except for thanksgiving offerings. He argues that the liturgy in the Sabbath and Festival *Musaph* (additional) service need not be understood as expressing a hope for the restoration of animal sacrifices. Rather, it can be interpreted as a recognition on our part of the devotion and dedication to God that our ancestors showed, and an expression of our hope that we may be inspired to show the same spirit of devotion in our own way.

24. Do you believe that flesh should not be served at Jewish functions and that all Jews should be vegetarians?

Because the realities of livestock agriculture are inconsistent with basic Jewish values, Jews should ideally be vegetarians and flesh should not be served at Jewish functions. But since the Torah does give permission for people to eat meat (as a concession to human weakness), people have been given the freedom to choose. In fact, the purpose of these questions and answers is to give Jews and others information to help them make a decision that is informed and based on Jewish teachings.

25. To improve health, wouldn't it be wiser to advocate that people reduce their meat consumption rather than that they become vegetarian? Doesn't Judaism advocate moderation, the golden mean, in such matters, rather than complete abstinence?

Certainly a reduction of meat consumption would be a step in the right direction. If many people did this, it would sharply reduce many of the problems that we have been discussing. However, as mentioned in Chapter 3, Rabbi Hirsch has stressed that "even the smallest unnecessary deprivation of strength is accountable to God. Every smallest weakening is partial murder. Therefore you should avoid everything which might possibly injure your health."[59]

Responding to a similar argument with regard to smoking, Rabbi Moses Auerbach, a teacher at Hebrew Teachers College in Baltimore, has stated that only deliberate self-delusion can persuade a person that there are "safe" limits in smoking. He adds that there is absolutely no safety in moderation, since even a limited intake of cigarette poison can seriously aggravate an existing condition of heart or lung disease that a person may not be aware of.[60] Rabbi Auerbach has also argued that even if there is a given point below which there is no risk, the peril of addiction and gradual increases beyond "safe" levels would remain.[61] The argument for moderate meat consumption would need to address similar concerns before asserting that such a diet is consistent with Jewish values.

26. What about the Chassidic view that, when one is pious and performs Torah *mitzvot*, you elevate an animal by consuming its flesh, since the energy produced from the animal is used to perform *mitzvot*, which the animal could not perform in any other way?[62]

This concept is related to the following *kabbalistic* teachings: during the Creation of the universe, the Holy Vessels (*Sephirot*) that were intended to contain the Divine Light were shattered. "Sparks" of holiness (*netzotzot*) fell to lower levels, ultimately becoming entrapped in material things. When done with the proper intention (*kavannah*) by a pious person, *mitzvot* can "elevate" these sparks back into their proper place in the universe. This process will culminate in the coming of the Messiah, and the restoration of spiritual harmony among all Creation. Kabbalists see meat-eating as part of this process, since they believe that animals are thus elevated into their proper levels of holiness.

There is also a reincarnational aspect to this teaching. According to the Kabbalists, sometimes a human soul is reincarnated as an animal, but retains its human consciousness, in order to atone for a specific sin. In *Shivchei Ha-Ari* (a 16th-century collection of stories about Rabbi Isaac Luria),[63] there are several tales about the Ari communicating with human souls in animal bodies. Similar stories are also recorded about the early Chassidic masters. In many of these cases, the soul in the animal asks the Rebbe to consume its meat and use the resultant strength for a specific *mitzvah*, in order to offset the sin and set the soul free to reincarnate as a human being once again. This, too, is part of the process of "elevating holy sparks."

Yonassan Gershom, a vegetarian Chassidic rabbi from Minnesota, believes that these concepts can be reconciled with vegetarianism. He notes that the process of raising sparks is cumulative, not a self-perpetuating cycle for all eternity. It is also an individualized process. Each human being is born with the mission to elevate specific sparks, and not others. As we come closer to the time of the Messiah, the process of raising sparks through the consumption of meat is also nearing completion. In his book, *Jewish Tales of Reincarnation*,[64] Rabbi Gershom cites the story of a Chassid who lost his taste for meat, and was later told in a dream that this was because he had completed the elevation of the specific sparks in meat that he was intended to elevate. The Chassid then became a vegetarian.[65]

Rabbi Gershom points to the recent increase in vegetarianism as a possible indicator that many people, like the Chassid in the story, are naturally losing their taste for meat precisely because they have already elevated the sparks assigned to them. In addition, he notes the very cruel treatment of animals today, which is not the way animals were raised and slaughtered in the days when the Chassidic stories originated. At that time, animals were treated as individuals. When the time came to butcher the family cow, the person eating the meat had personal interaction with the animal. Today, however, this relationship no longer exists. Most of us do not take our own cow or chicken to the *shochet* (ritual slaughterer), nor is there much interaction between the *shochet* and the animal.

After visiting a modern slaughterhouse and viewing current methods of meat production, Rabbi Gershom asserts that the *shochtim*, no matter how sincere and dedicated they may be, cannot maintain a spirit of holiness while slaughtering hundreds of animals under the mass-production conditions of today's slaughterhouses. In past centuries, an individual blessing was said with *kavannah* (intention) before slaughtering each animal. But, in today's high-speed industry, many *shochtim* can only make a single blessing for the whole day's quota of animals. If this is the case, how can there be proper *kavannah* for the elevation of the souls? Rabbi Gershom asserts that we are now left with the empty shell (*klippah*) of fleshpots without holiness.

Even in cases where the slaughtering is performed with the proper *kavannah*, the process does not necessarily go on forever. Rabbi Yehuda Hirsch of Strettana, a 19th-century Chassidic Rebbe (Rabbi), had once been a ritual slaughterer. So pure and holy was he that flocks of wild doves came of their own accord to lie down under his knife. The Seer of Lublin, upon seeing this miracle, urged Reb (Rabbi) Yehudah's teacher, Reb Urele of Strelisk, to ordain his disciple as a rabbi. But Reb Urele refused, saying that there were thousands of poor human souls reincarnated in the kosher species of animals, and that being a *shochet* was the proper work for Reb Yehuda. The time came, however, when the flocks of doves ceased to come. Reb Yehuda then gave up the butcher's business and was ordained as a rabbi.[66]

One is tempted to ask whether Reb Yehuda would have been willing to participate in the kosher meat industry as it exists today, given that he would scarcely have time to properly focus his thoughts before slaughtering each animal. It once happened that one of Rebbe Nachman of Breslov's followers was thinking about becoming a *shochet* and asked the Rebbe for his opinion. The Rebbe responded by giving lesson number thirty-seven of *Likutei Moharan*,[67] which explains that the soul of the animal is attached to the blood and that the *shochet* must have true *kavannah* in wielding the knife in order to raise the sparks properly. Failure to do so, says Reb Nachman, affects not only the animal, but the livelihood of the whole Jewish people because "where there is no Torah, there is no bread" (*Pirke Avot* 3:17). After hearing this lesson, the disciple decided against becoming a *shochet*.[68]

Rabbi Isaac Luria (the Ari) writes that "only a Torah scholar who is God-fearing and eats with proper intent can elevate the sparks of holiness within animals."[69] There is also a kabbalistic concern about the spiritual effect of meat-eating on the person. The Breslover Rebbe states that only a person who has reached a high spiritual level can be elevated by eating animal foods, and the opposite is also true: a person who lacks this high spiritual level may be further debased by eating animal foods.[70] Rabbi Chaim Kramer, a respected contemporary Breslover scholar, notes in his commentary to *Likutei Moharan* 37:6 that "when a person eats the meat of an animal which lacks proper *shechitah* (ritual slaughter), he also ingests the aspects of animal matter, darkness, foolishness, judgments, forgetfulness, and death." In the cases where a sinful soul has reincarnated as an animal, there is the additional danger that, if one is not holy enough to elevate the soul in the meat, then that soul may attach itself to you and, in turn, drag you down into sin. For this reason, Rabbi Moshe Cordovero, a major 16th-century kabbalist, expressed the opinion that one should eat a minimum of animal flesh.[71]

Not only is the sinner debased by eating animal foods, but the animals themselves are debased by misuse of their energy, for which the person who ate them will have to answer in the next life. In his book, My *Prayer*, Lubavitcher Chassid Rabbi Nissim Mindel notes that if one eats a chicken and then uses its energy to cheat or steal, the chicken can demand at the Heavenly Court, "By what right have you taken my life, and involved me in crime, which I would never have committed otherwise?"[72] Rabbi Gershom cites a similar story about animal souls which accused the false Messiah, Shabbetai Tzvi, before the Heavenly Court, complaining that he had used their energy to mislead the Jews into heresy.[73] These teachings strongly indicate that raising sparks through eating meat is not something to be taken lightly. This is why the Talmudic sages teach, "One who is ignorant of Torah is forbidden from eating meat."[74] This raises the question as to how many of us in this day and age are holy enough to eat meat with the proper consciousness to raise the sparks.

As a non-Chassid, I would respectfully observe that it seems hard to see how sparks of holiness can be elevated under modern conditions that involve so much cruelty to animals and do so much harm to people and the world. Also, based on recent nutritional studies, one would be better able to perform *mitzvot* and other sacred activities through a sensible, nutritious vegetarian diet, rather than by eating meat, with all its negative effects on health.

* * * * *

Questions for Vegetarians to Ask

Vegetarians, especially those who have recently changed their diets, are generally on the defensive. They must deal with many questions, such as the ones in this chapter. Those who eat meat have the support of society, and thus they never consider the consequences of their diet. It is vegetarians who are asked to explain the reasons for their diet, rather than those who support the cruel treatment and unnecessary slaughter of animals that an animal-centered diet requires.

Perhaps there are times when vegetarians should take the offensive in conversations with meat-eaters. Answers when questioned, and queries vegetarians put *to* their interrogators, can help show the benefits of vegetarianism and its consistency with Jewish values.

Here are some questions that can help vegetarians politely and respectfully "turn the tables" on non-vegetarians:

- Do you know how much cruelty is involved in raising animals for food today?
- Are you aware of the links between meat-eating and heart disease, cancer, and other degenerative diseases?
- Could you visit a slaughterhouse or kill an animal yourself?
- Do you know that while millions die annually of starvation, most grain grown in the United States and in most affluent countries is fed to animals destined for slaughter?
- Are you aware of the consequences of animal-centered diets with regard to pollution, destruction of tropical rain forests and other habitats, use of land, water, and other resources, and global climate change?
- Since Jews are only permitted to kill animals to meet an essential human need, and it is not necessary to consume animal products in order to maintain good health (the contrary is the case), can we justify the slaughtering of animals for food?
- Can we justify the force-feeding of ducks and geese to create pâté de foie gras? Can we justify taking day-old calves from their mothers so that they can be confined in cramped crates until they are killed, so that people can eat veal? Can we justify the killing of over 250 million male chicks immediately after birth at egg-laying hatcheries because they cannot produce eggs and have not been genetically programmed to have enough flesh to make it profitable to raise them for slaughter? Can we justify artificially impregnating cows every year so that we can continue to drink milk intended for their calves? Can we justify the many other horrors of factory farming?
- Since our sages state that we do not know the true value or reward for one *mitzvah* as compared with another, why do we seek to build extensive fences to expand certain ritual *mitzvot* while often ignoring broader *mitzvot* such as *tikkun olam* (repair the world), *bal tashchit* (do not waste resources), *bakesh shalom v'rodef shalom* (seek peace and

pursue it), and *tsa'ar ba'alei chayim* (do not cause "pain to living creatures")? By doing so, do we miss the forest for the trees?

- Do you know that vegetarianism is the diet most consistent with Jewish values?

When confronted with questions from people who are unthinkingly supporting current practices, it may be useful and effective to keep the focus on these wider concerns.

8: QUESTIONS & ANSWERS: GENERAL ISSUES

'Tis better thrice to ask your way
Then even once to go astray.[1]

QUESTIONS ON GENERAL VEGETARIAN-RELATED issues are considered in this chapter. Whole books can and have been written about some of these topics, but space concerns limit us to just brief introductions here. It is hoped that readers will use the discussions below as stepping stones to more detailed investigations, and will use the many valuable books in the Bibliography to investigate some of these questions more thoroughly.

1. If everyone became vegetarian, what would happen to butchers, *shochtim* (kosher slaughterers), and others dependent for a living on the consumption of meat?
There could be a shift from the production of animal products to that of nutritious vegetarian dishes. In England during World War II, when there was a shortage of meat, butchers relied mainly on the sale of fruits and vegetables. Today, new businesses could sell such food products as tofu, miso, felafal, soy burgers, and vegetarian *cholent* (Sabbath hot dish).

The change to vegetarianism would probably be gradual. This would provide time for a transition to other jobs. Some of the funds saved by individuals and groups because of lower food and health costs could be used to provide incomes for people during the retraining period.

The same kind of question can be asked about other moral issues. What would happen to arms merchants if we had universal peace? What would happen to doctors and nurses if people took better care of themselves, stopped smoking, improved their diets, and so on? Immoral or inefficient practices should not be supported because some people earn a living in the process.

2. What if everyone became vegetarian? Wouldn't animals overrun the earth?

This concern is based on an insufficient understanding of animal behavior, both natural and under present conditions. There are not millions of turkeys around at Thanksgiving because they want to help celebrate the holiday, but because farmers want them to exist. The breeders, not the animals themselves, control the breeding behavior and thus the number of animals. Throughout history, food supply and demand have kept animal populations quite steady. An end to the distortion of the sex lives of animals to suit our needs would lead to a decrease, rather than an increase, in the number of animals.[2] For example, dairy cows are artificially inseminated annually so that they will constantly produce milk. We are not overrun by the animals that we do not eat, such as lions, elephants, and crocodiles. The problem often is that of the extinction of animals, rather than their overpopulating the earth.

3. Instead of advocating vegetarianism, shouldn't we try to alleviate the evils of factory farming so that animals are treated better, less grain is wasted, and fewer health-harming chemicals are used?

The breeding of animals is big business, whose prime concern is profit. Animals are raised the way they are today because it is very profitable. Improving conditions, as suggested by this question, would certainly be a step in the right direction, but it has been strongly resisted by the meat industry since it would greatly increase already high prices. Here are two counter questions: Why not abstain from eating meat as a protest against present policies while trying to improve them? Even under the best of conditions, why take the life of a creature of God, "whose tender mercies are over all His creatures (Psalms 145:9)," when it is not necessary for proper nutrition (and, indeed, has many harmful effects)?

4. Isn't it important that we keep our priorities straight? How can we be so concerned about animals when there are so many critical problems facing people today?

Certainly many critical issues face the world today. I have written two other books, *Judaism and Global Survival* and *Mathematics and Global Survival*, which address current world problems. There is an ecological principle that "everything is connected to everything else." Every action has many ramifications. Hence, adopting vegetarian diets doesn't only reduce cruel treatment of animals. It also improves human health, reduces stress on threatened ecosystems, conserves resources, and provides the potential to reduce widespread hunger. In view of the many threats related to livestock agriculture, next to attempting to reduce the chance of nuclear war, working to promote vegetarianism may be the most important action one can take for global survival.

While there are some people who love animals and are cruel to people, the reverse is much more often the case: those who are cruel to animals are often also cruel to human beings. In fact, cruelty to animals among children is a strong predictor of violent criminal behavior later in life.

On the other hand, kindness to animals can lead to kindness to people. Some of history's greatest humanitarians were vegetarians and/or strong advocates of vegetarianism. These include: Plutarch, Leonardo da Vinci, Sir Isaac Newton, Jean Jacques Rousseau, General William Booth, Ralph Waldo Emerson, Percy Bysshe Shelley, Dr. J. H. Kellogg, Horace Greeley, Susan B. Anthony, Leo Tolstoy, Upton Sinclair, H. G. Wells, George Bernard Shaw, Albert Schweitzer, and Mahatma Gandhi.[3] Jewish humanitarian vegetarians include Isaac Bashevis Singer, Shmuel Yosef Agnon, Franz Kafka, and Isaac Leib Peretz, as well as several chief rabbis, as mentioned before (see their biographies in Chapter 11).

5. Haven't Jews historically had many problems with some animal rights groups which have often opposed *shechitah* (kosher slaughter) and advocated its abolishment?

Jews should work to improve conditions for animals not because of the views of animal rights groups (whether they are hostile to Jews or not) but because it is the approach most consistent with Jewish values. We can look to the Torah, not animal rights groups, to see how far the treatment of animals is from fundamental Jewish teachings.

While there are probably some extremists and anti-Semites in the animal rights movement (as in any movement), most vegetarian and animal rights advocates, a very high percentage of whom are Jewish, are people of good will. The fact that many people have misconceptions about Jewish practices is all the more reason for greater involvement by knowledgeable and committed Jews. It is important that the Jewish community engage in respectful dialogue with animal rights groups so that our teachings and our religious needs become better known to them.

The Jewish community should also consider how cruelty to animals can be reduced while meeting all *halachic* requirements. It is time for a commission of scholars and rabbis, along with experts in nutrition, health, ecology, agriculture, and other fields related to food, to consider how modern technology related to animals runs counter to many basic Jewish teachings.

6. Can't one work to improve conditions for animals without being a vegetarian?

Certainly. There are many areas where animals are abused today, and certainly there is much that needs to be done. However, one should keep in mind that the major area of animal abuse is related to factory farming. According to FARM (Farm Animal Reform Movement), "The number of warm-blooded animals brutalized and slaughtered each year is approximately seventy times the number of animals killed in laboratories, thirty times the number killed by hunters and trappers, and 500 times the number killed in pounds."[4] They also report that almost ten billion farm animals are killed annually to produce food. A typical animal welfare advocate who eats meat (like any non-vegetarian) is personally responsible for the slaughter of twenty-two warm-blooded animals per year,[5] 1,500 in a lifetime, and probably many more that are slaughtered for the advocate's meat-eating family.

7. What is the definition of a vegetarian diet? Can a vegetarian eat fish?

The generally accepted definition of a vegetarian diet is a diet that excludes flesh foods—that is, a diet without meat, poultry, or fish.[6] There are three types of vegetarian diets: the lacto-ovo-vegetarian diet, which includes dairy products and eggs; the lacto-vegetarian diet, which includes dairy products, but not eggs; and the vegan (pronounced "VEE-gan") diet, which uses no animal products at all.[7] Vegans also generally avoid using non-food animal products such as leather, wool, and fur. Many base their practice on a belief that it is ethically wrong to kill animals or exploit them in any way. Others feel that it is the healthiest diet and/or the diet that does the minimum harm to the environment, uses the least amount of natural resources, and is least harmful to the world's hungry people.

Vegetarians avoid fish because (1) they feel it is unnecessary to kill living creatures for food that is not necessary for proper nutrition; (2) fish are high in cholesterol, protein, and sometimes fat, and lack fiber and complex carbohydrates; (3) the extensive pollution of many bodies of water and the magnification of pollution effects through food chains make the consumption of fish dangerous to human health.[8]

Commercial fish farming (aquaculture) has grown rapidly in the past twenty-five years and now produces about one-third of all the fish humans eat.[9] While it has been advocated as a way to take pressure off rapidly dwindling stocks of wild fish, it has had the opposite effect, since it has raised demand for ocean fish (such as mackerel and anchovies) that are ground into meal to feed farmed fish. For each pound of farm salmon produced, two to five times that amount of ocean fish are caught to feed them. Fish farming also pollutes coastal areas with large amounts of animal waste.

8. If vegetarian diets are best for health, why don't most doctors recommend them?

While doctors are devoted to the well-being of their patients, unfortunately many doctors lack information about basic relationships between food and health, because nutrition is barely taught in medical schools. Also, many patients are resistant to making dietary changes. Hence, the accepted approach today seems to be to prescribe medications first, and, perhaps, recommend a diet as an afterthought. However, there now seems to be increasing awareness on the part of doctors about the importance of proper nutrition, and it is hoped that this will increase.

9. Why don't medical and governmental authorities recommend vegetarianism?

There have been some medical and governmental indications of the benefits of vegetarian diets. For example, as long ago as June 1961, an editorial in the *Journal of the American Medical Association* stated that a vegetarian diet can prevent ninety percent of strokes and ninety-seven percent of heart attacks. Also, as indicated in Chapter 3, the American Dietetic Association's 1997 "Position paper on Vegetarianism" illustrates the many benefits of plant-based diets. The U.S. Senate Select Committee on Nutrition and Human Needs recommended in February 1977 that Americans decrease their consumption of meat and increase their consumption of fruits, vegetables, and whole grains. Also, the 1988 report of the Surgeon General pointed out the many negative health effects of animal-centered diets and recommended an increase in the consumption of plant-based foods. Perhaps more will be done in the future, but the financial power of the beef and dairy lobbies and other groups who gain from the status quo prevents rapid changes.

10. What should a vegetarian eat to insure adequate nutrition?

There are a very large number of nutritious foods that vegetarians can eat from the plant kingdom. The Physicians' Committee for Responsible Medicine (PCRM) indicates that adequate nutrition can be obtained by eating a wide variety of foods from their "New Four Food Groups": (1) fruits, (2) vegetables, (3) whole grains, and (4) legumes. Recent recipe books (several are discussed in the Bibliography) contain a wide variety of delicious, nutritious vegetarian dishes.

11. How can a vegetarian get sufficient protein?[10]

This is the question most frequently asked of vegetarians. As Dr. Neal Barnard, director of the Physicians Committee for Responsible Medicine, points out, protein has been regarded with great awe in our society, almost as a fourth color of the flag: red, white, blue, and protein. However, the amount of protein that a person needs (as a percent of total calories) is actually relatively low: 4.5 percent, according to the World Health Organization of the United Nations; six percent, according to the Food and Nutrition Board of the U.S. Department of Agriculture; and eight percent, according to the U. S. National Research Council. It is extremely significant that during infancy, our period of most rapid growth, when infants double their birth weight in just six months, mother's breast milk provides only five percent of its calories from protein.

Most people get far too much protein, often several times the amount required, and this causes health problems. While the typical American consumes ninety to 120 grams of protein per day, recent studies indicate that twenty to thirty grams are sufficient. Adequate protein can easily be obtained from vegetarian, even vegan, diets. Protein is found in most plant foods as well as in animal foods. Green beans, for example, have over twenty percent of their calories from protein, and spinach has more than fifty percent.[11] It is almost impossible not to get adequate protein, even on a plant-based diet, provided that one is getting enough calories and consumes a reasonable variety of foods. Based on this, one might wonder why so many people think that getting sufficient protein is a major dietary concern. Perhaps the main reason is that much of our nutrition information has come from experiments on rats, and rats require far more protein than humans do; a rat mother's milk has about forty-seven percent of its calories from protein. The huge amount of money spent by the beef, dairy, and egg lobbies is also a major factor.

12. Do vegetarians have to "complement" proteins, that is, get a combination of different foods containing proteins at each meal to make sure that they get complete protein?

This was a theory first advocated by Frances Moore Lappé, who mistakenly argued in her very influential book, *Diet for a Small Planet*, that vegetarians should combine proteins in order to get the same "protein value" as meat. However, nutritionists no longer agree with that theory, and even Ms. Lappé indicated a change in her mind in later editions of her book. The

American Dietetic Association made clear in its 1992 paper, "Eating Well—The Vegetarian Way," that "Vegetarians do not need to combine specific foods within a meal as the old 'complementary protein' theory advised." The paper states: "The body makes its own complete proteins if a variety of plant foods—fruits, vegetables, grains, legumes, nuts, and seeds—and enough calories are eaten during the day."

13. How can a vegetarian get sufficient calcium? Don't we need milk and other dairy products in our diets to make sure that we are getting adequate calcium to reduce the risk of contracting osteoporosis?[12]
Osteoporosis, a disease generally related to aging, involves loss of bone mass which may result in one or more bones being broken, often under relatively little force. It is one of the most common bone diseases affecting women in affluent Western societies. The disease has commonly been associated with a lack of calcium, and the dairy industry has been promoting the consumption of a plentiful supply of dairy products as a way to prevent osteoporosis. However, scientific facts contradict this view. Worldwide, the countries with the highest levels of consumption of dairy products, including the United States, Israel, and several Scandinavian countries, are the ones with the highest rates of female osteoporosis. Eskimos, who have the highest dietary calcium intake of any people in the world, primarily from fish, have extremely high rates of osteoporosis. As mentioned in Chapter 3, while many Chinese people are lactose intolerant and consume no dairy products, their rate of osteoporosis is far lower than that for the U.S.

Recent research has linked osteoporosis to high animal-protein diets. It has been found that animal foods acidify the blood. In order to neutralize this excess acidity, calcium is drawn from the bones and later excreted. Vegetarians, even those who eat little or no dairy products, seldom get osteoporosis because they consume relatively little, if any, animal protein. Of course, it is important to consume plant foods that are rich in calcium and other vegetarian products, such as soy milk and cereals, that are enriched with calcium. Getting adequate exercise is another way to reduce the risk of getting osteoporosis.

Among the plant foods that are good sources of calcium are dark leafy greens (such as kale and mustard, collard, and turnip greens), broccoli, beans, dried figs, sunflower seeds, and calcium-fortified cereals and juices.[13] Dairy products are good sources of calcium, but they also contain large amounts of fat and animal protein.

According to the American Dietetic Association papers previously cited, vegans can usually obtain the calcium they need from plant foods alone, and studies have shown that vegetarians can absorb and retain more calcium from foods and have lower rates of osteoporosis than non-vegetarians.

14. What are other negative effects of getting too much animal protein?

Calcium lost due to high protein diets must be handled by the kidneys, and this may contribute to the formation of painful kidney stones. Excess dietary protein causes destruction of kidney tissue and progressive deterioration of kidney function. When people with partial loss or damage to their kidneys are placed on low-protein diets, they are often able to maintain much of their remaining kidney function.

People on animal-based diets not only get excessive protein, but also large amounts of hormones, fat, cholesterol, pesticides, antibiotics, and other harmful components of animal-source foods that place major burdens on the kidneys, liver, and digestive system.

15. How can a vegetarian get sufficient iron?[14]

There are many good plant food sources of iron. They include dried green vegetables, such as spinach and green beans, dried beans, pumpkin seeds, sesame seeds, black strap molasses, and iron-fortified breads and cereals. Foods high in vitamin C, such as broccoli, citrus fruits and juices, tomatoes, and green pepper, help the body absorb iron from plant sources. Vegans seldom suffer from iron-deficiency anemia.

16. Does a vegetarian need to have an extensive knowledge of nutrition?

Naturally, the more information a person has about nutrition, the better. But one need not be an expert on nutrition to be sure of getting adequate nutrition on a vegetarian diet. If one has a balance of foods from the "New Four Food Groups" (fruits, vegetables, whole grains, and legumes), avoids empty calories, and gets adequate rest and exercise, one can be very healthy. The avoidance of the excessive fat, cholesterol, and protein associated with flesh/dairy centered diets is a major positive step toward improved health.

Of course, once one moves toward vegetarianism, he or she might wish to learn more by reading books (see Bibliography), attending meetings, and speaking to knowledgeable people.

17. Don't vegetarians (especially vegans) have to be concerned about getting sufficient vitamin B$_{12}$, and can't the absence of this vitamin cause irreversible nerve damage?[15]

This is the one nutrition issue that should be of concern to vegans, because plant foods grown by modern chemical-based agriculture do not contain vitamin B$_{12}$. Vegetarians who consume dairy products and/or eggs will generally get adequate amounts of this essential nutrient because cows and chickens are high on the food chain and concentrate the vitamin in their tissues. With regard to vegans, some positive factors are (1) many studies have indicated that very little (about two micrograms [millionth of a gram]) of vitamin B$_{12}$ is needed daily; (2) while there are and have been millions of vegans who do not consume any animal products at all, cases of vitamin B$_{12}$ deficiency-related problems among them are rare. Still, vegans should not ignore this potential danger. Fortunately, many soy milk products and cereals are fortified with vitamin B$_{12}$. Also, it can be obtained through non-animal-based vitamin B$_{12}$ pills. When in doubt, a trusted medical professional should be consulted and/or one's B$_{12}$ level should be checked.

18. Can a vegetarian diet be unhealthy?

Yes, if it is extremely unbalanced. For example, if a person eats only or primarily fruits, or has a diet based almost completely on one food, such as rice, or consumes a great deal of candy bars and other sweets and empty calories from diet sodas, one can have a diet that lacks essential nutrients.

But a well-balanced diet with an adequate mix of fruits, vegetables, whole grains, and legumes, provides optimum health.

19. What health problems are associated with the consumption of dairy products?

The basic dairy product, cow's milk, is an ideal food—for the calf. For human beings, it can lead to several health problems. It is high in fat, protein, and cholesterol, low in carbohydrates, and devoid of fiber. Because dairy products and meat are so similar in many nutrients, John McDougall, M.D. asserts that dairy foods can be thought of as "liquid meat." Like flesh products, dairy products have been linked to several degenerative diseases, including heart disease, stoke, and diabetes.[16]

Due to extensive advertising campaigns by the dairy lobby, most people erroneously believe that dairy foods are good for human health. Many believe that it is "nature's perfect food." However, in addition to the recent medical evidence against dairy products, we can observe how other animals use milk. In its natural environment, no other young animal drinks the milk of another species or drinks milk after it is weaned. Humans are the only species to do both.

How about skim milk and other low-fat dairy products? These are lower in fat, which is positive. However, when the fat is skimmed from the milk, there is an increase in the relative proportions of protein and lactose, the same ingredients that cause many of the health problems associated with dairy products, such as food allergies and lactose intolerance. These low-fat products also have other nutritional deficiencies, including a complete lack of dietary fiber and low amounts of some vitamins and minerals.

20. What is an ideal cholesterol level?

Probably no one has done more work on connections between cholesterol and heart disease than William Costelli, M.D., Director of the Framingham (Massachusetts) Heart Study, the largest epidemiological study of heart disease. He states:

We've never had a heart attack in Framingham in thirty-five years in anyone who had a cholesterol under 150. Three-quarters of the [world's people] never have a heart attack. Their cholesterols are all around 150.[17]

It is important to note that for every decrease of one percent in the cholesterol level, there is a two percent decrease in the risk of heart attack.[18] Hence a reduction in cholesterol level is a very effective way to reduce risk of heart problems.

Cholesterol is only found in meat and other animal products, but never in plant foods. Eggs are extremely high in cholesterol having as much as 250 mg. The consumption of eggs can cause rapid and dramatic increases in people's cholesterol levels.

21. Is a change from beef to chicken and fish a positive step for improved health?

There may be some improvement in terms of lower fat, but chicken and fish still have high levels of protein and cholesterol. For example, 3.5 ounces of broiled lean flank steak are fifty-six percent fat, forty-two percent protein, with seventy mg of cholesterol, while the same amount of light or dark chicken, with the skin, is fifty-one percent fat, forty-six percent protein, and eighty-eight mg of cholesterol.[19] The high protein in fish and chicken can cause health problems, as discussed above.

Many people feel a false sense of security when they change from red meat to a primarily chicken and fish diet. The previously discussed study by Dr. Dean Ornish showed dramatic improvements in the condition of patients with severe heart problems who switched to vegetarian, almost vegan, very low-fat diets. It also showed that those who followed diets recommended by medical groups, such as the American Heart Association, which involve thirty percent of calories from fat, and include chicken without the skin, fish, and some dairy products, showed little improvement, and in most cases stayed the same or became worse.

22. Is vegetarianism an effective approach to weight loss?

Generally, yes. Many nutritionists believe that more important than the amount of food eaten is the type of food eaten. The reason is the calorie content of different nutrients: every gram of carbohydrates contains four calories; every gram of protein contains four calories; but every gram of fat contains nine calories. Hence, the typical high fat standard American animal-based diet is a prime contributor to obesity. Since vegetarians generally have lower fat diets than meat-eaters, they tend to be slimmer.

An effective long-term weight control program should include plenty of foods from the "new four food groups"—fruits, vegetables, whole grains, such as breads, rice, and pasta, and legumes, such as beans. It should exclude (or at least minimize) meats, poultry, fish, high-fat dairy products, fried foods, and added oils, such as salad dressings and margarine. It is important to read food labels and select foods with low fat content. Remember that every gram of fat, whether from an animal product or a vegetable product contains nine calories.

Recently high-protein low-carbohydrate diets have become very popular because people can temporarily lose large amounts of weight eating the high fat foods they enjoy so much. It is important to note, however, that when these diets are successful, it is because of caloric restriction when following the plan, and not because of the types of food consumed. There are serious health risks associated with these diets, because they promote the types of foods that have been strongly linked to a wide variety of degenerative diseases. Because of these factors, these diets have been opposed by many medical groups, including the World Health Organization, the American Cancer Society, the American Heart Association, the Surgeon General of the United States, the American Institute for Cancer Research, and the American Dietetic Association.[20]

23. Isn't it true that many people in nations that don't get enough meat suffer from malnutrition?

Yes, but they suffer not because they don't eat meat. They don't get enough calories. It has been estimated that twenty million people are dying annually because of a lack of adequate nutrition. Animal-based diets contribute to this, because, as noted previously, over seventy percent of the grain grown in the United States (and over one-third of all grain grown worldwide) is fed to animals destined for slaughter, and the U.S. and other developed countries import food from countries where people are severely malnourished.

Actually, there are two faces of malnutrition in the world today: one is in the less-developed countries, where people lack sufficient food, and the second in developed countries, like the U.S., where people suffer from degenerative diseases due to too much rich food, such as meat and dairy products. According to a recent Worldwatch Institute report, the number of overweight people in the world (about 1.2 billion) now equals the number of people suffering from malnutrition due to inadequate food intake.[21]

24. While vegetarianism may be fine for adults, don't children need to consume meat, dairy, products, and eggs?

Children can get all the protein, calcium, carbohydrates, vitamins, and other nutrients from plant-based foods. Meat is a good source of iron and protein, but it is also high in saturated fat and cholesterol, and the high amount of protein that it contains depletes calcium from the bones.

Children raised on strict vegetarian diets are generally healthy. A good source for further information is *Pregnancy, Children, and the Vegan Diet* by Michael Klaper (see Bibliography).

25. Don't meat producers take good care of their animals since their profits depend on it?

Profits depend on obtaining the maximum output in terms of pounds of meat, gallons of milk, or number of eggs produced, with the least expenditure in terms of such factors as feed and energy. Producers have found that crowding animals into very small spaces increases profits, until the point where the crowding is so great that the number of animals that die prematurely becomes too costly. This is similar to the transportation of slaves: it was considered "economical" to crowd slaves on the slave ships, even though many died during the trip.

26. Aren't animals raised for the kosher food market treated more compassionately than other food animals?

Unfortunately, animals raised for the kosher market are generally raised under the same conditions as nonkosher animals. It is usually only the process of slaughter that differs.

27. Doesn't humane legislation ensure the welfare of farm animals?

On both state and federal levels, the raising of animals for food is specifically exempted from anti-cruelty laws and humane legislation. Strong opposition from the powerful farm lobby has defeated legislative efforts to even study the treatment of farm animals.

28. Since animals kill each other in nature, why should we be concerned about killing animals for food?

Predator animals have no choice. They must eat other animals in order to live. Perhaps this is the way that nature takes care of old and weak animals that would not be able to survive much longer anyway. But human beings do have a choice, and we now know that we can be very healthy on a vegetarian diet, in fact far healthier than on a animal-based diet. Hence, there is no good reason to raise and slaughter animals for food.

29. Shouldn't people who abstain from eating meat also avoid consuming eggs and milk?

Many of the arguments made for not eating meat are valid with regard to eggs and milk, although to a lesser degree in some cases. And the vegan diet (non-use of any animal products) is a more humane diet. However, an estimated ninety percent of vegetarians today are lacto-ovo vegetarians. Many hope to become vegans eventually and some are moving toward that goal.

I prefer to look at vegetarians who consume eggs and milk as people who have made an important ethical decision, but who have not yet gone as far as possible. One can become a vegan by degrees. What is important is to take the first step and then progress toward improvements.

30. Aren't vegetarians who use leather shoes and other leather products being inconsistent?

It depends upon one's reasons for being a vegetarian. If it is based upon health, rather than concern for animals, for example, it would not be inconsistent.

Some vegetarians use leather products because these are byproducts of slaughter, rather than prime causes of it. Many vegetarians have changed to shoes of natural or synthetic non-animal materials. It has become easier to get such products recently as the demand for them has increased. Some vegetarians continue to wear leather products until they wear out and then purchase non-leather products.

31. Aren't there also problems related to eating vegetables? Aren't vegetables also sprayed with chemicals?

The concept of concern for plants is actually a strong positive point for vegetarianism. Because animals have to eat about ten times as much vegetable food to return a single unit of food value as meat, a vegetarian diet means less destruction of plants. Also, most vegetarian food can be obtained without killing the plant; this includes ripe fruits and nuts, berries, melons, seeds, legumes, tomatoes, squash, cucumbers, and pumpkins.

It is good that people are starting to think that plants have a certain state of sensitivity because this may lead to a greater awareness that animals are not unfeeling things. And certainly any consciousness in plants is of a different quality than that in humans and animals.

Unfortunately, it is true that many vegetables are sprayed with chemicals. It is important to wash them well. Also, efforts should be made to reduce unnecessary spraying of pesticides. But here, too, vegetarianism is beneficial because, as indicated previously, the movement of chemicals up the food chain leads to far greater amounts of pollutants in meat and fish.

32. What are the effects of the consumption of meat and other animal products on the onset of puberty and sexual maturity of females?[22]

This is one of the most negative effects of animal-based diets. Several studies have shown a decrease in the average age of puberty for females from about seventeen years of age in the middle of the 19th century to an average of about twelve years today. This shows how unnatural animal-centered diets, especially with all the added hormones and other chemicals, are for human beings. There is strong evidence that the sharp drop in the age of puberty is due to the steady increase in hormone-treated animal products in typical Western diets. In areas of China where people still consume plant-based diets, the average onset of puberty ranges from fifteen to nineteen years, and averages seventeen years. Migration studies also show a drop in the age of puberty in the next generation when people change from plant-based diets to the typical animal-based diets in their new country.

Experts indicate that physical maturity does not necessarily mean emotional maturity. As Laurence Steinberg, co-author of *You and Your Adolescent* (Harper Perennial, 1997) says, "A girl may look like a woman long before she [can act] like one."

Many girls face difficult, highly emotional situations at a time when they are not emotionally mature enough to react properly. Hence, in addition to its many other health and environmental benefits, a shift to well balanced vegetarian diets, without artificial hormones, would help prevent early pregnancies and the many social and emotional problems related to early sexual awareness and activities. A related concern is that early puberty has been linked to increased risk of breast cancer.

33. Is it important for vegetarians and everyone else to eat organic foods?

Certainly. EarthSave lists sixteen healthy reasons to eat organic.[23] these include: organic vegetarian foods have less residue from herbicides, pesticides, fungicides, toxic nitrates, and toxic metals; have no hormones or antibiotics; have more essential and trace minerals and other healthy agents; taste far better and enable the eating of the plant's skin; are better for children (children receive an average of four times greater exposure to at least eight widely used cancer-causing pesticides in non-organic foods);

are better for farm workers (according to a National Cancer Institute Study, farmers exposed to pesticides had a six-times greater risk of contracting cancer than non-farmers); are better for the environment since there is less soil erosion, water pollution, and loss of diversity; and are better for small farmers who are being squeezed by the technologies being used by agribusiness.

34. How serious are food-borne diseases?

They are very serious. The following summary is based on documented facts from John Robbins's *The Food Revolution: How Your Diet Can Help Save Your Life and Our World* (see Bibliography). The primary source of E.Coli O157:H7 infections is hamburgers and other sources of ground beef. A very conservative estimate (since many cases are not reported or are misdiagnosed) is that about 200 people in the United States become sick from E.Coli and several die daily. Long term afflictions suffered by many survivors of E.Coli O157:H7 poisoning include epilepsy, blindness, kidney failure, and lung damage.

The leading cause of food-borne illness in the United States is Campylobacter, a bacteria found in contaminated chicken flesh; an estimated seventy percent of American chickens and ninety percent of American turkeys are contaminated by this bacteria. It is estimated that more than 5,000 people in the United States become ill with Campylobacter daily and that there are fifty fatalities annually. Each year over 650,000 Americans are sickened from eating Salmonella-tainted eggs annually, and this causes about 600 deaths. Among symptoms of Salmonella poisoning are fever, headache, nausea, abdominal cramps, vomiting, and diarrhea. While the dangerous bacteria discussed above have also been found in non-animal products, they are far more often found in animal products. In virtually every investigated case in which these bacteria were found in fruits and vegetables, the cause has been traced to animal agriculture, usually a result of water contaminated by animal waste.

35. Wasn't Hitler a vegetarian?[24]

Is it really relevant what Hitler ate or did not eat? Would anyone cite Hitler's abstinence from smoking to discredit non-smokers? However, Hitler's alleged vegetarianism is brought up so often that it invites a response.

Because he suffered from excessive sweatiness and flatulence, Hitler sometimes went meatless. However, he generally continued to eat meat. In his definitive biography, *The Life and Death of Adolph Hitler*, the historian Ralph Payne mentions Hitler's special fondness for Bavarian sausages (p. 346). Other biographers, including Albert Speer, point out that he also sometimes ate ham, liver, and game.[25] Hitler not only ate meat, but he also banned vegetarian organizations in Germany and the occupied countries, even though vegetarian diets would have helped solve Germany's food shortage during the war.

36. I enjoy eating meat. Why should I give it up?

If one is solely motivated by what will bring pleasure, perhaps no answer to this question would be acceptable. But Judaism is motivated by far more: doing *mitzvot*, performing good deeds, sanctifying occasions, helping feed hungry people, pursuing justice and peace, and so on. This book attempts to show that people who take Jewish values seriously should be vegetarians.

Even if one is primarily motivated by considerations of pleasure and convenience, the negative health effects of an animal-centered diet should be taken into account. One cannot enjoy life when one is not in good health.

9: B'TAY-AVON:
HAVE A HEARTY APPETITE!

And you shall eat and be satisfied and bless the Lord your God for the good land He has given you. (Deuteronomy 8:10)

PREVIOUS CHAPTERS HAVE DOCUMENTED MANY REASONS why Jews (and others) should adopt sensible, well-balanced, nutritious vegetarian diets. This chapter will provide some suggestions on practical ways to practice this diet effectively.

A. Vegetarianism—A Way of Life

Some suggestions for making the transition to vegetarianism and a healthier lifestyle easier follow. You know yourself best; adopt suggestions and a pace of change most comfortable for you.

1. Many people become vegetarians instantly, totally giving up meat, poultry, and fish overnight. Others make the change gradually. Do what works best for you.

2. It is important to supply your nutritional needs by eating a wide variety of foods in season rather than depend on a limited selection of foods with which you were previously familiar. Experiment with new foods; dare to improvise!

3. If possible, plan menus in advance. Take time to build attractive meals using foods you enjoy. Many sources for recipes for tasty meals are given later. Generally aim to have simple meals with quick and easy preparation. Simplicity in diet has many advantages, including health and saving time.

4. Approach each meal with positive expectations. Enjoy your food. Don't consider yourself an ascetic. Realize that your diet is best for life— your life and that of spared animals, hungry people, and the environment.

5. Learn principles of sound nutrition. Read books on vegetarianism and natural health. Start to build a home library that you can use to seek responses to questions as well as to lend books to friends. Subscribe to health magazines, such as *Health Science*, *Vegetarian Voice*, *Vegetarian Journal*, and *Vegetarian Times*. Attend vegetarian and natural health meetings and conferences.

6. Become familiar with vegetarian restaurants in your area. Find out which restaurants offer salad bars with a wide variety of fresh vegetables. If their vegan selection is small, ask them to offer more of these choices.

7. Associate with other vegetarians and become friendly with health-minded people for mutual support and reinforcement. This is valuable even if socialization is mostly by telephone or the Internet. It is especially important for children—they should know that there are others with diets similar to theirs.

8. Become familiar with local health food stores, co-ops, ethnic stores, and the natural food section of your supermarket. However, many "natural food" products may be overpriced and not all that healthy. You don't have to shop in a special store to obtain healthy vegetarian foods. However, new foods can add variety to your diet. Here are some special items that you should get to know.

- Tofu—soy bean curd, which is a high-protein product that can be adapted to many vegetarian dishes.
- Tamari—a natural soy sauce prepared without caramel coloring or chemicals. Most brands are high in sodium although several low sodium options are available. Generally, tamari is wheat-free.
- Tahini—natural sesame butter.
- Rice cakes—puffed brown rice pressed to form round cakes, which are crisp and crunchy.
- Unsulfured, unsweetened, dried fruits.
- Unsalted shelled nuts and seeds.

While no special equipment is essential for vegetarian diets, the following may be very valuable: a vegetable juicer, blender, food processor, pressure cooker, and a stainless steel steamer (with perforated "wings" that open to any size pot and three legs, so water does not touch the vegetables).

9. Increase consumption of fruits, vegetables, and their freshly squeezed juices. See to it that a good variety of these foods, as well as seeds, raisins, and nuts, are always available at home.

10. As long as sufficient calories are consumed daily, protein needs can be easily met by all healthy vegetarians and vegans.

Maintaining a healthy diet is not difficult. The important thing is to eat a variety of wholesome plant-based foods, including some protein-rich foods, and consume sufficient calories.

A few good sources of plant-based protein are nuts, seeds, lentils, tofu, and tempeh. Many common foods such as whole grain bread, broccoli, spinach, potatoes, corn, and peas add to protein intake.

11. Use healthier substitutes. Instead of polished rice, use brown rice. Instead of white flour, use whole wheat or brown rice. Instead of sugar or an artificial sweetener, use rice bran syrup, or blackstrap molasses. Instead of margarine, use grapeseed or sesame oil (in recipes) or tahini dressing as a spread. Instead of commercial oils, use cold-pressed, pure grapeseed, sunflower, sesame, canola, or olive oil.

12. When you are invited to a wedding, bar/bat mitzvah, or dinner at someone's home, respectfully let your hosts know beforehand that you eat only vegetarian food. Generally, they comply cordially and often enjoy preparing a special meal for you and other guests. If they ask, "why?," use this as an opportunity to respectfully educate them, using the information in this and other vegetarian books.

If you feel it would be an imposition for your host to prepare something special for you, offer to bring a vegetarian or vegan dish. This will not only relieve the pressure on the host, but will also provide the opportunity to introduce the host and the other guests, whose knowledge of and experience with vegetarian food may be limited, to something really wonderful! Situations such as this can often lead to stimulating discussions on why one chose to be vegetarian.

13. Here are some additional suggestions for healthy eating: become a label reader; pay special attention to small print and nutritional data on food packages; minimize use of products with food colorings, preservatives, stabilizers, and artificial flavors; avoid frying, if possible; you might want to

minimize and possibly avoid the use of foods that contain caffeine, such as coffee, cola drinks, chocolate, and regular tea.

Ideally, a healthy vegetarian diet should contain a minimum of canned products, refined sugar and flour, artificial sweeteners, and salt. However, when you first adopt a vegetarian diet, you may wish to reduce consuming these products gradually.

14. Use substitutes for animal products while working with familiar recipes to make them as healthy and humane as possible. Here are some examples:

- Tofu, tempeh, textured vegetable protein, nuts, and refrigerated or frozen soy "burgers," "hot dogs," and other mock meats may be used in main dishes and other recipes instead of meat products.

- There are many delicious substitutes for dairy products, including soy-based milks, almond milk, rice milk, oat milk, and their associated cheeses, yogurts, and ice creams. Cheeses made from any of these various milk substitutes may be used for melted cheese sandwiches and pizzas. A good source for alternatives to dairy products is *The Uncheese Cookbook: Creating Amazing Dairy Substitutes* and *Classic Uncheese Dishes*, by Joanne Stepaniak (Summertown, Tennessee: Book Publishing Co.).

- Regular sour cream can be replaced by soy yogurt or a non-dairy sour cream substitute. Cheeses made from milk substitutes can replace high-fat dairy-based cheeses. You can further limit your fat intake by choosing lower fat substitutes.

- There are a variety of good substitutes for an egg, including a mashed banana, two tablespoons of cornstarch or arrowroot, or quarter of a cup of tofu. A powdered vegan egg replacer is also available in health food stores. A valuable source of information on this subject, as well as for many eggless recipes, is *Instead of Chicken, Instead of Turkey: A Poultryless "Poultry" Potpourri* by Karen Davis, founder and director of United Poultry Concerns (www.upc-online.org).

An excellent source of information on everything in this chapter as well as other vegetarian-related issues is the Vegetarian Resource Group (VRG), www.vrg.org.

These suggestions are just a beginning. As you read more about vegetarianism, attend meetings, and interact with like-minded individuals, you will expand your horizons and find the lifestyle ideal for you.

B. Recipes

There is an abundance of very comprehensive recipe books, including some written primarily for the Jewish community, which can be found in the Bibliography.

A valuable internet source of recipes is www.Foodtv.com, the official website of the "TV Food Network." By clicking on their "meatless/vegetarian" box in the "Advanced Recipe Search" section, you can find many vegetarian recipes from celebrity chefs. For special occasion meals, you can check out the five-course vegetarian menu, which changes weekly.

For locating vegetarian restaurants, the website http://VegDining.com provides more than 700 listings for vegetarian restaurants worldwide. At this site, you can also: find links to national and international vegetarian groups; join an ongoing vegetarian dining discussion group to receive news and talk about vegetarian restaurants in different cities; learn about special events coming up at vegetarian restaurants; and learn about a special international vegetarian card. There is an impressive index of over 1,600 vegetarian restaurants and health food stores scattered across the globe at www.happycow.net/. Vegetarians heading to Jerusalem, Santiago, London, Paris, or pretty much anywhere may want to give the "Happy Cow" a look before leaving.

Since vegetarianism is sprouting up in so many areas, it should be no surprise that there is a vegetarian cyber-superstore on the web at www.planetveggie.com. This site offers sections about all aspects of vegetarianism and vegetarian living, including information about vegetarian supplements and cruelty-free products (such as non-leather shoes, belts, and wallets) at discount prices and tips for healthy living, cooking, and how to purchase herbs and other natural foods.

C. Mixed Marriages: When Only One of You Is a Vegetarian

There are a number of factors that will affect how well a couple with dietary differences gets along:

1. Was there a change in the diet of either spouse after the wedding?

2. How strongly does the vegetarian hold his/her view? Does she/he regard it as a moral crusade or only as a personal preference? Is he/she revolted at the sight of meat?

3. How strongly does the non-vegetarian hold his/her view? Does she/he deeply resent it when a strong case is made for vegetarianism? Or does he/she respect the vegetarian position and perhaps even agree with it, but just feel unable to adopt that diet?

While the above factors should be considered, it is hoped that the following suggestions will be helpful in most situations:

Suggestions for Both Spouses

1. Recognize that the issues you agree on are far greater than those on which you disagree;

2. Recognize that your spouse did not adopt her/his diet to hurt you or make life more complicated for you. Try to respect his/her decision, whether it is based on what she/he regards as great moral principles, on convenience, on conformity, or on habit.

3. You might both want to take advantage of the many increasingly available vegetarian substitutes for hot dogs, hamburgers, and other animal-based meals.

4. Try to be creative in experimenting with new dishes that do not compromise your position.

5. Never attack your spouse's point of view, especially in public.

6. Compensate for any friction related to dietary differences by stressing important areas of agreement.

7. Try to find restaurants where you can eat together, without either spouse feeling that her/his principles are being violated.

Suggestions for the Vegetarian Spouse

1. Play an active role in shopping and preparing meals. Try to show that vegetarian meals can look appealing and be tasty.

2. Invest in a few good cook books (see Bibliography) and try to come up with perhaps seven or eight easy recipes that you can both enjoy.

3. If you lack time for meal preparation, you might find valuable ideas and recipes in *Meatless Meals for Working People: Quick and Easy Vegetarian Recipes* by Debra Wasserman and Charles Stahler and *Conveniently Vegan* by Debra Wasserman (see Bibliography).

4. Try to be a positive role model. Try to let your good health, cheerful attitude, and tolerance serve as a positive example of a vegetarian life.

5. Don't talk about your diet and the many benefits of vegetarianism unless your spouse is interested.

6. Use your improved health and vigor to be a better spouse.

7. If meat is not served in the house, be understanding if your spouse feels that he/she needs to eat meat outside sometimes.

8. If appropriate, have vegetarian books and magazines around the house, so that your spouse may pick them up and learn about the benefits and other aspects of vegetarian diets.

Suggestions for the Non-Vegetarian Spouse

1. Try to see the positive side of your spouse's diet. Recognize that she/he may be having a hard time defending his/her diet outside the home and that some support at home can be very helpful.

2. Don't say "how much easier life could be if you could just throw a steak in the oven (or on the grill)."

3. Appreciate any improved health and increased vitality your mate has due to a vegetarian diet.

4. Recognize that if you eat vegetarian food you are not compromising any principle or belief, while your spouse would be doing so if she/he ate meat. Consider, for example, that all meals served by the Israeli military are kosher, even though many Israeli soldiers do not normally observe the kosher laws, so that nobody's beliefs will be violated. (Vegetarian food is also available for Israeli vegetarian soldiers.)

5. Try to find some good vegetarian recipes that you find convenient and enjoyable, and that you can share together.

In conclusion, recognize that, while eating is one of life's great pleasures, it is not all of life, so please don't let any disagreements get in the way of your enjoying your life together.

10: JEWISH VEGETARIAN GROUPS AND ACTIVITES[1]

Vegetarians are sprouting up all over.
(Slogan on T-shirt)

A **International Groups.** The international center for Jewish vegetarian activities is "The International Jewish Vegetarian and Ecological Society," often referred to as the "International Jewish Vegetarian Society" (IJVS), or just the "Jewish Vegetarian Society" (JVS). Its headquarters are at Bet Teva in London. The society has published a quarterly magazine, *The Jewish Vegetarian*, since September 1966. Generally, each issue includes an editorial, articles relating Judaism to vegetarianism, information about vegetarianism in Israel, local issues, Jewish vegetarian groups and individuals, announcements of society and related events, book reviews, recipes, and news about the society and its members.

The Jewish Vegetarian Society sponsors many events and activities related to its goals. Its motto, which appears on the masthead of *The Jewish Vegetarian*, comes from Isaiah's prophecy about the future ideal age: "They shall not hurt nor destroy in all My holy mountain" (Isaiah 11:9). The Society has branches in many parts of the world, and is a member of both the European Vegetarian Union and the International Vegetarian Union.

The Society publishes and distributes many articles showing the relationship between Judaism and vegetarianism. It has an official cookbook, *Jewish Vegetarian Cooking*, by Rose Friedman (see Bibliography for information about this and other books mentioned in this chapter). There are two types of membership available: one for practicing vegetarians, who do not eat flesh foods, and another for non-vegetarians who are in sympathy with the movement.

The origins of the society show how one person, one letter, one simple act can have a great influence. Vivien Pick wrote a letter about vegetarianism to the *London Jewish Chronicle* in 1964, in which she asked people interested in joining a Jewish vegetarian group to contact her. The response was great, and the result was the Jewish Vegetarian Society.

From the start of the Society in 1964 until his death in 1992, Philip Pick, Vivien's father, was its president and editor of *The Jewish Vegetarian*. After many years of devoted service, he was made honorary life president. He was a passionate vegetarian who campaigned vigorously for the vegetarian cause. Largely through his efforts, the Society grew from a handful of people to an international organization with chapters in sixty-five countries. He wrote many powerful articles and editorials and spoke at conferences all over the world furthering vegetarianism from a positive Jewish perspective. He also edited *The Tree of Life*, a collection of articles and editorials which appeared in the magazine. An example of his many strong editorials and other writings is given below:

Shall we participate in the use of poisoned carcasses of birds and beasts for food, and ask for a perfect healing? Above all, shall we harden our hearts to the cries of tormented creatures reared in the captivity and darkness of factory farms, and ask for pity and compassion for ourselves and our infants?[2]

On October 31, 2000 I gave the first annual "Philip Pick Memorial Lecture at Bet Teva.

According to the March 2000 issue of *The Jewish Vegetarian*, the patrons of the Jewish Vegetarian Society are Rabbi Raymond Apple (Australia), Justice Zvi Berenson (Israel), former Knesset member Mordecai Ben Porat (Israel), Haifa Ashkenazic Chief Rabbi Shear Yashuv Cohen (Israel), The Count Gentile, K.O.C., K.O.L. (U.K.), Rebbetzin Goren (Israel), Prof. Alex Hershaft (U.S.), Dr. Michael Klaper (U.S.), Prof. Richard Schwartz (U.S.), Rt. Hon. The Lord Wetherill, P.C., D.L. (U.K.), and Prof. Louis Berman (U.S.).

In 2000 the JVS International Council members were Naomi Fellerman (Chairperson), Harry Binstock, Laurie Binstock, Jonathan Briggs, Michael Freedman, Jeffrey Goldberg, Minna Pick, Hon Secretary

Shirley Labelda, Julie Rosenfield, John Schlackman, Margaret Toch, Henry Toch, and Leonard Waxman. Naomi Fellerman is currently the editor of *The Jewish Vegetarian.*

Because of recent expansions, the Society has three regional presidents: Stanley Rubens, LL.B., of Melbourne, Australia, is President of the southern regions; Rabbi Noach Valley (to be discussed later) is President for North America; Rabbi David Rosen (see "Biographies of Famous Jewish Vegetarians") is President for Israel and the East.

The IJVS office is run by Shirley Labelda and Ruth Hyman. From 1994 to 1999, *The Jewish Vegetarian* was edited by Julie Rosenfield (who also contributed many articles), with help from Shirley Labelda. Additional information about IJVS and other groups discussed in this chapter is in the Appendix.

The IJVS has supported the Orr Shalom Children's Homes in Israel for many years, centers where homeless children receive loving care within a family atmosphere. Meals at the homes are strictly vegetarian and it is hoped that the home will help spread vegetarian ideas and ideals throughout Israel. The homes were established by Hal and Shelly Cohen, who recognized the need for an alternative to the traditional system for deprived children.

Orr Shalom is now helping about 180 at-risk children to become contributing men and women in Israeli society. They are seeking additional funds to enable them to continue their recent expansion.

B. Vegetarianism in Israel

A center for the International Jewish Vegetarian Society was established in 1992 at 8 Balfour Street (adjacent to the French Square) in the heart of Jerusalem. This was the fulfillment of Philip Pick's dream of over a quarter of a century and many years of hard work.

There was a "Housewarming Ceremony" at the Center on April 2, 1992. Rabbi Shear Yashuv Cohen, Ashkenazic Chief Rabbi of Haifa and Patron of the Society, was out of the country but sent a message of congratulations and good wishes. Mark Weintraub, then chairman of the Israel Jewish Vegetarian Society, opened the proceedings and welcomed the eighty-five people present at the historic event. In his address to the gathering, Rabbi David Rosen, President of the Israel Jewish Vegetarian Society and former Chief Rabbi of Ireland, told the assembly that "the sublimest of our Jewish teachings are expressed through authentic Jewish vegetarianism and will be a source of redemptive light in keeping with prophetic vision that will shine forth from Jerusalem." Philip Pick, founder and President Emeritus of the International Society, said that the Society had made impacts in all parts of the world and expressed his dream that the historic occasion would be "the forerunner of the days when the movement shall encompass all the people of Israel in their adherence to the divine will of compassion for all creation, when the war against nature will cease."

The hundredth issue of *The Jewish Vegetarian* (March, 1992) informed members of the new Jerusalem Center. In an editorial in that issue, Philip Pick wrote: "Although the road to Jerusalem has been long and arduous, it is with joy that we embark on the next stage of our efforts, in the knowledge that once again the message will go out from Jerusalem to foster love and compassion for all living creatures and a diminishment of the current war against creation."

The Jerusalem Center is increasingly involved in important activities, including setting up lectures by local and visiting experts; having an annual *Tu B'Shvot* program; becoming a center for vegetarian-related books, magazines, videos and other material; and becoming a source for nutritional and general dietary information. It is hoped that it will become a center for a number of interns and other volunteers who can carry out valuable projects, such as translating material from Hebrew and into Hebrew, organizing letter writing campaigns to newspapers and other media outlets, and organizing additional projects to help spread information related to the Jewish vegetarian cause.

From 1995 to 2000, the Assistant Director of the Center was Aden Bar-Tura. In 2000, Elihu Menzin took over that position.

Vegetarianism is an active movement in Israel today. Its increasing popularity is indicated by the rapid growth of health food stores and vegetarian restaurants, and increasing interest in such topics as nutrition, health, animal rights, and ecology. In addition, most supermarkets and many corner grocery stores carry granolas, whole-wheat flour, brown rice, and other natural foods.

A valuable resource for vegetarian restaurants and health food stores in Israel is the *Guide to Vegetarian Restaurants in Israel*, edited by Mark Weintraub, the first director of the Jerusalem Vegetarian Center, and published by the Vegetarian Resource Group. In addition to its information about and ratings of restaurants and listing of health food stores, the book has a list of animal rights, vegetarian/vegan, and environmental groups in Israel, a short vegetarian Hebrew–English dictionary, a discussion of vegetarian foods commonly found in Israel, and information about the Jewish Vegetarian Society and Jewish vegetarian books. For a free copy of this important resource, send two dollars to cover postage and handling to the Vegetarian Resource Group (see Appendix).

Amirim is a completely vegetarian community (*moshav*) in Israel. Located in the Galilee, near the city of Safed, its high elevation enables residents and visitors to see both the Mediterranean Sea and the Sea of Galilee. Many of the eighty vegetarian and naturalist families in Amirim provide lodging and vegetarian meals to vacationers. Visitors can eat at a variety of homes to sample different types of meals and meet a variety of people. The village store contains a full range of organic foods but no meat, poultry, fish, or cigarettes. There is a swimming pool and other recreational facilities available for vacationers, and some members of the community provide massages and other health therapies. Among the potential activities for visitors and residents are hikes, visits to Safed, tours of the Galilee, and visits to gravesites of famous Jewish leaders and scholars, such as Rabbi Shimon Bar Yochai.

A valuable source of information about animal issues and groups, primarily in Israel, is *ProAnimal* magazine. Each of its issues discusses activities of Israeli animal rights and animal welfare groups and has an extensive list of the groups, along with contact information. The editor and publisher is Suzanne Trauffer.

In January 1994, Israel passed an "Animal Protection Act." The complete text of the act was printed in the January 1995 issue of *ProAnimal* magazine. Among the provisions of the act are that no person shall "torture an animal nor be cruel to an animal, nor ill-treat an animal in any way," nor "organize animal fighting contests," nor "work an animal which is not capable of doing so due to its physical condition." While the legislation marks a major step forward, "the law does not apply to killing animals intended for human consumption" and "does not apply to animal experiments," where other legislation applies. The application of the law to current intensive factory farming methods is being tested by a suit brought to the Israeli Supreme Court by Israeli animal rights activists who argue that the production of pâté de foie gras violates the law.

CHAI (Concern for Helping Animals in Israel) is a non-profit, tax-exempt organization established in 1984 by American animal activist Nina Natelson to assist animal protection efforts in Israel. CHAI sends funds and veterinary medical supplies to Israel's animal shelters and helps build new shelters; sponsors humane education seminars and materials for teachers around the country. It built the "Isaac Bashevis Singer Humane Education Center" at the SPCA in Tel Aviv. The Singer Center is becoming the source for an extensive library of books and videos about animals and animal issues. It also conducts educational programs, including CHAI's "Living Together" program that brings Jewish and Arab children together to learn about and help animals. CHAI is currently raising funds to help reduce the number of animals currently killed due to the inability to provide sufficient shelter. CHAI has also funded a scientist to develop a humane alternative to the practice of killing male chicks at birth.

Among CHAI's other accomplishments are: it helped draft Israel's first "Animal Protection Law" (discussed above); it replaced the routine strychnine poisoning of animals at municipal pounds with humane methods; it focused media attention on the benefits of the oral rabies vaccine in humanely controlling rabies instead of the strychnine poisoning of animals in the fields; and it urged the government to distribute the vaccine (the distribution began in March 2000).

CHAI has organized many campaigns that stopped abuses and changed policy in many areas. It convinced the Army to switch to alternatives instead of operating on dogs in paramedic training classes and urged them to make a similar switch in emergency medicine classes for doctors. It stopped the Ministry of Tourism's practice of offering free tickets and transportation to the spectacle of the sacrificing of lambs by the Samaritans; it organized support in the U.S. Congress and Senate and the Israeli Knesset to change the Ministry of Finance's practice of imposing huge customs duties on animal ambulances donated to animal shelters while allowing similar ambulances donated to human hospitals to enter the country duty-free (the first animal ambulance was donated by CHAI to the new SPCA Tiberias and entered the country duty-free).

CHAI also co-sponsored, with the Ministry of Education, Israel's first countrywide humane education contest—the first governmental initiative to promote humane values. CHAI has held many ground-breaking conferences which have brought media attention and public awareness for the first time to the issues, including: a conference co-sponsored by the Ministry of Education on the link between violence toward animals and toward people and the need for humane education; an international medical conference about alternatives to animals in laboratories (the proceedings were distributed worldwide); and humane education seminars for teachers countrywide, which empower teachers to reach thousands of students nationwide on the connections between animal overpopulation, factory farming, vivisection, vegetarianism, human health, and the environment.

A relatively new animal rights group that has been very active in Israel is Anonymous for Animal Rights. With David Massey as founder and Yossi Wolfson as coordinator, Anonymous has established an "Animal Rights and Education Center" at 93 Dizingoff Street in Tel Aviv (after many years at 48a Ben Yehuda Street), which has become a base for activities, meetings, and research. The center contains more than 200 books, over forty videos, and a large variety of journals and other publications. These resources are valuable tools for the many visiting students who come to do research on animal-related topics.

Anonymous has organized and participated in hundreds of activities in its first six years, including demonstrations in front of fur shops and fast food meat establishments, such as McDonald's and Burger Ranch, marches and other protests against animal experiments, involvement in various school projects, and the distribution of printed material. Its campaign to ban animal circuses has had positive results, with a *de facto* ban on such circuses in Israel. Cooperating with other animal protection organizations, Anonymous has helped stop a plan to establish a breeding facility in the south of the country for monkeys raised for experiments. The group was also instrumental in a campaign that led Yossi Sarid, former Minister of Education, to ban animal dissection in all Israeli state-run schools. The group plans to focus increasingly on vegetarianism and veganism. To further these causes the group uses both traditional methods, such as publishing and distributing literature, and innovative ones, such as street theater.

Avi Pinkas, an Israeli engineer, has started a group called *Hai-meshek*, (Israeli Society for the Prevention of Cruelty to Farm Animals). Its primary function has been to improve the treatment of farm animals on Israeli farms.

An Israeli animal rights umbrella group is Noah, the Federation of Animal Protection Societies in Israel. The organization was formally established in 1993, as the brainchild of Israeli animal rights Knesset member Avraham Poraz, a vegetarian lawyer, who wanted to see all of Israel's animal welfare groups working together. Noah has approximately twenty member societies, including groups concerned about dogs, cats, horses, donkeys, farm animals, and laboratory animals. Noah has given the animal welfare movement in Israel a boost, since it represents so many organizations and has earned the respect of many groups (e.g., municipal and government bodies and the media).

Noah coordinates an annual "Knesset Day," on which Israeli Knesset members address animal rights advocates on relevant animal issues. The group recently held a conference at which Israeli judges and law enforcement officials discussed legal issues related to punishing people who mistreat animals. Noah also is spearheading a campaign to get the Israeli Supreme Court to ban the force feeding of geese to create foie gras.

An active vegetarian group is the Vegetarians and Vegans Society, centered in Tel-Aviv. Recently, the society has become much more active, publishing new material and organizing outreach activities. An important recent activity took place in Tel-Aviv on December 22, 1999. Under the title "Meatout: A Wonderful Day Without Meat," the Society organized an evening of lectures and videos on different aspects of vegetarianism.

There are a number of additional vegetarian and animal rights/welfare groups, and animal shelters in many Israeli cities. Information about these groups and how to contact them can be found in each issue of *ProAnimal* magazine.

In the mid-1990s, I started a campaign for a "vegetarian-conscious Israel by 2000," with the aim of increasing the awareness of Israelis to vegetarian-related issues and Jewish teachings on these issues. To further the campaign, I have spoken to many groups throughout Israel, had letters published in the *Jerusalem Post*, and have met with several chief rabbis and other Israeli leaders. An article on these activities appeared in the August 10, 1995 issue of the *Jerusalem Post*.

C. North American Groups and Activities

The Jewish Vegetarians of North America (JVNA) is affiliated with the International Jewish Vegetarian Society. It has several hundred members and its current president is Rabbi Noach Valley, spiritual leader of the Actor's Synagogue in New York City. Rabbi Valley also helps coordinate a vegetarian group in Manhattan, which frequently has meetings with speakers and activities, and he coordinates a weekly vegetarian *kiddush* at his synagogue after Sabbath services. He often contributes articles to the JVNA newsletter, edited by Eva Mossman, assisted by her husband Israel and daughter Ziona. Israel Mossman is coordinator of The Jewish Vegetarians of North America and handles the membership in the USA and Canada.

The periodic JVNA newsletter keeps members informed about Jewish vegetarian activities in various communities and also includes articles, book reviews, and information about Jewish vegetarian contacts. A large number of American rabbis receive the newsletter.

In 1998, JVNA sent to over 3,500 North American congregational rabbis a special issue of its newsletter, which included a letter to the rabbis, urging them to put vegetarianism on their synagogues' agendas. The letter was signed by over twenty rabbis, and many doctors, nutritionists, other professionals, and vegetarian activists. Included with the letter were fact sheets showing contradictions between the realities of animal-based diets and basic Jewish mandates and this author's article, "What Diet Does God Prefer for People." The group also plans to sponsor an annual "Vegetarian Shabbat."

Charles Stahler and Debra Wasserman were instrumental in the early years of the JVNA. They ran the group and edited the newsletter for many years, before turning over their responsibilities to the Mossmans, when Charles and Debra founded and ran the Vegetarian Resource Group, an important and influential national vegetarian information organization. Charles and Debra were extremely active in planning Jewish vegetarian conferences and in distributing literature at street fairs in various communities. Their diligent efforts provided the glue that kept the society functioning vibrantly and creatively for many years.

Another person who was extremely important in the formation and early years of the JVNA is Jonathan Wolf. The group was founded in his living room in 1975, shortly after Jonathan and several other Jewish vegetarians attended the World Vegetarian Congress in Orono, Maine. Jonathan wrote articles and flyers for the JVNA beginning in 1976 advocating Jewish vegetarianism based on compassion for animals, concern for the environment, feeding the hungry, and preserving health. He is a committed Orthodox Jew, who told the *New York Times* in 1976 that all the reasons for people becoming vegetarian have roots in Jewish teachings. He has held many Jewish vegetarian events in his home and at synagogues in Manhattan, and he has periodically taught a unique course, "Judaism and Vegetarianism," at Lincoln Square Synagogue in New York. In this course (which the author attended and from which many of the ideas and sources in this book derive) he examines connections between vegetarian and Jewish values, utilizing material from the Torah and Talmud, modern *responsa*, Jewish legal codes, the writings of Rav Kook, Joseph Albo, and other Jewish scholars, and fiction by vegetarian authors such as Isaac Bashevis Singer.

Jonathan has been extremely creative in connecting vegetarian values and menus to the calendar of Jewish holidays. For many years he hosted up to sixty guests for annual vegetarian Passover *seders*. Especially interesting is the vegetarian *Tu B'Shvot seder* which he has conducted since 1975 in his home, following and expanding the tradition of the 16th-century kabbalists of Safed (who loved trees and tasted a variety of fruits, but were not vegetarians). The *Tu B'Shvot seders* include a tasting of the seven species of grains and fruits of the land of Israel mentioned in the Torah, Prophets, Talmud, *Midrash*, and other holy writings, with four special cups of wine. The *seders* involve much singing, merriment, good feeling, warmth, community, games, and blessings of thanks. Jonathan has also often hosted vegetarian Sabbath and holiday meals, as well as discussions on vegetarian and environmental issues in his home.

Local chapters of the Jewish Vegetarians of North America have become active in many communities in the U.S. and Canada. A listing of groups and contact people can be found in the group's newsletter.

Roberta Kalechofsky is founder and leader of Jews for Animal Rights (JAR). This group attempts to make Jews and others aware of Jewish values related to compassion for animals as contrasted with what the group regards as the "unprecedented modern abuse of animals." The group produces literature and postcards related to Jewish teachings on treatment of animals.

Roberta has been prolific in producing Jewish vegetarian materials. Through her Micah Publications, which specializes in vegetarian and animal rights books, she has written or edited and published *Vegetarian Judaism, The Jewish Vegetarian Year Book, Haggadah for the Liberated Lamb, Haggadah for the Vegetarian Family, Judaism and Animal Rights, Rabbis and Vegetarianism,* and *A Boy, A Chicken, and the Lion of Judea: How Ari Became a Vegetarian* (see Bibliography). For many years, she produced a Jewish vegetarian calendar ("The Jewish Vegetarian Year"), which contained many recipes, ideas, and appropriate quotations. She has also published a series of "Green Mitzvah Booklets," which relate Jewish values to a number of vegetarian and animal rights issues.

The JVNA presents a "Jewish Vegetarian of the Year Award" at its conferences. The first award was presented to the late Isaac Bashevis Singer in 1986. Since then, the award has been received by myself, the late Florence Mitrani, Roberta Kalechofsky, Rabbi Noach Valley, and Jay Lavine, M.D.

I recently gave a course on "Judaism and Vegetarianism" through e-mail and over 700 students registered. E-mail addresses of these students are on an e-mail distribution list, and this provides a group of interested people throughout the United States and several other countries who can help promote vegetarianism and provide feedback about articles and proposed vegetarian activities and projects. The author also has about 100 vegetarian-related articles and book reviews on the Internet at schwartz.enviroweb.org. He sends these articles out periodically to individuals and various e-mail distribution lists; for example, articles relating Jewish holidays to vegetarianism are sent before each holiday to an e-mail list of Jewish media.

Two major books relating Judaism and vegetarianism were originally published in the 1980s: this book (Exposition Press, 1982; Micah Publications, 1988, second edition) and *Vegetarianism and the Jewish Tradition* by Louis Berman (K'tav, 1982). Berman, professor of psychology and staff counselor at the Student Counseling Service, University of Illinois, Chicago Circle, has lectured on vegetarianism in Chicago, New York, Denver, Los Angeles, and Dayton, Ohio, and has taught an evening adult education class in vegetarian cooking in his home town of Evanston, Illinois. He has also published a *Haggadah for Tu B'Shvot*, which incorporates many vegetarian themes.

In summary, many exciting things are happening in the Jewish vegetarian world, and there is much about which to be optimistic. By actively seeking ways to build on these and other significant events and projects, there is great potential for increased progress toward a cruelty-free world.

11: BIOGRAPHIES OF FAMOUS JEWISH VEGETARIANS

Aside from the fact that both the original Garden of Eden and the messianic vision of the future reflect the vegetarian ideal in Judaism, it is of course such a dietary lifestyle that is most consonant with the goal and purpose of Torah to maximize our awareness, appreciation, and sensitivity to the Divine Presence in the world. It is therefore only natural for us to affirm as did Rav Kuk [Kook], the first Ashkenazi Chief Rabbi in Israel, that a redeemed world must perforce be a vegetarian world.[1]—Rabbi David Rosen (Biography in this chapter)

THIS CHAPTER PROVIDES BRIEF BIOGRAPHIES OF famous Jews who were vegetarians for all or a substantial part of their lives.[2] The author would appreciate hearing about other Jewish vegetarians who have not been included and/or significant facts that have been omitted from these biographies.

Agnon, Shmuel Yosef (1888–1970)

Shmuel Yosef Agnon was a central figure in modern Hebrew fiction. He wrote many novels and short stories about major contemporary spiritual concerns. He won the Israel Prize for Literature in 1954 and 1958 and the Nobel Prize in Literature in 1966, the first time that this honor was given to a Hebrew writer. His folk epic, *The Bridal Canopy*, was widely recognized as one of the cornerstones of modern Hebrew literature.

Agnon was a devout Jew who spent much of his life in Israel. He was extremely devoted to vegetarianism. He wove vegetarian themes into many of his stories, as in the following excerpt:

He received the Sabbath with sweet song and chanted the hallowing tunefully over raisin wine. The table was well spread with all manner of fruit, beans, greenstuffs and good pies,...but of flesh and fish there was never a sign. The old man and his wife had never tasted flesh since reaching maturity.[3]

Agnon's great sensitivity to all creatures can be seen in the following excerpt from his speech upon receiving the Nobel Prize for Literature:

> Lest I slight any creature, I must also mention the domestic animals, the beasts, and the birds from whom I have learned. Job said long ago (35:11): "Who teacheth us more than the beasts of the earth, and maketh us wiser than the fowls of heaven?" Some of what I have learned from them I have written in my books, but I fear that I have not learned as much as I should have done, for when I hear a dog bark, or a bird twitter, or a cock crow, I do not know whether they are thanking me for all I have told of them or calling me to account.[4]

Cohen, Rabbi David (The Nazir of Jerusalem) (1887–1973)

Rabbi David Cohen, the famous kabbalist and renowned Jewish philosopher, was born near Vilna, capital of Lithuania. He made a major contribution to Jewish vegetarianism by collecting and editing the Jewish vegetarian ideas of Rav Kook.[5] He was known as "The Nazir of Jerusalem" because he adopted all the obligations of the Nazarite as described in the Torah; he did not drink wine or cut his hair for a specific period. He was also a strict vegetarian. He was the father of the present Chief Rabbi of Haifa, Rabbi Shear Yashuv Cohen, and of the wife of the former Ashkenazic Chief Rabbi of Israel, Rabbi Shlomo Goren.

Cohen, Rabbi Shear Yashuv[6]

Rabbi Shear Yashuv Cohen, an important modern scholar and religious leader, has been a vegetarian from birth and is a patron of the Jewish Vegetarian Society. He graduated in 1947 from Rav Kook's Universal Yeshiva in Jerusalem and was ordained a rabbi by the late Chief Rabbi Herzog. From 1948 to 1953, he was chaplain in the Israeli Defense Forces and Chief Chaplain of the Israeli Air Forces (1952–53). His many positions include President of the Harry Fischel Institute for Research in Jewish Law and Seminary for Rabbis and Rabbinical Judges; member of the City Council of Jerusalem; Deputy Mayor of Jerusalem (1965–75); Chief Rabbi of Haifa (since 1975); and Chancellor of the Ariel United Israel Institutes (since 1973). In 1999 he received an Honorary Doctorate from Bar-Ilan University.

Gordon, Aaron David (1856–1922)

Aaron David Gordon was a Hebrew writer who wrote numerous articles on labor, Zionism, and Jewish destiny. As a strong advocate of the *kibbutz* (collective settlement) approach, his writings influenced the Jewish Labor Movement throughout the world. He hoped that *kibbutzim* would be vegetarian settlements, dependent on the land for their produce.

Gordon believed that Zionism would obtain self-fulfillment through working the land. He came to Israel at the age of forty-eight and spent many years farming. He saw the state of Israel as a challenge to Jews to make a contribution to humanity. He believed that the Jews would be tested through their attitudes and behavior toward the Arabs.

The importance that Gordon placed on vegetarianism can be seen in the following selection:

> The attitude toward vegetarianism...the attitude toward living creatures is...the clearest test of our attitude towards life and toward the world as it really is....The ethical regard toward living creatures that involves no hope of reward, no utilitarian motive, secret or open, such as honor, shows us...the significance of righteousness and all the other desired traits...[How can we have] righteousness, truth, and the like [along with] eating living creatures!"[7]

Goren, Rabbi Shlomo (1917–1994)

Rabbi Shlomo Goren was the Ashkenazic Chief Rabbi of Israel from 1972 to 1982. He was formerly Ashkenazic Chief Rabbi of Tel Aviv–Jaffa and Chief Rabbi of the Israeli Defense Forces. In the latter capacity, he was the first person to conduct a religious service at the liberated Western Wall in Jerusalem in 1967.

Rabbi Goren wrote many *responsa* on issues related to modern technology and conditions of modern warfare. He also wrote and published many volumes on *Halacha* and Jewish philosophy. His comprehensive commentary on the section *Berachot* of the Jerusalem Talmud won the Israel Prize in 1961.

The Rabbi's wife is a life-long vegetarian, having been reared in the Orthodox vegetarian home of "The Nazir of Jerusalem."[8]

Kacyzne, Alter (1885–1941)

Alter Kacyzne was born in Lithuania but spent most of his creative years in Warsaw, where many of his plays were successfully staged. His works include many dramatic poems, ballads, short stories, and one full length novel, *The Strong and the Weak*, which won much praise for its great historical and political significance. His writing often dealt with people's inhumanity. Kacyzne became a vegetarian at the age of eighteen, after a curious dream in which he was forced to eat a roasted child. His vegetarian beliefs were well known in Poland. He and his wife hosted well-attended vegetarian receptions. He was beaten to death with sticks and clubs by Nazis in Ukraine in 1941 and then buried in a mass grave.[9]

Kafka, Franz (1883–1924)

Franz Kafka was a Czech-born, German novelist whose writing had great influence on Western literature and art. His many books include *The Castle*, *The Trial*, and *The Great Wall of China*. His novels have been translated into many languages, including Hebrew, and have been adapted for movies, plays, and operas. The action in his books generally centers around the hero's search for identity.

Kafka was attracted to vegetarianism for health and ethical reasons. While viewing fish at an aquarium, he said, "Now I can look at you in peace; I don't eat you anymore." He had little faith in conventional doctors; he was interested in the benefits of nature-cure and raw-foods diets. He was also involved in anti-vivisection activities.[10]

Kook (Kuk), Rabbi Abraham Isaac Hakohen (1865–1935)

Rabbi Abraham Isaac Hakohen Kook (Rav Kook) was the first Ashkenazic Chief Rabbi of pre-state Israel during the British mandate. He was a very beloved person who helped inspire many people to move toward spiritual paths. He urged religious people to become involved in social questions and efforts to improve the world.

Rav Kook's philosophy of vegetarianism is in "A Vision of Vegetarianism and Peace," edited by Rabbi David Cohen. As discussed previously, Rav Kook believed strongly that God permitted people to eat meat as a concession. He taught that the many prohibitions related to the slaughtering and eating of meat were meant as an implied scolding and as a reminder that people should have reverence for life, and this would eventually bring people back to vegetarianism in the days of the Messiah. Rav Kook was reportedly not a complete vegetarian, but there is no doubt that he was a leading advocate for vegetarianism.

Leftwich, Joseph (1892–1984)

Joseph Leftwich was an author, editor, and anthologist, who was considered an authority on Jewish and Yiddish literature. He translated works by Shalom Asch, Max Brod, I. L. Peretz, Zalman Schneur, and Stefan Zweig. He also edited several influential anthologies: *Yisroel, The First Jewish Omnibus* (1933, rev. 1963), which has a wide selection of Jewish literature from many countries; *Golden Peacock* (1939), translations of Yiddish poetry; and *The Way We Think* (2 vols., 1969), Yiddish essays in English translation. Leftwich was an active vegetarian and a patron of the Jewish Vegetarian Society. He wrote brief biographies of vegetarian writers, which appeared in *The Jewish Vegetarian* and an introduction to *The Tree of Life*, a collection of essays selected and edited by Philip Pick that discuss Judaism and vegetarianism (see the Bibliography).

Maccoby, Chaim Zundel (The Kamenitzer Maggid)[11] (1858–1916)

Rabbi Chaim Zundel Maccoby was born in Kamenitz, Russia. He settled in London in 1890 and preached Torah, religious Zionism, and vegetarianism in the streets of that city. He taught people how to have compassion for all living creatures and how to remain healthy with little money. He was known by many as a great and saintly preacher and was a dedicated vegetarian who wore cloth shoes all year long to show his abhorrence of leather. In 1975, the Hall of Education Library opened at Bar Ilan University, Ramat Gan, Israel, dedicated to his memory.

Peretz, Isaac Leib (1852–1915)

I. L. Peretz was a prolific and versatile writer of Hebrew and Yiddish stories and poems who was one of the founders of modern Yiddish literature as well as an important figure in Hebrew literature. He had many original ideas and used his rich imagination to champion the cause of the oppressed and common people. His compassion and sensitivity encouraged many aspiring authors. He wrote much about the lives of the Chassidim, and the Jewish socialist movement was greatly influenced by his ideas.

Ravitch, Melech (1893–1976)[12]

Melech Ravitch was considered the dean of Yiddish poetry. His poems occupy nearly a dozen pages in the Yiddish poetry anthology, *The Golden Peacock* (edited by Joseph Leftwich). He compiled an 850-page anthology of material about Jewish Warsaw called *The Warsaw That Was* and wrote about 200 short portrait sketches of Yiddish writers. Ravitch's poems and essays expressed universal values. He was a vegetarian most of his life and a patron of the Jewish Vegetarian Society.

Rosen, Rabbi David[13]

Rabbi Rosen was Chief Rabbi of Ireland from 1979 to 1985. He completed his advanced rabbinic studies in Israel where he received his rabbinic ordination. In addition to military service in the armed corps of the Israeli Defense Forces (IDF), he served as chaplain in the Western Sinai. Rabbi Rosen is an Honorary President of the International Jewish Vegetarian Society for Israel. He, his wife, and two daughters are vegetarians, which they find completely compatible with Orthodox Judaism.

Rabbi Rosen and his family currently live in Jerusalem where he directs the Israel office of the Anti-Defamation League and is the ADL's co-liaison to the Vatican. He was formerly the Dean of the Sapir Jewish Heritage Center in Jerusalem and Professor at the Jerusalem Center for Near East Studies on Mt. Scopus. He is President of the International Council of Christians and Jews and President of the World Conference on Religion and Peace, an all-encompassing world inter-faith body, He was also a key negotiator of the accord that established full relations between the Vatican and Israel. Many of his outspoken statements supporting vegetarianism are cited in this book.

Singer, Isaac Bashevis (1904–1991)

I. B. Singer was born in Poland and came to the United States in 1935. He was a writer for the New York *Yiddish Daily Forward* under the pen name of Isaac Warshavsky. He wrote many short stories and novels, including *The Family Moskat, Satan in Goray, The Magician of Lublin, Gimpel the Fool, The Spinoza of Market Street, The Slave, Enemies: A Love Story*, and *Shadows on the Hudson*. He won the Nobel Prize for Literature in 1978. The protagonists of many his novels and short stories are either vegetarians or thinking about becoming vegetarian.

He was a vegetarian for the last thirty years of his life, primarily because of compassion for animals. He was a patron of the Jewish Vegetarian Society and in July 1979 received an award from the Vegetarian Information Service for his contributions to literature and vegetarianism. He also received a "Jewish Vegetarian of the Year" award from the Jewish Vegetarians of North America in 1986. He was very devoted to the vegetarian cause and was frequently quoted as saying, "I am a vegetarian for health reasons—the health of the chicken."

The following excerpt is from Singer's short story, "The Slaughterer":

Barely three months had passed since Yoineh Meir had become a slaughterer, but the time seemed to stretch endlessly. He felt as though he were immersed in blood and lymph. His ears were beset by the squawking of hens, the crowing of roosters, the gobbling of geese, the lowing of oxen, the mooing and bleating of calves and goats; wings fluttered, claws tapped on the floor. The bodies refused to know any justification or excuse—every body resisted in its own fashion, tried to escape, and seemed to argue with the Creator to its last breath.[14]

Singer's strong feelings with regard to vegetarianism are indicated in the following selection:

The longer I am a vegetarian, the more I feel how wrong it is to kill animals and eat them. I think that eating meat or fish is a denial of all ideals, even of all religions. How can we pray to God for mercy if we ourselves have no mercy? How can we speak of right and justice if we take an innocent creature and shed its blood? Every kind of killing seems to me savage and I find no justification for it.[15]

12: SUMMARY

*The dietary laws are intended to teach us compassion and lead
us gently to vegetarianism.* (Rabbi Shlomo Riskin)[1]

J UDAISM MANDATES COMPASSION, NOT JUST FOR JEWS,
but for the stranger, and even for enemies; not just for people, but for
all of God's creatures. Compassion is one of the characteristics
associated with being a descendant of Abraham, the first Jew. Jews are
to consider the welfare of animals and to avoid *tsa'ar ba'alei chayim*,
inflicting pain on any living creature.

Judaism stresses the preservation of life and health. This is so
important that if it might help preserve a life, Jews are commanded to set
aside most commandments, including those related to the Sabbath,
kashrut, and fasting on Yom Kippur.

Judaism places great emphasis on reducing hunger. A Jew who helps
feed a hungry person is considered, in effect, to have fed God. Related to
helping the hungry are the important Jewish concepts of pursuing justice,
giving charity, being compassionate, supporting policies that reduce
poverty, and sharing food and other resources.

Judaism teaches that people are to be co-workers with God in
preserving and improving the earth. We are to be stewards and to use God's
bounties for the benefit of all. Nothing that has value can be wasted or
destroyed unnecessarily.

Judaism emphasizes the need to seek and pursue peace. Great is peace
for it is one of God's names, all God's blessings are contained in it, it must
be sought even in times of war, and it will be the first blessing brought by
the Messiah.

Vegetarianism is the diet most consistent with these important Jewish ideals:

A vegetarian diet does not require the raising of animals in closed, cramped spaces, where they are denied exercise, fresh air, sunlight, and fulfillment of their natural instincts.

- A vegetarian diet is consistent with our body structure and chemistry, and is least likely to lead to heart disease, cancer, stroke, and other degenerative diseases.

- A vegetarian diet does not require the wasteful use of grain, land, water, pesticides, fertilizer, and fuel while millions of people die annually from hunger and its effects.

- A vegetarian diet is most consistent with the concepts that "the earth is the Lord's," that we are to be partners with God in preserving and enhancing the world, and that we are not to waste or unnecessarily destroy anything of value.

- A vegetarian diet, by not wasting scarce resources and by not requiring the daily slaughter of helpless creatures of God, is most likely to lead to that day of harmony and peace when "nations shall beat their swords into plowshares and their spears into pruning hooks, and not study war anymore." (Isaiah 2:4)

The negative effects of animal-centered diets are interconnected: the cruel methods used to raise animals lead to unhealthy animals, which in turn affects human health; the feeding of seventy percent of the grain grown in the United States to livestock contributes to global hunger; the tremendous amounts of grain grown for animal feed require large amounts of fertilizer and pesticides, whose manufacture and use cause extensive air and water pollution and depletion of soil fertility; waters polluted by pesticides, fertilizers, and other chemicals result in fish that are unhealthy to eat; animal-based agriculture contributes to food, energy, and water shortages, which increase the potential for violence and war. Everything is connected to everything else.

Although vegetarianism is an important step in the right direction, it is not the complete answer to current critical problems:

- Jews should also work to eliminate violations of *tsa'ar ba'alei chayim* related to raising animals for food, scientific testing, the use of animals for furs, and the abuse of animals for sport and entertainment.
- Although a vegetarian diet is a positive step for preserving health, Jews should also strive to improve their health through exercise, elimination or reduction of the consumption of highly processed foods, and other positive lifestyle changes.
- Jews should work to see that food and other resources saved through vegetarian diets are used to help hungry people; they should also strive for better social and economic conditions to enable people in poor countries to produce the food that they need for survival.
- In addition to improving the environment through vegetarian diets, Jews should work for better energy, transportation, industrial, and residential systems consistent with the Torah concepts of stewardship and *bal tashchit*.
- Finally, consistent with Torah mandates, Jews should seek and pursue peace by working for more equitable sharing of the earth's resources, more harmonious relations among nations, and a reduction of arms budgets, which take funds from critical human needs such as education, shelter, employment, health, and proper nutrition.

Much of this book can be summed up by the following statement by Rabbi David Rosen:

> We must clearly advocate dietary practices that are truly in consonance with the sublimest values of the Torah, and today more than ever before these are overwhelmingly incompatible with carnivorous indulgence.[2]

Based on this statement and all the material previously discussed, at the close of this book one respectful question will be addressed to Jews who plan to continue to eat meat: In view of strong Jewish mandates to be compassionate to animals, preserve our health, help feed the hungry, preserve and protect the environment, conserve resources, and seek and pursue peace, and the very negative effects animal-centered diets have in each of these areas, will you now become a vegetarian, or at least sharply reduce your consumption of animal products?

APPENDIX

U NTIL 1978, I WAS A "MEAT AND POTATOES" MAN. MY mother would be sure to prepare my favorite dish, pot roast, whenever I came to visit with my wife and children. It was a family tradition that I would be served a turkey drumstick every Thanksgiving. Yet, I not only became a vegetarian, but I now devote a major part of my time to writing, speaking, and teaching about the benefits of vegetarianism. What caused this drastic change?

In 1973 I began teaching a course, "Mathematics and the Environment" at the College of Staten Island. The course uses basic mathematical concepts and problems to explore current critical issues, such as pollution, resource scarcities, hunger, energy, population growth, the arms race, nutrition, and health. While reviewing material related to world hunger, I became aware of the tremendous waste of grain associated with the production of beef at a time when millions of the world's people were malnourished. In spite of my own eating habits, I often led class discussions on the possibility of reducing meat consumption as a way of helping hungry people. After several semesters of this, I took my own advice and gave up eating red meat, while continuing to eat chicken and fish.

I then began to read about the many health benefits of vegetarianism and about the horrible conditions for animals raised on factory farms. I was increasingly attracted to vegetarianism, and on January 1, 1978, I decided to join the International Jewish Vegetarian Society. I had two choices for membership: (1) practicing vegetarian (one who refrains from eating any flesh); (2) non-vegetarian (one who is in sympathy with the movement, while not yet a vegetarian). I decided to become a full practicing vegetarian, and since then have avoided eating any meat, fowl, or fish.

After that decision, besides learning much about vegetarianism's connections to health, nutrition, ecology, resource usage, hunger, and the treatment of animals, I also started investigating connections between vegetarianism and Judaism. Through background reading and Jonathan Wolf's course "Judaism and Vegetarianism" at Lincoln Square Synagogue in New York in 1979, I learned that the first biblical dietary law (Genesis 1:29) is strictly vegetarian, and I became convinced that important Jewish mandates to preserve our health, be kind to animals, protect the environment, conserve resources, share with hungry people, and seek and pursue peace all point to vegetarianism as the best diet for Jews (and everyone else). To get this message to a wider audience I wrote this book, *Judaism and Vegetarianism*, which was first published in 1982. (A second expanded edition was published in 1988.)

Increasingly, as I learned about the realities discussed in this book and their inconsistency with Jewish values, I came to see vegetarianism as not only a personal choice, but a societal imperative, an essential component in the solution of many national and global problems. I have recently been spending much time trying to make others aware of the importance of switching toward vegetarian diets, both for themselves and for the world.

I have always felt good about my decision to become a vegetarian. Putting principles and values into practice is far more valuable and rewarding than hours of preaching. When people ask me why I gave up meat, I welcome the opportunity to explain the many benefits of vegetarianism.

While my family was initially skeptical about my change of diet, they have become increasingly understanding and supportive. In 1993 my younger daughter was married in Jerusalem at a completely vegetarian wedding. My wife has also become a vegetarian, and recently we have moved toward veganism, by giving up dairy products and eggs in most cases.

Recently, I have noted signs of increased interest in vegetarianism, and a growing number of people are concerned about dietary connections to health, nutrition, animal rights, and ecology.

Yet, McDonald's has recently opened outlets in Russia, China, and Israel, and it and other similar fast food establishments continue to expand worldwide. And there is still a predominance of meat served at weddings, bar and bat mitzvahs, and other Jewish celebrations, and for lunches at Jewish day schools and camps. So there is much that still needs to be done. My hope is to be able to keep learning, writing, and speaking about vegetarianism, to help bring closer that day when, in the words of the motto of the International Jewish Vegetarian Society, "no one shall hurt nor destroy in all of God's holy mountain." (Isaiah 11.9)

A. Action-Centered Ideas

As this book (and many other books) illustrate, vegetarianism is increasingly a societal imperative because of the many negative environmental and economic effects of the mass production and widespread consumption of animal products. Hence, since it is essential that people shift toward vegetarianism, here are some suggestions to promote plant-based diets:

1. Become well informed. Learn the facts about vegetarianism from this and other books (see Bibliography), the Internet (see websites listed later in this Appendix), and other sources. Learn how to effectively answer questions about vegetarianism, and use such questions as an opportunity to inform others.

2. Help educate others about vegetarianism. Wear a button. Put a bumper sticker on your car. Make up and display posters. Write timely letters to the editors of your local newspapers. Set up programs and discussions. There are a wide variety of interesting vegetarian slogans on buttons, bumper stickers, and T-shirts and sweat shirts. For example:

Love animals. Don't eat them.
Vegetarianism is good for life.
Happiness is reverence for life. Be vegetarian.

Use the world vegetarian symbol on correspondence. This will help the vegetarian movement obtain publicity that it badly needs and, because of prohibitive costs, cannot be easily obtained otherwise. Stickers and rubber stamps with the world vegetarian symbol can be obtained from the International Jewish Vegetarian Society.

3. Use the material in this and other vegetarian books in discussions with doctors. Help increase their knowledge of the many health benefits of a vegetarian diet.

4. Ask the rabbi of your synagogue if Jews should eliminate or at least sharply reduce their consumption of meat today because of important Jewish principles such as *bal tashchit*, *tsa'ar ba'alei chayim*, and *pikuach nefesh* that are being violated. Ask if these concepts can be included in sermons and classes.

5. Request that meat or fish not be served at synagogue and Jewish organizational functions and celebrations. Ask school principals and school directors to provide students with nutritious vegetarian options.

6. Ask the rabbi and/or head of a Hebrew school to organize a trip to a slaughterhouse so that people can observe for themselves how animals are slaughtered. A trip to a factory farm to see how cattle, chickens, and other animals are raised would also be very instructive.

7. Arrange synagogue and Jewish organizational sessions where vegetarian dishes are sampled and recipes exchanged.

8. Speak or organize an event with a guest speaker on the advantages of vegetarianism and how vegetarianism relates to Judaism.

9. Get vegetarian books into public and synagogue libraries by donating duplicates, requesting that libraries purchase such books, and, if you can afford it, by buying some and donating them. Ask local librarians to set up special exhibits about vegetarian foods and vegetarian-related issues.

10. Work with others to set up a vegetarian food co-op or restaurant or help support such places if they already exist. Encourage people to patronize such establishments.

11. Register yourself with a community, library, or school speakers' bureau. Take advantage of your increased knowledge and awareness to start speaking out.

12. Contact the food editor of your local newspaper and ask that more vegetarian recipes be included.

13. When applicable, raise awareness by showing how values of the Sabbath and festivals are consistent with vegetarian concepts. For example: Point out that the *kiddush* recited before lunch on the Sabbath indicates that animals are also to be able to rest on the Sabbath day; on *Sukkot*, note that the *sukkah* (temporary dwelling place) is decorated with pictures and replicas of fruits and vegetables (never with animal products); on Yom Kippur, consider the mandate expressed in the prophetic reading of Isaiah to "share your bread with the hungry," which can be carried out best by not having a diet that wastes large amounts of land, grain, water, fuel, and other agricultural resources.

14. Join the International Jewish Vegetarian Society, the Jewish Vegetarians of North America (addresses given later), and local vegetarian groups.

15. Support groups that are working to reduce world hunger, especially, these groups that generally go beyond merely providing charitable aid to the needy, but rather strive, in accordance with Maimonides' concept of the highest form of charity, to make people self-reliant in producing their own food.

16. If people are not willing to become vegetarians, encourage them to at least make a start by giving up red meat and having one or two meatless meals a week (perhaps Mondays and Thursdays, which were traditional Jewish fast days).

17. Do not concentrate only on vegetarianism. It is only part of the pursuit of justice, compassion, and peace. Become aware and try to affect public policy with regard to the issues raised in this book: preserving health, showing compassion for animals, saving human lives, conserving resources, helping hungry people, and seeking and pursuing peace.

If you ever feel overwhelmed by the many crises facing the world today and the difficulties of trying to move people toward vegetarian diets, please consider the following:

Jewish tradition teaches, "It is not for you to complete the task, but neither are you free to desist from it."[1] We must make a start and do whatever we can to improve the world. Judaism teaches that a person is obligated to protest when there is evil and to proceed from protest to action (see Question 17, Chapter 7). Each person should imagine that the world is evenly balanced between good and evil and that his or her actions can determine the destiny of the entire world.

Even if little is accomplished, trying to make improvements will prevent the hardening of your heart and will affirm that you accept moral responsibility. The very act of consciousness raising is important because it may lead to future changes.

B. Resolution on Judaism and Vegetarianism
A Jewish Vegetarian Conference in Toronto, Canada, which took place in July, 1993 passed the resolution below (slightly modified). It is hoped that other groups will use this as a model for similar resolutions.

Whereas,

1. Judaism mandates that people be very careful about preserving their health and their lives (*v'nishmartem me'od l'nofshotechem*, Deuteronomy 4:15), but animal-centered diets have been linked to heart disease, stroke, several forms of cancer, and other illnesses, and this has led to sharp increases in medical expenditures in the United States, and

2. Judaism stresses that we are to share our bread with hungry people, but over seventy percent of the grain grown in the United States and two-thirds of the grain exported by the United States is fed to animals destined for slaughter, as an estimated twenty million people die annually from hunger and its effects, and

3. Judaism teaches that "the earth is the Lord's" and that we are to be partners with God in preserving the world, but animal-based diets contribute significantly to soil erosion and depletion, extensive air and water pollution related to chemical fertilizer, pesticides, and "mountains of manure," the destruction of tropical rain forests and other ecological systems, global warming, and

4. Judaism mandates that we are not to waste or unnecessarily destroy anything of value (*bal tashchit*—Deuteronomy: 20:19, 20), but livestock agriculture requires up to twenty times as much land and ten times as much energy and water as the production of vegetarian foods, as well as vast amounts of pesticides, fertilizer, and other resources, and

5. Judaism emphasizes compassion for animals (*tsa'ar ba'alei chayim*), but animals are raised for food today under cruel conditions, in crowded, confined cells, denied fresh air, exercise, and any fulfillment of their instinctual needs, and fed and injected with chemicals and hormones, and

6. Judaism stresses that we must seek and pursue peace and that violence results from unjust conditions, but animal-centered diets, by wasting valuable resources, help to perpetuate the widespread hunger and poverty that eventually lead to instability and war, and

7. God's first dietary law was vegetarian (Genesis 1:29), and

8. Rabbi Abraham Isaac Hakohen Kook, the first Ashkenazic Chief Rabbi of pre-state Israel, stated that in the messianic period people will again be vegetarians, fulfilling the prophecy of Isaiah: "The wolf shall dwell with the lamb...the lion shall eat straw like the ox...and none shall hurt nor destroy in all of God's holy mountain" (Isaiah 11:6–9), and

9. according to the Talmud (*Pesachim* 109a), since the destruction of the Temple, Jews need not eat meat in order to rejoice, and

10. the realization of Judaism's vision and the welfare and survival of the world require more than ever that Jews be "a light unto the nations," with regard to such issues as ecology, human health, world hunger, conservation of resources, and proper treatment of animals, and this can best be carried out through vegetarian diets, and

11. vegetarian diets can help Jews fulfill their challenge to be compassionate children of compassionate ancestors, and

12. for too long the Jewish community has generally paid insufficient attention to ways in which animal-based diets deviate from basic Jewish teachings and threaten human health, hungry people worldwide, and our environmental future,

we respectfully resolve to make facts and concepts on the moral issues related to animal-centered diets more widely known in the Jewish community;

we urge Jews to consider the many benefits of a vegetarian diet and the ways it reflects and embodies central Jewish values;

we urge rabbis to explore these issues, and to pursue them with their congregations, students, colleagues, and families;

we urge principals of yeshivas, day schools, and Talmud Torahs to see that these issues are included in their curricula;

we urge Jewish groups to refrain from serving meat at communal functions;

we urge Jewish families to celebrate their simchas with vegetarian meals;

we urge camp directors to see that vegetarian options are available at all meals;

we encourage the Jewish media to give extensive coverage to the many moral issues related to our diets;

we resolve to evaluate progress toward these goals periodically and to consider ways to improve our efforts.

C. The Service of the Heart

Since the destruction of the Temple and the end of animal sacrifices, prayer, called the service of the heart, has played a major role in Judaism. The following questions related to vegetarianism should be considered as we prepare for prayer:

- Might our prayers for compassion be answered more favorably if we showed greater compassion for God's defenseless creatures?
- Might our prayers for sustenance be responded to more positively if our eating habits helped needy people obtain an adequate portion of God's bounteous harvests?
- Might our prayers for good health receive a more favorable response if we did not consume animal products with high doses of pesticides, antibiotics, and other chemicals, as well as cholesterol, saturated fat, and animal protein?
- Might our prayers for rain to nourish our crops produce better results if much of that rain was not used primarily to grow feed crops for animals destined for slaughter, while many people lack adequate food and water?
- Might our prayers for peace (*Sim Shalom*)[2] be answered more favorably if we shared God's provisions more equitably, thereby reducing the prospects for war and violence?
- Might our chant every Sabbath morning, "The soul of all living things shall praise God's name..." (*Nishmat Kol Chai T'va'rech Et Shim'Chah*),[3]

be better received if we do not have a diet that depends on treating living creatures as machines whose sole purpose is to feed our stomachs?

There are many prayers in the *Siddur* which stress concern for compassion to animals. In addition to those previously mentioned, every synagogue service contains a recitation of the words, *Baruch ha'm'rachem al ha'briyot* (blessed is the One [God] who has compassion on the creatures) and *kol ha'n'shamah t'hallel Kah* (every soul, including animals, shall praise God). Judaism teaches that God will show special mercy to the person who treats animals mercifully.[4]

Are the following words of Isaiah valid today if we fail to show compassion to animals as well as people?

I cannot endure iniquity and solemn assembly;
Your new moons and your appointed feasts,
My soul hates.
They have become a burden to me,
That I am weary to bear.
When you spread forth your hands,
I will hide my eyes from you,
Even though you make many prayers,
I will not listen.
Your hands are full of blood. (Isaiah 1:12–15)

The following lines from a poem by Coleridge are also applicable:

He prayeth best who loveth best
all things both great and small
For the dear God who loveth us
He made and loveth all.[5]

The previously told story of Rabbi Israel Salanter placing compassion for animals ahead of Yom Kippur evening prayers reinforces these teachings.

Rabbi Abraham Joshua Heschel, an outstanding 20th-century Jewish philosopher, stated that more than worship is required by God. "Worship without compassion is worse than self-deception; it is an abomination."[6] The word "prayer" (t'filah) comes from the Hebrew word l'hitpallel, which means self-evaluation. Perhaps our self-evaluation would be enhanced if we acted with compassion toward hungry people and defenseless creatures.

D. Imitation of God

The Jewish tradition asserts that we are to imitate God's qualities of kindness, compassion, and forbearance. This is related to the biblical account of the creation of people in the image of God (Genesis 1:26). Other biblical sources for the commandment to imitate God are found in the statement that we are to be holy as God is holy (Leviticus 19:2) and that we are to walk in God's ways (Deuteronomy 10:12).

A rabbinic statement that we should imitate God is that of Hama bar Hanina in his commentary on the verse, "After the Lord your God you shall walk" (Deuteronomy 13:5):

How can man walk after God? Is He not a consuming fire? What is meant is that man ought to walk after (imitate) the attributes of God. Just as the Lord clothes the naked, so you shall clothe the naked. Just as He visits the sick, so you shall visit the sick. Just as the Lord comforts the bereaved, so you shall also comfort the bereaved; just as He buried the dead, so you shall bury the dead.[7]

As the Lord is our shepherd, we are shepherds of voiceless creatures. As God is kind and compassionate to us, we should be considerate of animals. By showing compassion to animals through a vegetarian diet, we help fulfill the commandment to imitate God's ways.

E. Our Wedding Vow to God

The Prophet Hosea stated that we have, in effect, a wedding vow to God. What are the conditions of our betrothal?

I will betroth you unto me forever;
I will betroth you unto me in righteousness
    and in justice, in loving kindness and in compassion.
I will betroth you unto me in faithfulness,
    and you shall know the Lord. (Hosea 2:21–2)

Observant Jews recite these words every weekday morning as they wrap the *tefillin* strap around their fingers as a symbolic wedding ring.

It is interesting to note that the above "wedding vows" appear in the writings of Hosea immediately after the covenant that God made with animals (Hosea 2:20) which was cited in Chapter 2. Perhaps this is to indicate that one can only be bound up with God if one is living as harmoniously as possible with animals.

This above wedding vow echoes and reinforces much of what we have said elsewhere in this book. We are to be co-workers with God, and the traits that we are to exhibit are righteousness, justice, loving-kindness, and compassion. These important traits, which constitute our wedding vow to God, are echoed in other statements of the prophets:

What does the Lord require of you
but that you act justly, love kindness,
and walk humbly with your God. (Micah 6:8)

"Let not the mighty man glory in his might,
Let not the rich man glory in his riches,
Let not the wise man glory in his wisdom,
but let him who glories, glory in this,
That he understands and knows me,
That I am the Lord,
Who practices kindness, justice, and righteousness, in the earth,
For in these things I delight,"
Thus says the Lord. (Jeremiah 9:22–23).

It is not enough just to know that there is a God, but to know and imitate His ways of kindness, justice, compassion, and righteousness. These characteristics are consistent with vegetarian diets:

- We work for righteousness when we eat in such a way that there is no violence toward either humans or non-human animals.
- We work for justice when our diets are such that all can get their just share of God's bountiful harvests.
- We show loving-kindness to all people when our diets do not make it more difficult for them to get sufficient nourishment.
- We show compassion for animals when our diets do not require their mistreatment and slaughter.

F. Morality Beyond the Requirements of the Laws

Judaism distinguishes between normative law and *lifnim me-shurat ha-din*, ethical conduct above and beyond the minimum requirements of the law. According to most Jewish authorities, the Jewish moral imperatives that establish standards stricter than the law should prompt people to renounce cruelty to animals, even in many cases where the procedure considered appears to have benefits to people.

Some examples may help illustrate the Jewish stress on going beyond the minimum requirements of the law. Rabbi Moses Ben Israel Isserles (the Rema), a 16th-century *halachic* authority, ruled that the law permits plucking feathers from a live bird for use as quill pens; however, he adds that people refrain from doing so, thus going beyond the requirements of the law, because of the inherent cruelty involved in this practice.[9] The previously related story of Rabbi Judah the Prince's insensitive treatment of a cow being led to slaughter is another example. A person of his stature and abilities was expected to show greater compassion, although this was not strictly required by Jewish law. His failure to do so led to his punishment at the Hand of Heaven.

The principle of *lifnim me-shurat ha-din* may be applied to our diets. While one cannot find a prohibition against eating meat in Jewish law, Jews who are to be *rachmanim b'nei rachmanim*, compassionate children of compassionate ancestors, should eliminate or at least sharply reduce their consumption of animal products.

G. Key Jewish Vegetarian and Vegetarian-Related Groups

Amirim
Philip Campbell, contact, or Sarah Peleg, accommodations
Moshav Amirim, Bikat Beit Hakarem
Karmiell 20115, Israel
Tel.: (06) 989-045; Fax: (06) 980-772

Anonymous For Animal Rights
Yossi Wolfson, coordinator
PO Box 6315
Tel Aviv 61062, Israel
Tel.: (03) 525-4632; fax: (03) 525-8599
e-mail reyo@netvision.net.il.

CHAI (Concern for Helping Animals in Israel)
Nina Natelson, founder and director
PO Box 3341
Alexandria, VA 22302
Tel.: 703-658-9650; fax: 703-941-6132
e-mail: chai_US@compuserve.com; website: www.chai-online.org

Hai-meshek
Avi Pinkas, founder and director
8 Geulim Street
Rishon Letzion 75280, Israel
Tel./Fax: (03) 962-4086; e-mail: pinkasav@internet-zahav.net.

International Jewish Vegetarian Society (IJVS) also **Jewish Vegetarian Society** (JVS)
Bet Teva, 855 Finchley Road
London, NW11 8LX, England
Tel.: 020-8455-0692; fax: 020-8455-1465
e-mail: ijvs@yahoo.com; website: www. ivu.org/jvs/

The Jerusalem Center
8 Balfour Street, Jerusalem.
Tel.: (02) 561-1114; e-mail: ijvsjlem@netmedia.net.il.

The Jewish Vegetarians of North America (JVNA)
Israel Mossman, coordinator
6938 Reliance Road
Federalsburg, MD 21632
Tel.: 410-754-5550; e-mail: imossman@skipjack.bluecrab.org
website: www.orbyss.com/jvna.htm.

Jews For Animal Rights (JAR) and **Micah Publications**
Roberta Kalechofsky, founder and director
255 Humphrey Street
Marblehead, MA 01945
Tel.: 781-631-7601; fax: 781-639-0772
e-mail: micah@micahbooks.com; website: www.micahbooks.com.

Mazon
12401 Wilshire Blvd., Suite 30
Los Angeles, CA 90025-1015
Tel.: 310-442-0020; e-mail: mazonmail@aol.com.

Noah
Andre Menache, director
Tel./Fax: (09) 765-9311; phone: (09) 766-1502 or (052) 945-272
e-mail: menache@netvision.net.il.

Orr Shalom
PO Box 1837/20 Harsav Street
Mevasseret-Zion 90805, Israel
Tel.: (02) 533-7059.

ProAnimal
Suzanne Trauffer, editor

2211 N. Berkshire Road
Charlottesville, VA 22901
Fax: 804-296-1096; e-mail: stramak@aol.com
Erez Ganor, Israeli contact
PO Box 1032
B'nei Ayish 79845 Israel
Fax: (07) 651-9591; e-mail: erezganor@barak-online.net

Vegetarians and Vegans Society
Tel.: (03) 560-7744; fax (03) 560-4582.

H. Some Significant Websites

Note: There are literally hundreds, if not thousands, of valuable sites related to vegetarian groups, publications, information, and issues. Rather than trying to list many of them, several especially valuable ones and some with links to other valuable sites are listed.

http://jewishveg.com (contains a wide variety of material related to Judaism and vegetarianism, as well as valuable links).
www.vrg.org/links (Vegetarian Resource Group).
www.ivu.org/articles/net/judaism.html (International Vegetarian Union material on Judaism)
www.ivu.org/ (International Vegetarian Union)
www.vegsource.com (excellent source of information and links)
www.farmusa.org (Farm Animal Reform Movement [FARM])
www.purefood.org (information on irradiated foods, genetically modified foods, and related topics.)
www.pcrm.org (Physicians Committee for Responsible Medicine [PCRM])
www.nlm.nih.gov/ (The National Library of Medicine [NLM])
http://schwartz.enviroweb.org (Richard H. Schwartz's internet articles; many issues considered in this book are addressed in these articles.)

NOTES

1: A Vegetarian View of the Bible

1. Rashi's commentary on Genesis 1:29. All dates of birth and death indicated are according to the Common Era (C.E.) unless otherwise noted.
2. Quoted in Nehama Leibowitz, *Studies in Bereshit* (Genesis), Jerusalem: World Zionist Organization (3rd edition), 1976, 77.
3. *Sanhedrin* 59b. (Note that references to the Babylonian Talmud are identified herein by tractate, folio number, and side of the page (a or b).
4. Nachmanides, commentary on Genesis 1:29.
5. Joseph Albo, *Sefer ha-Ikkarim*, 3:15.
6. Rabbi J. H. Hertz, *The Pentateuch and Haftorahs* (London: Soncino Press, 1958), 5; also see Nehama Leibowitz, *Studies in Deuteronomy*, Jerusalem: World Zionist Organization (3rd Edition), 1976, 137.
7. Nachmanides commentary on Genesis 5:4.
8. Rabbi Abraham Isaac Hakohen Kook, *A Vision of Vegetarianism and Peace*, Sections 1 and 4.; also see Leibowitz, *Studies in Deuteronomy*, 138.
9. From Rav Kook's *Tallelei Orot* (*Dewdrops of Light*), cited by Leibowitz, *Studies in Deuteronomy*, 138.
10. Kook, *A Vision*, Sections 7, 12; Rabbi Samuel H. Dresner, *The Jewish Dietary Laws: Their Meaning for Our Time*, New York: Burning Bush Press, 1959,21–25; Cassuto, commentary on Genesis 1:27.
11. Kook, *A Vision*, Sections 1–7; see also Leibowitz, Studies in Bereshit, 77.
12. Joseph Albo, *Sefer ha-Ikkarim*, Vol. III, Chapter 15.
13. Rabbi Isaak Hebenstreit, *Graves of Lust* (Hebrew), Rzeszow, Poland, 1929, 6.
14. Samson Raphael Hirsch's commentary on Genesis 9:2.
15. Dresner, *The Jewish Dietary Laws*, 29.
16. Quoted by Leibowitz, *Studies in Bereshit*, 77.
17. Rashi, based on *Midrash Rabbah*; also *Baba Kamma* 91b.
18. This speculation is considered by Philip Pick,"The Source of Our Inspiration," 3.
19. See Rabbi Elijah J. Schochet, *Animal Life in Jewish Tradition*, New York: K'tav, 1984, 290; also see S. Clayman, "Vegetarianism, The Ideal of the Bible," *The Jewish Vegetarian* (Summer, 1967): 136–137, and Hebenstreit, *Kivrot Hata'avah*, 7.
20. Hertz, *Pentateuch and Haftorahs*, 276.

21. Talmudic sage Ben Zoma teaches as follows: "Who is rich? The person who rejoices in his or her portion" (*Pirke Avot* 4:1).

22. Reverend A. Cohen, *The Teaching of Maimonides*, New York: Bloch Publishing Co., 1927, 180.

23. See Leibowitz, *Studies in Deuteronomy*,135.

24. Schochet, *Animal Life*, 300.

25. Rabbi J. David Bleich, "Vegetarianism and Judaism," *Tradition*, Vol. 23, No. 1, (Summer, 1987), 86.

26. Ibid, 87.

27. Leibowitz, *Studies in Deuteronomy*, 136.

28. Ibid. Also see Kook, *A Vision*, Sections 1, 2, and 4.

29. Hebenstreit, *Kivrot Hata'avah*, 9.

30. *Chulin* 84a.

31. *Pesachim* 49b.

32. Kook, *A Vision*, Section 4; also see the discussion in Joe Green, "Chalutzim of the Messiah—The Religious Vegetarian Concept as Expounded by Rabbi Kook," 2.

33. Kook, *A Vision*, Section 4; also see the discussion in Green, "Chalutzim," 2, 3.

34. Kook, "Fragments of Light," in *Abraham Isaac Kook*, ed. and trans. Ben Zion Bokser, New York: Paulist Press, 1978, 316–21.

35. Quoted in Abraham Chill, *The Commandments and Their Rationale*, New York, 1974, 400. Among the sources listed by Rabbi Chill for positive vegetarian messages are *Hullin* 9a, 10b, 27a, 28a, 31a, 84a; *Menahot* 29a; *Midrash Sifre Re'eh* 78; *Midrash Rabbah*, *Lekh Lekha* ch. 44, Section 9, ch. 84, Section 7; *Midrash Tanchuma* Re'eh, ch. 6; *Maimonides, Mishneh Torah, Hilchot Shechitah* ch. 1; *Sefer ha-Mitzvot* (Aseh) 146; *Sefer Mitzvot Gadol* (Aseh) 63; *Sefer Mitzvot Katan* 197; *Shulchan Aruch Yorah De'ah* ch. 1; *Sefer Ha-Hinnukh, Mitzvah* 451.

36. Rabbi Pinchas Peli, *Torah Today*, Washington, DC: B'nai B'rith Books, 1987, 118.

37. Kook, *A Vision*, Sections 1, 2, 4, 6, and 32; also see Rabbi Alfred Cohen, "Vegetarianism from a Jewish Perspective," *Journal of Halacha and Contemporary Society*, Vol. 1, No. II, (Fall, 1981), 45.

38. Hertz, *Pentateuch and Haftorahs*, 5; also see Kook, *A Vision*, Sections 6, 32.

39. Green, "Chalutzim of the Messiah," 1.

40. *Shabbat* 118b.

2: Tsa'ar Ba'alei Chayim—Judaism and Compassion for Animals

1. *Shabbat* 133b.

2. Chafetz Chayim, *Ahavat Chesed*, 2:2, 182.

3. Rabbi Samson Rafael Hirsch, *Nineteen Letters*, Jerusalem/New York: Feldheim (Rabbi Joseph Elias edition), 1969, Letter 4.

4. Ibid.

5. *Shabbat* 77b.

6. Malbim, *Commentary on Proverbs* 12:10.

7. Maimonides, *Guide of the Perplexed*, 3:17.

8. *Sefer Chasidim* (ed. Reuben Margolies), No. 666.
9. *Baba Metzia* 32b; *Shabbat* 128b.
10. Rabbi Solomon Ganzfried, *Code of Jewish Law*, New York: Hebrew Publishing Co., 1961, book 4, ch. 191, 84.
11. Rabbi Samson Raphael Hirsch, *Horeb*, Dayan Dr. I. Grunfeld, trans., London: Soncino Press, 1962, Vol. 2, 293 (Section 60, No. 417).
12. *Choshen Mishpat* 338.
13. Hirsch, *Horeb*, Vol. 2, 293 (Section 60, No. 417).
14. Rashi's commentary on Deuteronomy 25:4.
15. Hertz, *Pentateuch and Haftorahs*, 854.
16. William E. H. Lecky, *History of European Morals*, 3rd ed. rev., New York: Appleton-Century-Crofts, 1903, Vol. 2, 162.
17. *Kilayim* 8:2–3; *Baba Metzia* 90b.
18. *Shulchan Aruch, Yoreh De'ah* 297:2.
19. Hirsch, *Horeb*, vol 2., 287 (Section 57, No. 409).
20. *Sefer Hachinuch, Mitzvah* 550.
21. *Gittin* 62a; *Berachot* 40a.
22. *Jerusalem Talmud Ketuvot* 4:8 and *Yevamot* 15:3.
23. *Shulchan Aruch, Orach Chayim* 167:6; *Berachot* 40a; also see Magen Avraham 18, and the Or Ha'Chayim's commentaries on Genesis 24:19 and Numbers 20:11.
24. Rashi's commentary on Exodus 23:12.
25. Hertz, *Pentateuch and Haftorahs*, 298.
26. Rabbi Eli Munk, *The Call of the Torah*, New York: ArtScroll, 1992, 268.
27. *Midrash Leviticus Rabbah* 27:11.
28. Maimonides, *Guide of the Perplexed*, 3:48.
29. Ibid.
30. Ibid.
31. Ibid.
32. Rabbi E. J. Schochet, *Animal Life in Jewish Tradition*, New York: K'tav, 1984, 216.
33. Abraham Chill, *The Commandments and Their Rationale*, New York, 1974, 114.
34. Ibid.
35. *Abot de R. Nathan*, ch. 23.
36. *Shabbat* 128b; *Baba Metzia* 32b.
37. Hirsch, *Horeb*, Section 72, No. 482.
38. Hagahot Hatam Sofer, *Baba Metzia* 32b. See also Vol. 3 of *Contemporary Halachic Problems* by Rabbi J. David Bleich, 203.
39. In his article, "Judaism and Animal Experimentation" in *Animal Sacrifices*, Tom Regan, ed., Philadelphia: Temple University Press, 1993, fn. 30. Rabbi J. David Bleich cites many sources that prohibit recreational hunting; also see the *Encyclopedia Judaica* 8:1111.
40. *Avodah Zarah* 18b.
41. *Yorah Deah*, Second Series, 10.
42. Schochet, *Animal Life*, 283–287.

43. Joe Green, *The Jewish Vegetarian Tradition*, Johannesburg, South Africa: Joe Green, 1969, 15, based on the teaching of the Rema.

44. Dresner, *Jewish Dietary Law*, 33–34.

45. *Shulchan Aruch, Orach Chayim* 223:6.

46. Ganzfried, compiler. *Code of Jewish Law*, Vol. 2, 29.

47. *Shabbat* 128b.; for a discussion of sources for *tsa'ar ba'alei chayim*, see Rabbi J. David Bleich, "Judaism and Animal Experimentation" in *Animal Sacrifices*, op. cit., 65–69.

48. *Shulchan Aruch, Orach Chayim* 316:2.

49. Ibid. 332:2.

50. Ibid. 332:3.

51. Ibid. 332:4.

52. Ibid. 305:19.

53. S. Y. Hirsch, *Horeb*, Chapter 60, No. 416.

54. *Midrash Exodus Rabbah* 2:2.

55. *Midrash Tanchuma*, Noah 3; cited by Schochet, *Animal Life*, 148. Joseph was also considered a *tzaddik* because of his resistance to sexual temptations.

56. *Midrash Genesis Rabbah*; Noah 31:14.

57. *Baba Metzia* 85a; *Midrash Genesis Rabbah* 33:3.

58. Noah J. Cohen, *Tsa'ar Ba'alei Chayim—The Prevention of Cruelty to Animals, Its Bases, Development and Legislation in Hebrew Literature*, Jerusalem: Feldheim, 1976, 4–5.

59. Ibid.

60. Rabbi Alfred Cohen, "Vegetarianism from a Jewish Perspective," *The Journal of Halacha and Contemporary Society*, Vol. I., No. II, (Fall, 1981), 48.

61. S. Y. Agnon, *Days of Awe*, Jerusalem: Shocken, 1939.

62. Martin Buber, *Tales of the Chasidim*, Vol. 1, 249.

63. Mordecai Ben Ammi (1854–1932), quoted by Joe Green, *The Jewish Vegetarian Tradition*, 19–20.

64. Cited by Schochet, *Animal Life*, 147.

65. *Yalkut Shimoni* to Psalm 36.

66. A very thorough treatment of how chickens are raised under factory conditions is given by Karen Davis, *Prisoned Chickens, Poisoned Eggs*, Summertown, TN: Book Publishing Co., 1997.

67. www.wspa.org.uk/foiegras/foiegras.html; "Pets or Pâté," *The Jewish Vegetarian* 23 (Spring, 1972): 7–8.

68. "Foie Gras from Israel Vies With The French," *New York Times*, Sept. 10, 1980; a 1999 *Jerusalem Post* article indicated that Israel is the number one producer of foie gras.

69. Feinstein, Rabbi Moshe, *Igrot Moshe, Even Haezer*, Part 4, B'nai B'rak, 1985, end of Section No. 92, 164–165. Also see the *responsum* by Rabbi David Golinkin, "Is it Permissible for Jews to Purchase and Eat Veal?," *Moment*, February, 1993, 26, 27.

70. Rabbi A. Spero, "An Update on White Veal and its *Halachic* Implications," *The Jewish Press*, Oct. 8, 1982, 27, and Oct. 15, 1982, 19.

71. Nathaniel Altman, *Eating for Life*, Wheaton, IL.: Theosophical Publishing House, 1977, 76–77.

72. Robbins, John, *Diet For a New America*, Stillpoint Publishing: Walpole, NH, 1987, 62–63.

73. Ruth Harrison, *Animal Machines*, London: Vincent Street, 1964, 54–55.

74. Ibid., 54.

75. Ibid., 110–112.

76. Ibid., 12.

77. John Harris, "Killing for Food," in *Animals, Men, and Morals*, S. R. Godlovitch and John Harris, eds. New York: Taplinger Publishing Co., 1972, 98.

78. Harrison, *Animal Machines*, 3.

79. Hirsch, *Horeb*, Chapter 60, Section 415.

80. Carmell, Rabbi Aryeh, *Masterplan: Judaism—Its Programs, Meanings, Goals*, New York/Jerusalem: Feldheim, 1991, 69.

81. Rosen, Rabbi David, "Vegetarianism: An Orthodox Jewish Perspective," in *Rabbis and Vegetarianism: An Evolving Tradition*, Roberta Kalechofsky, ed., Marblehead, MA: Micah Publications, 1995, 53.

82. Ibid, 54.

3: Judaism, Vegetarianism, and Health

1. Rabbi Samson Raphael Hirsch, *Horeb*, Dayan Dr. I. Grunfeld, trans. London: Soncino Press, 1962, (Section 62, No. 428).

2. For a more extensive consideration of the Jewish approach to health care, see "Prevention: Torah Perspectives on Maintaining Health" by Yosef Ben Shlomo Hakohen, published by Nishma, Toronto, Torah paper No. IX, and "An Ounce of Prevention: The Jewish Approach to Maintaining Health" by Yosef Ben Shlomo Hakohen and Richard H. Schwartz, *Emunah Magazine*, Fall, 1995, 44–46.

3. Also see *Sota* 14a.

4. *Yalkut Lekach Tov, Shmot, B'shalach.*

5. *Sanhedrin* 73a.

6. *Shabbat* 54b.

7. *Chulin* 9a; *Choshen Mishpat* 427; *Yoreh De'ah* 116.

8. *Pesachim* 25a; Maimonides, *Mishneh Torah, Yesodei ha Torah*, 7.

9. *Yoma* 85b; *Sanhedrin* 74a.

10. Maimonides, *Mishneh Torah, Hilchot Deot* 4:1.

11. Rabbi Samson Raphael Hirsch, *Horeb*, Dayan Dr. I. Grunfeld, trans. London: Soncino Press, 1962, Vol. 2, 298 (Section 62, No. 427).

12. *Baba Batra* 2:9.

13. *Yalkut Shimoni* 184.

14. *Sanhedrin* 17b.

15. *Ta'anit* 11a,b.

16. *Chulin* 84a; *Berachot* 40a; *Avodah Zarah* 11a.

17. *Shabbat* 140b.

18. *Shabbat* 50b.

19. *Shulchan Aruch, Orach Chayim* 4:18.

20. *Chulin* 105a,b.
21. *Midrash Leviticus Rabbah* 34:3.
22. Rabbi J. H. Hertz, *The Pentateuch and Haftorahs*, London: Soncino Press, 1958, 843.
23. Ibid; also see *Babba Kamma* 4:9, 15b, and 46a; *Ketuvot* 41b.
24. Maimonides, *Hilchot Rotze'ach*, ch. 11, part 4.
25. Fred Rosner, *Modern Medicine and Jewish Law*, New York: Bloch, 1972, 28.
26. Ibid.
27. *Ta'anit* 20b.
28. *Sanhedrin* 4:5.
29. *Shabbat* 151b.
30. *Sefer Chasidim*, No. 724.
31. Cited by Rosner, *Modern Medicine*, 30.
32. Ibid, 31.
33. Mikkel Hindhede, *American Journal of Epidemiology*, 100, No. 5:394.
34. Nathaniel Altman, *Eating for Life*, Wheaton, IL: Theosophical Publishing House, 1977, 22.
35. John A. Scharffenberg, *Problems with Meat*, Santa Barbara, CA: Wadsworth, 1977), 28.
36. Ibid.
37. R. L. Phillips, "Role of Lifestyle and Dietary Habits in Risk of Cancer among Seventh Day Adventists," *Cancer Research* 35 (November 1975): 3513.
38. Morton Mintz, "Fat Intake Increasing Cancer Risk," *Washington Post*, September 10, 1976.
39. B. Armstrong et al, "Blood Pressure in Seventh Day Adventists," *American Journal of Epidemiology* 105, No. 5 (May 1977): 444–9.
40. Ibid.
41. Gene Marine and Judith Van Allen, *Food Pollution: The Violation of Our Inner Ecology*, New York: Holt, Rinehart and Winston, 1972, 19.
42. Paul Dudley White, *American Heart Journal* (December, 1964): 942.
43. For much of this section I am indebted to Emanuel Goldman, Ph.D., Professor of Microbiology and Molecular Genetics, New Jersey Medical School, Newark, NJ, USA. and to material in *The Food Revolution* by John Robbins.
44. Stuart Levy of Tufts University School of Medicine, citing a 1998 Institute of Medicine report described in *The Scientist*, July 5, 1999 (Vol. 13, No. 14).
45. For example, Denise O'Grady, "Bacteria Cases in Denmark Cause Antibiotics Concerns in U.S.," *New York Times*, November 4, 1999.
46. For example, Stuart Levy, "The Challenge of Antibiotic Resistance," *Scientific American*, March 1998.
47. "World Health Organization Meeting on the Medical Impact on the Use of Antimicrobial Drugs in Food Animals, Berlin, Germany, October 4, 1997," WHO Press Release, October 7, 1997.
48. *Science*, 1998; 279: 996–997.

49. Glynn K., et al, "Emergence of Multidrug-resistant *salmonella enterica* serotype typhimurium DT104 infections in the United States," *New England Journal of Medicine* (1998) 338: 1333–1338.

50. Speech before Irvington Trust, New York City, February 8, 1994.

51. Rabbi Alfred Cohen, "Vegetarianism from a Jewish Perspective," *Journal of Halacha and Contemporary Society*, Vol. 1, No. II, (Fall, 198 1), 61.

52. Rosen, Rabbi David, "Vegetarianism: An Orthodox Jewish Perspective," in *Rabbis and Vegetarianism: An Evolving Tradition*, Roberta Kalechofsky, ed., Marblehead, MA: Micah Publications, 1995, 54.

4: Judaism, Vegetarianism, and Feeding the Hungry

1. Testimony before the Ad Hoc Senate Committee on World Hunger.

2. *Baba Batra* 9a.

3. *Midrash Tannaim.*

4. Passover *Haggadah.*

5. Gary Gardner and Brian Halweil, "Underfed and Overfed—The Global Epidemic of Malnutrition," Worldwatch paper No. 150, March 2000, 11.

6. Ibid, 12.

7. Ibid, 13.

8. Frances Moore Lappé, et al, *World Hunger: Twelve Myths.*, New York: Grove Press, 1998, 2.

9. Based on calculations using data from the "2000 World Population Data Sheet," Population Reference Bureau, Washington, D.C.

10. Rifkin, Jeremy, *Beyond Beef*, New York: Dutton, 1992, 177.

11. *Philadelphia Inquirer*, 13 Oct, 1974, 9B.

12. Lester R. Brown, *In the Human Interest*, New York: Norton, 1974, 21.

13. A detailed analysis of the waste related to livestock agriculture is in *Diet For a Small Planet* by Frances M. Lappé, Twentieth Anniversary Edition, New York: Ballantine, 1991.

14. *Food First Resource Guide*, San Francisco: Staff of the Institute for Food and Development Policy, 1979, 7.

15. James Parsons,"Forest to Pasture: Development or Destruction?" *Revista de Biologia Tropical*, Vol. 24, supplement 1, 1976, 124, cited by Frances M. Lappé, *Diet*, 63.

16. "Still More Bull!" T. Colin Campbell, Ph.D., *EarthSave Magazine*, Volume 11, Number 1, p.3. ; "World Bank versus World Health," Neal D. Barnard, M.D., *Satya*, February 2000, 25.

17. Rabbi Emanuel Rackman, "Torah Concept of Empathic Justice Can Bring Peace," *The Jewish Week* (April 3, 1977), 19.

18. Ibid.

19. *Sukkot* 45b.

20. *Ketubot* 68a.

21. Maimonides, *Mishneh Torah, Hilchot Matnot Aniyim* 7:10.

22. Ibid., 10:7.

23. *Shabbat* 63a.
24. *Midrash Exodus Rabbah, Mishpatim* 31:14.
25. *Pirke Avot* 3:21.
26. *Betza* 32a.
27. *Eruvim* 41.
28. *Nedarim* 64b.
29. Genesis 18:2; *Abot de Rabbi Nathan* 7:17a,b.
30. Maimonides, *Mishneh Torah Hilchot Shabbat* 2:3.
31. *Bezah*, 32b.
32. *Yebamot* 79a; *Midrash Numbers Rabbah* 8:4.
33. Rashi's commentary on Genesis 41:50, based on *Ta'anit* 11a.
34. Rabbi Samson Raphael Hirsch, *Horeb*, Dayan Dr. I. Grunfeld, trans., London: Soncino Press, 1962, Vol. 1, 54–55 (Section 17, Nos. 126, 127).
35. *Pirke Avot* 1:14.
36. *Berachot* 55a.
37. Paper on world hunger by Mazon, ad hoc Jewish Committee on hunger, 1975.
38. Class before Pesach given at Young Israel of Staten Island, attended by author.
39. Jay Dinshah, *The Vegetarian Way*, Proceedings of the 24th World Vegetarian Conference, Madras, India, 1977, 34.
40. "The Energy–Food Crisis: A Challenge to Peace—A Call to Faith" statement from the Inter religious Peace Colloquium held in Bellagio, Italy, May 1975.
41. Rifkin, Jeremy, *Beyond Beef*, New York: Dutton, 1992, 160, 163.
42. Ibid., p. 160; estimates vary. In her book, *Diet for a Small Planet*, New York: Ballantine, 1991, 445, 446, Frances Moore Lappé calculates that it takes sixteen pounds of grain and soy to produce one pound of edible feedlot beef.
43. Ibid, 163.
44. 1992 Census of Agriculture, Table OA, U, S. Department of Commerce, Bureau of the Census.
45. Robbins, John, *The Food Revolution*, unpublished manuscript, 105.
46. Ibid.
47. Joanne Stepaniak, *The Vegan Sourcebook*, Los Angeles: Lowell House, 1998, 59.
48. Robbins, John, *Diet for a New America*, 352.

5: Judaism, Vegetarianism, and Ecology

1. *Shabbat* 10a; *Sanhedrin* 7.
2. *Ecclesiastes Rabbah* 7:28.
3. *Kiddushin* 4:12, 66d.
4. *Mishneh Baba Batra* 2:8.
5. Ibid. 2:8–9.
6. *Berachot* 30:5.
7. Story told by Rabbi Shlomo Riskin in "Biblical Ecology, A Jewish View," a television documentary, directed by Mitchell Chalek and Jonathan Rosen.
8. *Sefer Hachinuch* 530.

9.   *Kiddushin* 32a.

10. *Baba Kamma* 91b.

11. *Berachot* 52b.

12. *Shabbat* 67b.

13. Rabbi Samson Raphael Hirsch, *Horeb*, Dayan Dr. I. Grunfeld, trans., London: Soncino Press, 1962, Vol. 2, 282 (Section 56, No. 401).

14. Ibid., 280 (Section 56, No. 399).

15. *Midrash Ecclesiastes Rabbah* 1:18.

16. Cited by David Miller, *The Secret of Happiness*, New York: Rabbi David Miller Foundation, 1937, 9.

17. Michael Brower and Warren Leon, *The Consumer's Guide to Effective Environmental Choices: Practical Advice From the Union of Concerned Scientists*, New York: Three Rivers Press, 1999, 59.

18. Lappé, *Diet*, 76, based on presentation of agronomist Georg Borgstrom to the Annual meeting of the American Association for the Advancement of Science (AAAS), 1981.

19. "Facts of Vegetarianism," Booklet of the North American Vegetarian Society (PO Box 72, Dolgeville, NY 13329), 3.

20. Joanne Stepaniak, *The Vegan Sourcebook*, Los Angeles: Lowell House, 1998, 63.

21. Ibid.

22. Tom Aldridge and Herb Schlubach, "Water Requirements for Food Production," Soil and Water, No. 38 (Fall, 1978), University of California Cooperative Extension, 13–17; Paul and Anne Ehrlich, *Population, Resources, Environment*, San Francisco: Freeman, 1972, 75–76.

23. "The Browning of America," *Newsweek*, Feb. 22,1981, 26ff, cited in Lappé, *Diet*, 76.

24. John S. and Carol E. Steinhardt, "Energy Use in the U. S. Food System," *Science* (April 19, 1974).

25. Lappé, *Diet*, 10.

26. Ibid., pp. 74, 75, based on work of Drs. Marcia and David Pimentel at Cornell University.

27. Ibid, 74.

28. Alan B. Durning, "Cost of Beef for Health and Habitat," *Los Angeles Times*, September 21, 1986, 3.

29. Raw Material in the United States Economy 1900–1977," *Technical Paper* 47, U. S. Department of Commerce, U. S. Department of Interior, Bureau of Mines, p. 3, cited by Lappé, *Diet*, 66.

30. Ibid, Table 2, 86.

31. Joanne Stepaniak, *The Vegan Sourcebook*, Los Angeles: Lowell House, 1998, 64.

32. Ibid, 65. This same source indicates that one agricultural textbook, *Modern Livestock and Poultry Production*, estimates that at least two billion tons of manure are produced annually on U. S. farms.

33. Georg Borgstrom, *The Food and People Dilemma*, Duxbury Press, 1973, p. 103, cited by Lappé, *Diet*, 84.

34. Jeremy Rifkin, *Beyond Beef*, New York: Dutton, 1992, 203.

35. Stepaniak, *The Vegan Sourcebook*, 61.

36. Lappé, *Diet*, 80.

37. Ibid., 81.

38. Keith Akers, *A Vegetarian Sourcebook*, New York: G. Putnam, 1983, 87; 120–124.

39. Albert Gore Jr., introduction to new edition of *Silent Spring* by Rachel Carson, Boston, MA: Houghton Mifflin, 1994, xix.

40. Stepaniak, *The Vegan Sourcebook*, 62.

41. Pamphlet of RainForest Action Network, 300 Broadway, San Francisco, CA 94133.

42. *Newsweek*, Sept. 14, 1987, p.74; Julie Enslow and Christine Padoch, People of the Tropical Rainforest, Berkeley: University of California Press, 1988, 169.

43. Extensive coverage of this issue can be found by contacting the Union of Concerned Scientists (UCS) (www.ucsusa.org). There are increasingly frequent news reports about rising temperatures and climate change-related events, including droughts, severe storms, and melting of glaciers and ice caps.

44. Michael Brower and Warren Leon, *The Consumers Guide...*, 50.

45. Jeremy Rifkin, *Beyond Beef*, New York: Dutton, 1992, 1, 2.

46. Union of Concerned Scientists pamphlet (www.ucsusa.org).

6: Judaism, Vegetarianism, and Peace

1. *Midrash Leviticus Rabbah* 9:9.

2. *Pirke Avot* 1: 12.

3. *Yalkut Shimoni, Yithro* 273.

4. *Midrash Leviticus Rabbah* 9:9.

5. *Gittin* 59b.

6. *Midrash Genesis Rabbah* 38:6.

7. *Pirke Avot* 5: 11.

8. Rabbi Maurice Eisendrath, "Sanctions in Judaism for Peace," in *World Religions and World Peace*, Homer A. Jack, ed., Boston, MA: Beacon, 1968.

9. Rabbi J. David Bleich, "Vegetarianism and Judaism," *Tradition*, Vol. 23, No. I (Summer, 1987).

10. Nachmanides' commentary on Deuteronomy 22:6.

11. Maimonides, *Guide of the Perplexed*, 3:17.

12. *Sefer Ha Chinuch, Mitzvah* 596.

13. Rabbi Elijah J. Schochet, *Animal Life in Jewish Tradition*, New York: K'tav, 1984), 217.

14. Rabbi Samson Raphael Hirsch, *Horeb*, Dayan Dr. 1. Grunfeld, trans., London: Soncino Press, 1962, Vol. 2, Chapter 68. Section 454.

15. Ibid.

16. Quoted by Francine Klagsbrun, *Voices of Wisdom*, New York: Pantheon Books, 1980, 458.

17. G. S. Arundale, "The World Crucifixion," *The Vegetarian Way*, Proceedings of the 24th World Vegetarian Conference, Madras, India (1977),145.

18. Quoted by Barbara Parham, *Why Kill for Food?*, Denver, CO: Ananda Marga, 1979, 54.

19. Plato, *Republic* 2. A historical review of the relationships among war, food production, and consumption is given by Dudley Giehl, *Vegetarianism: A Way of Life*, New York: Harper and Row, 1979, 95–101.

20. Quoted in *The Vegetarian Way*, 12.

21. Quoted in *The Vegetarian Way*, 19th World Vegetarian Congress, 1967.

22. Mark Hatfield, "World Hunger," *World Vision* 19 (February 1975): 5.

23. *Staten Island Advance*, article by Susan Fogg, July 13, 1980, 1.

24. Jeremy Rifkin, *Beyond Beef*, New York: Dutton, 1992, 2.

25. Joanne Stepaniak, *The Vegan Sourcebook*, Los Angeles; Lowell House, 1998, 68, based on a statement by agricultural expert David Pimentel at the 1997 annual meeting of the Canadian Society of Animal Science.

7: Questions and Answers/Jewish issues

1. *Pesachim* 109a.

2. *Baba Batra* 60b.

3. Ibid.

4. Rabbi J. David Bleich, "Vegetarianism and Judaism," Vol. 23, No. 1 (Summer, 1987), 87. Other sources that indicate that there is no necessity to eat meat at any time today are cited by *S'dei Chemed*, Volume 5, (*Inyon Achilah*) and Volume 6 (*basar*); Rabbi David Rosen (*Rabbis and Vegetarianism*, pages 53 and 57); and Dovid Sears, (*A Vision of Eden* [unpublished manuscript]).

   These cited sources include: *Kiddushin* 3b; *Reisheet Chochma* 4, 129 (of Rabbi Elijah de Vidas; *Teshuvot Rashbash*, 176; *Magen Avraham, Orach Chayim* 696:15; *Sh'nei Luchos HaBris*, as cited in *Pischei Teshuvah, Yoreh Deah* 18:9; *Be'er Heitev* (quoting Isaac Luria (the "Ari") on *Shulchan Aruch, Orach Chayim* 134:1; *Kerem Shlomo Yoreh Deah*, 1; *Shulchan Aruch, Orach Chayim*, 288.

5. Rabbi Alfred Cohen, "Vegetarianism From a Jewish Perspective," *Journal of Halacha and Contemporary Society*, Vol. 1, No. II, (Fall 1981): 41, 43.

6. Ibid, 43.

7. Rabbi Moshe Halevi Steinberg, "A Collection of *Responsa*" (questions and answers concerning conversion and converts), *Responsa* No. 1, 2.

8. Kook, *Vision*, Sections 1–7.

9. *Shabbat* 119; *Sanhedrin* 7.

10. *Sanhedrin* 59b.

11. Kook, *Vision*, Section 2; Also see J. Green, "Chalutzim of the Messiah: The Religious Vegetarian Concept as Expounded by Rabbi Kook" (lecture given in Johannesburg, South Africa), 2.

12. Ibid.

13. Rabbi Samson Raphael Hirsch's commentary on Genesis 1:26.

14. Reverend A. Cohen, *The Teaching of Maimonides*, New York: Bloch Publishing Co., 1927, 178.

15. Ibid, based on Maimonides, *Guide to the Perplexed* 3:32; Maimonides did believe that the Temple sacrifices would be reestablished during the messianic period.

16. Ibid, 178–79.
17. Ibid, 179.
18. Rabbi J. H. Hertz, *The Pentateuch and Haftorahs*, London: Soncino Press, 1958, 562.
19. Ibid.
20. Ibid, 559.
21. Rashi's commentary on Isaiah 43:23.
22. Commentary of David Kimchi on Jeremiah 7:22–23.
23. Rev. Dr. A. Cohen, *Soncino Chumash*, London: Soncino Press, 647.
24. In *Olat Rayah*, 2: 292, Rav Kook stated: "In the future, the spirit of enlightenment will spread and reach even the animals. Gift offerings of vegetation will be brought to the Holy Temple, and they will be acceptable as were the animal sacrifices of old"; also see Hertz, *Pentateuch and Haftorahs*, 562.
25. *Midrash Vayikra Rabbah* 9:7; also see Hertz, *Pentateuch and Haftorahs*, 562.
26. *Berachot* 17a.
27. Morris Laub, "Why the Fuss over Humane Slaughter Legislation?," Joint Advisory Committee Paper, January 26,1966, 1. Also see the extended discussion in Rabbi E. J. Schochet's *Animal Life in Jewish Tradition*, New York: K'tav, 1985, 283–287.
28. Ibid, 2.
29. Laub, "Why the Fuss?"; Resolution of the Rabbinical Council of America, No. 16, (27th Annual National; Convention, June 24–27, 1963.)
30. Quoted in *The Extended Circle*, Jon Wynne-Tyson, ed., Fontwell, Sussex: Centaur Press, 1985, 28.
31. Ibid, 16.
32. Rabbi Samson Raphael Hirsch, *Horeb*, Dayan Dr. I. Grunfeld, trans., London: Soncino Press, 1962, Chapter 17, Section 125.
33. Cohen, "Vegetarianism...," 62.
34. Ibid.
35. Josephus, *Wars of the Jews*, Vol. I, Cambridge, MA: Loeb Classical Library, Harvard University Press, 1926, 7.
36. II Maccabees 5:27.
37. Cohen, "Vegetarianism...," 47.
38. Quoted in SANE (Committee for a Sane Nuclear Policy) slide show, "The Race Nobody Wins."
39. Cohen, "Vegetarianism...," 50.
40. This speculation is based on a statement by Rabbi Zalman Schachter, foreword to Louis A. Berman's *Vegetarianism and the Jewish Tradition* (New York: K'tav, 1982), xv.
41. Maimonides, *Mishneh Torah*, Laws of Festivals, 6:18.
42. See "Involvement and Protest," Chapter 1 of *Judaism and Global Survival*, Richard H. Schwartz, New York: Atara, 1987.
43. *Shabbat* 54b.
44. *Shabbat* 55a.
45. *Tanchuma to Mishpatim*.
46. *Ta'anit* 11a.

47. *Pesachim* 114b.

48. Also see Diana K. Appelbaum, "Vegetarian Passover *Seder*," *Vegetarian Times*, 37 (April 1980): 44, and S. Strassfeld *et al.*, *The (First) Jewish Catalog*, Philadelphia: Jewish Publication Society, 1973, 142.

49. *Baba Batra* 75a; *Midrash Leviticus Rabbah* 13:3; 22: 10; *Sanhedrin* 99a.

50. *The Jewish Encyclopedia*, New York: K'tav, Vol. 8, 38.

51. Ibid.

52. Ibid.

53. *Shabbat* 108a and "Tosefot S. V. 'Aizeh.''

54. Rabbi J. David Bleich, "Vegetarianism and Judaism," *Tradition*, Vol. 23, No. I (Summer, 1987).

55. Ibid.

56. Steinberg, *Responsum* No. 1,3.

57. Ibid.

58. Rabbi David Rosen, "Vegetarianism: An Orthodox Jewish Perspective," in *Rabbis and Vegetarianism: An Evolving Tradition*, Roberta Kalechofsky, ed., Marblehead, MA: Micah Publications, 1995, 59–60.

59. Rabbi Samson Raphael Hirsch, *Horeb*, Dayan Dr. I. Grunfeld, trans., London: Soncino Press, 1962, Chapter 62, section 428.

60. Rabbi Moses Auerbach, "Smoking and the *Halacha*," *Tradition*, 10 (3) (Spring, 1969), 50.

61. Ibid.

62. This question is included here because it is often raised, especially by Chassidim. For the response I am greatly indebted to Rabbi Yonassan Gershom, author of *Jewish Tales of Reincarnation* (Northvale, NJ: Jason Aronson, 1999), and to Rabbi Dovid sears for his careful review and many valuable suggestions. Rabbi Sears also covers these issues in greater depth in a his forthcoming book, tentatively entitled, *Compassion for Animals in Jewish Law and Mysticism*.

63. Klein, Aaron and Jenny, Eds, and trans., *Tales in Praise of the Ari*, New York: Jewish Publication Society, 1970.

64. *Jewish Tales of Reincarnation*, Northvale, NJ: Jason Aronson, 1999.

65. Gershom, *Jewish Tales*, 75–77.

66. Langer, Jiri, *Nine Gates to the Chassidic Mysteries*, ed. and trans. by Stephen Jolly, James and Clark. New York. 1961, pp. 100–01.

67. Mykoff, Moshe (trans.) and Chaim Kramer (annotator), *Likutei Moharan*, Breslov Research Institute, Jerusalem, 1997, Volume 5.

68. *Siach Sarfei Kodesh* 1–190.

69. *Sha'ar haMitzvot, Ekev,100*, as preserved by Rabbi Chaim Vital.

70. *Sefer HaMidot*, II: 1.

71. *Shiur Komah*.

72. Mindel, *My Prayer*, 280.

73. Gershom, 73–75.

74. *Pesachim* 49b.

8: Questions and Answers/General Issues

1. Guiterman, *A Poet's Proverbs*, 1924, 50.
2. J. Harris, "Killing for Food," in S. R. Godlovitch and John Harris, eds., *Animals, Man, and Morals*, New York: Taplinger Publishing Co., 1972, 109.
3. A list of famous vegetarians is in Nathaniel Altman, *Eating for Life*, Wheaton, IL: Theosophical Pub. House, 1977, 6.
4. Pamphlet of FARM (Farm Animal Reform Movement); PO Box 30654, Bethesda, Maryland 20824 (www.farmusa.org), 1-888-FARM-USA.
5. Ibid.
6. Victor Sussman, *The Vegetarian Alternative*, Emmaus, PA: Rodale Press, 1978, 2.
7. Ibid. For a very thorough discussion of vegan diets, see *The Vegan Sourcebook* by Joanne Stepaniak (see Bibliography).
8. For a more detailed discussion of why vegetarians do not eat fish, see Richard H. Schwartz, "Do You Eat Fish?," *Tikkun*, November/December, 1999, 24–26.
9. This paragraph is based on information in the *Anchorage Daily News*, Associated Press: Rick Callahan, "Aquaculture Taking Its Toll," June 29, 2000.
10. A comprehensive discussion of protein needs for humans is in Marc Sorensen, *MegaHealth*, Irvins, UT: National Institute of Fitness, 1993, 278–287, as well as the other vegetarian books in the Bibliography.
11. Percents of calories from protein in vegetable foods can be found in *MegaHealth*, 281–286.
12. The analysis of dairy products and osteoporosis is based on material from *MegaHealth*, 172–176, 179, and other vegetarian books.
13. Calcium contents of typical plant and animal foods are presented in *MegaHealth*, 181–182.
14. The analysis of iron requirements is based on material from *MegaHealth*, 249–250.
15. The analysis of vitamin B_{12} requirements is based on material from *MegaHealth*, 293–295, and other vegetarian books.
16. An extensive discussion of the negative effects of dairy products is in John A. McDougall, M.D., *The McDougall Plan* (Clinton, NJ: New Win Publishing, 1983), 49–62.
17. Quoted by Neal D. Barnard, M.D., *The Power of Your Plate*, Summertown, TN: Book Publishing Company, 1990, 16.
18. Ibid, 18.
19. Andrew Nicholson, M.D., "Chicken is Not a Health Food," *Good Medicine*, PCRM, Autumn, 1994, 14.
20. For more information, please see ADA's position paper on weight management which is posted at their website (www.eatright.org). Also see John Robbins, *The Food Revolution* (unpublished manuscript), 28.
21. Gary Gardner and Brian Halweil, "Underfed and Overfed—The Global Epidemic of Malnutrition," Worldwatch Paper 150, Washington, D. C.: Worldwatch institute, March 2000, 7.

22. Much of the information for this section is from "Discuss puberty with girls early on," Susan Spaeth Cherry, *Staten Island Advance*, June 8, 1999, p. D3 and "More Girls Experience early puberty," by Jennifer Haupt, CNN, March 31, 2000. More information on connections between high fat diets and the decreasing age of puberty can be found in *Diet for a New America* by John Robbins (Walpole, NH: Stillpoint Publishing, 1988, 266–267), and *The Power of Your Plate* by Dr. Neal Barnard (Summertown, TN: Book Publishing Co., 1990, 60–61).

23. "Earthsave: Healthy People, Healthy Planet," Spring 2000, Volume II, No. 2, 11.

24. I am indebted to Ralph Meyer for this information related to Hitler's alleged vegetarianism, including copies of pages from several biographies which refer to Hitler eating meat. For more information, Ralph Meyer, Box 3301, Santa Monica, CA 90408.

25. See John Toland's *Adolph Hitler* (New York: Doubleday. 1992), 30, 54, 107, and 256 and Albert Speer's *Inside the Third Reich*, 89.

10: Jewish Vegetarian Groups and Activities

1. Information for this chapter was obtained primarily from the Jewish Vegetarianism, *ProAnimal* magazine, and the Newsletter of the Jewish Vegetarians of North America. Information about these publications is given in the chapter. Whenever possible, the material was verified with the individuals and groups discussed.

11: Biographies of Famous Jewish Vegetarians

1. Rosen, Rabbi David, "Vegetarianism: An Orthodox Jewish Perspective," in *Rabbis and Vegetarianism: An Evolving Tradition*, Roberta Kalechofsky, ed. (Marblehead, MA: Micah Publications, 1995), p. 57.

2. Information for this chapter was obtained from the *Encyclopedia Judaica* in addition to the sources noted.

3. S. Y. Agnon, *The Bridal Canopy*, 222–23.

4. Philip Pick, "Agnon, Teller of Tales," in Philip Pick, ed., *The Tree of Life*, (New York: A. S. Barnes, 1977), 56.

5. Joe Green, "Chalutzim of the Messiah" (lecture given in Johannesburg, South Africa, 1.)

6. Personal message from Rabbi Cohen.

7. *Jewish Vegetarian.*

8. *Jewish Vegetarian*, 29 (August 1973): 42.

9. *Jewish Vegetarian*, 44 (Spring 1978): 19.

10. *Jewish Vegetarian*, 40 (December 1976): cover.

11. *Jewish Vegetarian*, 33 (Autumn 1974): 27.

12. *Jewish Vegetarian*, 40 (December 1976): 14–16.

13. *Jewish Vegetarian*, 51 (Winter 1979): 10; further information was obtained from material sent by Rabbi Rosen to the author.

14. I. B. Singer, "The Slaughterer," short story in *The Seance and Other Stories*, New York: Farrar, Straus, & Giroux, 1968.

15. *Jewish Vegetarian.*

12: Summary

1. Rabbi Shlomo Riskin, "A Sabbath Week—Shabbat Ekev," *The Jewish Week*, Aug. 14, 1987, 21.
2. Rosen, Rabbi David, "Vegetarianism: An Orthodox Jewish Perspective," in *Rabbis and Vegetarianism: An Evolving Tradition*, Roberta Kalechofsky, ed., Marblehead, MA: Micah Publications, 1995, 59.

Appendix

1. *Pirke Avot* 2:21.
2. Conclusion of *Amidah*, prayer in Sabbath morning services.
3. Sabbath morning prayer.
4. *Shabbat* 151b.
5. Samuel T. Coleridge, "The Ancient Mariner."
6. Rabbi A. J. Heschel, The Insecurity of Freedom, New York: Farrar, Straus, & Giroux, 1967, 87.
7. *Sota* 14a.
8. See Bleich, Rabbi J. David, "Judaism and Animal Experimentation," in *Animal Sacrifices*, Tom Regan, ed., Philadelphia: Temple University Press, 1986, 84–89.
9. *Shulchan Aruch, Even Haezer* 5:14; also see Bleich, 84.

BIBLIOGRAPHY

A. Jewish Books and Articles Related to Vegetarianism

Berman, Louis. *Vegetarianism and the Jewish Tradition.* New York: K'tav, 1982. (A comprehensive review of connections between Judaism and vegetarianism.)

Bleich, Rabbi J. David, "Vegetarianism and Judaism," *Tradition,* Vol. 23, No. 1 (Summer, 1987).

Cohen, Rabbi Alfred, "Vegetarianism From a Jewish Perspective," *Journal of Halacha and Contemporary Society,* Vol. I, No. II (Fall, 1981).

Cohen, Noah J. *Tsa'ar Ba'alei Chayim—The Prevention of Cruelty to Animals, Its Bases, Development, and Legislation in Hebrew Literature.* New York: Feldheim, 1979. (Survey of the laws and lore relating to animals and their treatment in the Jewish tradition. Defense of *shechitah,* ritual slaughter.)

Green, Joe. "Chalutzim of the Messiah—The Religious Vegetarian Concept as Expounded by Rabbi Kook" (text of a lecture given in Johannesburg, South Africa. Outline of some of Rabbi Kook's vegetarian teachings.)

——. *The Jewish Vegetarian Tradition.* Johannesburg, South Africa: 1969. (Fine discussion of many aspects in the Jewish tradition, such as compassion for animals, which point toward vegetarianism as a Jewish ideal.)

Kalechofsky, Roberta. *A Boy, A Chicken, and The Lion of Judea—How Ari Became a Vegetarian.* Marblehead, MA: Micah Publications, 1995. (How a Jewish boy in Israel overcomes family and peer-pressure to "take charge of his stomach.")

——. *Haggadah for the Liberated Lamb.* Marblehead, MA: Micah Publications, 1985. (Resource material for conducting a vegetarian Passover *seder,* with supplementary readings.)

——. *Haggadah For the Vegetarian Family.* Marblehead, MA, Micah Publications, 1988. (Good material for families with children.)

——. *Vegetarianism and the Jewish Holidays.* Marblehead, MA: Micah Publications, 1993. (Green Mitzvah Booklet) (Questions and answers about vegetarian connections to Jewish festivals. Recipes are included.)

——. *Vegetarian Judaism.* Marblehead, MA: Micah Publications, 1998. (Updated, comprehensive analysis of reasons Jews should adopt vegetarianism.)

215

——., editor. *Judaism and Animals Rights: Classical and Contemporary Responses.* Marblehead, MA: Micah Publications,1992. (A wide varieties of articles on animal rights, vegetarianism, animal experimentation, from the perspective of Judaism.)

——., editor. *Rabbis and Vegetarianism: An Evolving Tradition.* Marblehead, MA: Micah Publications, 1995. (Articles on vegetarianism by seventeen rabbis from different backgrounds and perspectives.)

Kook, Rabbi Abraham Isaac. "Fragments of Light: A View as to the Reasons for the Commandments," in Abraham Isaac Kook, a collection of Rabbi Kook's works, Ben Zion Bokser, trans. and ed., New York; Paulist Press, 1978. (A summary of Rav Kook's thoughts on vegetarianism.)

——. *A Vision of Vegetarianism and Peace* (Hebrew). (There is an English translation by Rabbi Jonathan Rubenstein. The vegetarian philosophy of this great Jewish leader and thinker.)

Pick, Philip, ed. *The Tree of Life: An Anthology of Articles Appearing in "The Jewish Vegetarian,"* 1966–1974. New York: A. S. Barnes, 1977. (A wide variety of essays and editorials from the Jewish Vegetarian on many aspects of the relationship between Judaism and vegetarianism.)

Raisin, Jacob A. *Humanitarianism of the Laws of Israel: Kindness to Animals.* Jewish Tract 06, Cincinnati, OH: Union of American Hebrew Congregations. (Concise summary of laws in the Jewish tradition relating to kindness to animals.)

Schochet, Rabbi Elijah J. *Animal Life in Jewish Tradition.* New York: K'tav, 1984. (Thorough, well-documented consideration of all aspects of animal issues, from the perspective of the Jewish tradition.)

Schwartz, Richard H. *Judaism and Animal Issues.* Marblehead, MA: Micah Publications, 1993. (Green Mitzvah Booklet)

——. *Judaism, Health, Nutrition, and Vegetarianism.* Marblehead, MA: Micah Publications,1993. (Green Mitzvah Booklet)

Sears, Dovid. *The Vision of Eden: Animal Welfare and Vegetarianism in Jewish Law and Mysticism.* (Unpublished manuscript by a Breslov Chassid that has a wealth of quotations and insightful essays relating Judaism to animal issues and vegetarianism.)

Weintraub, Mark. *Guide to Vegetarian Restaurants in Israel.* Baltimore, MD: Vegetarian Resource Group, 1996. (Reviews and background information about vegetarian restaurants in Israel, Also lists health food stores in major cities.)

Wolf, Jonathan and Richard Schwartz. "Judaism, Vegetarianism, and *Tu B'Shvot*," in *Trees, Earth, and Torah: A Tu B'Shvot Anthology.* Arthur Waskow, *et al.*, eds. (Philadelphia: Jewish Publication Society, 1999), 403–410.

B. General Books on Vegetarianism

Akers, Keith. *A Vegetarian Sourcebook.* Arlington, VA: Vegetarian Press, 1985, 1993.

Altman, Nathaniel. *Eating for Life.* Wheaton, IL: Theosophical Publishing House, 1977.

Coats, David C. *Old McDonald's Factory Farm.* New York: Continuum, 1989.

Davis, Karen. *Prisoned Chickens, Poisoned Eggs*. Summertown, TN: Book Publishing Co., 1997. (Comprehensive, insightful analysis of all aspects of the chicken and egg industries.)

Eisman, George L. *The Most Noble Diet*. Miami, FL: Diet-Ethics, 1984.

Eisnitz, Gail A. *Slaughterhouse: The Shocking Story of Greed, Neglect, and Inhumane Treatment Inside the U.S. Meat Industry*. Amherst, NY: Prometheus Books, 1997. (Graphically exposes the horrors of modern slaughterhouses. None of her examples involve ritual slaughter.)

Giehl, Dudley. *Vegetarianism: A Way of Life*. New York: Harper and Row, 1979. (Introduction by Isaac Bashevis Singer.)

Harrison, Ruth. *Animal Machines*. London: Vincent Stuart, 1964. (Classic analysis of the evils of factory farming. Foreword by Rachel Carson.)

Havala, Suzanne and Robert Pritikin. *The Complete Idiot's Guide to Being Vegetarian*. New York: MacMillan, 1999. (Shows how to become a vegetarian for a long, healthy life, with meal planning guides and sample menus.)

Hur, Robin. *Food Reform: Our Desperate Need*. Austin, TX: Heidelberg, 1975.

Lappé, Frances Moore. *Diet for a Small Planet*. New York: Ballantine Books, 1992 (20th anniversary edition). (Update of classic book that pioneered vegetarian concepts.)

Lyman, Howard. *Mad Cowboy: Plain Truth From the Cattle Rancher Who Won't Eat Meat*. New York: Scribner, 1998. (Fascinating story of how Lyman shifted from a Montana cattle rancher to one of today's most outspoken and eloquent vegetarian activists.)

Marcus, Erik. *Vegan: The New Ethics of Eating*. Ithaca, NY: McBooks Press, 1998. (Benefits of veganism covered mainly through discussions of the work of key personalities, including Dean Ornish, M.D., T. Colin Campbell, and Lori and Gene Bauston.)

Mason, Jim and Peter Singer. *Animal Factories*. New York: Harmony Books, 1990. (The horrible realities of factory farming.)

Moran, Victoria. *Compassion: The Ultimate Ethic*. Wellingborough, Northamptonshire, U.K.: Thorsons, 1985.

Null, Gary. *The Vegetarian Handbook: Eating Right for Total Health*. New York: St. Martin's Press, 1987.

Parham, Barbara. *What's Wrong With Eating Meat?* Denver, CO: Ananda Marga Publications, 1979.

Rifkin, Jeremy. *Beyond Beef: The Rise and Fall of the Cattle Culture*. New York: Dutton, 1992. (Powerful analysis of the many negative effects related to the raising of cattle and the consumption of beef.)

Robbins, John. *Diet For a New America*. Walpole, NH: Stillpoint Publishing, 1987. (Popular book that documents health, animal rights, and ecological reasons for not eating flesh, eggs, and dairy foods.)

———. *The Food Revolution: How Your Diet Can Help Save Your Life and Our World*. Berkeley: Conari, 2001. (Update and expansion of *Diet for a New America*.)

Singer, Peter. *Animal Liberation*. New York Review of Books Publishers, 1990. (Powerful argument for vegetarianism. Considers cruelty to animals in factory farming and scientific experimentation in great detail.)

Walters. Kerry S. and Lisa Portress, editors. *From Pythagorus to Peter Singer*. New York: State University of New York Press: 1999. (Anthology of historical moral arguments for vegetarianism.)

Wynne-Tyson, Jon. *Food For a Future: How World Hunger Could Be Ended By the 21st Century*. London: Thorsons, 1988.

C. Health and Nutrition Issues

American Natural Hygiene Society. *The Greatest Health Discovery*. Chicago: Natural Hygiene Press, 1972. ("Natural Hygiene and Its Evolution, Past, Present, and Future.')

Barnard, Neal D., M.D. *The Power of Your Plate: A Plan for Better Living*. Summertown, TN: Book Publishing Company. 1990. ("Eating well for better health—17 experts tell you how!")

Campbell, T. Colin, Ph.D. and Christine Cox. *The China Project: Keys to Better Health, Discovered in Our Living Laboratory*. Ithaca, NY: New Century Nutrition, 1996.

Diamond, Harvey and Marilyn Diamond. *Fit For Life*. New York: Warner Books, 1985. (Introduction to natural hygiene. Many recipes, best selling diet and health book ever.)

——. *Fit For Life. II—Living Health*. New York: Warner Books, 1987.

Esser, William, M.D. *Dictionary of Natural Foods*. Bridgeport, CT: Natural Hygiene Press, 1983. (Beautifully illustrated listing and discussion of fruits, vegetables, nuts, and seeds.)

Fuhrman, Joel, M.D. *Fasting and Eating for Health: A Medical Doctor's Program for Conquering Disease*. New York: St. Martin's Press, 1995. (Many valuable suggestions for healthier living.)

Harris, William, M.D. *The Scientific Basis of Vegetarianism*. Honolulu: Hawaii Health Publishers, 1995. (Many graphs and charts make a very strong case for the health benefits of vegetarianism.)

Klaper, Michael, M.D. *Vegan Nutrition: Pure and Simple*. Umatilla, FL: Gentle World, 1995.

——. *Pregnancy, Children, and the Vegan Diet*. Umatilla, FL: Gentle World, 1988. (Excellent for new or expectant mothers.)

Kradjian, Robert M., M.D. *Save Yourself From Breast Cancer: Life Choices That Can Help You Reduce the Odds*. New York: Berkeley Publishing Group, 1994. (Convincing case by a veteran cancer surgeon that breast cancer risks can be sharply reduced by a shift to vegetarianism.)

McDougall, John A., M.D. *McDougall's Medicine—A Challenging Second Opinion*. Piscataway, NJ: New Century Publishers, 1985. (Challenges currently accepted treatments for many degenerative diseases.)

McDougall, John A., M.D. and Mary A. McDougall. *The McDougall Plan*. Piscataway, NJ: New Century Publishers, 1983. (A gold mine of information on all aspects of nutrition. Recipes.)

Messina, Mark and Virginia. *The Dietitians' Guide to Vegetarian Diets: Issues and Applications*. Wilmington, DE: Aspen Publishers, 1996. (Valuable for dietitians counseling patients or as a textbook.)

Ornish Dean, M.D. *Dr. Dean Ornish's Program for Reversing Heart Disease*. New York: Ballantine, 1990. (How heart disease can be reversed through a very low-fat diet, exercise, meditation, and stress reduction. Many recipes.)

Sorensen, Marc, Ed.D. *MegaHealth*. Irvins, UT: National Institute of Health, 1993. (Thorough, well-documented discussion of the links between diet and health.)

D. Recipe Books

Benjamin, Alice and Corrigan, Harriet. *Cooking With Conscience: A Book for People Concerned About World Hunger*. New York: Seabury, 1978.

Dinshah, Freya. *The Vegan Kitchen*. Malaga, New Jersey: American Vegan Society, 1987.

Friedman, Rose. *Jewish Vegetarian Cooking*. New York: Thorsons, 1985. (The official cookbook of the International Jewish Vegetarian Society. Lacto-ovo vegetarian recipes.)

Gentle World. *The Cookbook for People Who Love Animals*. Umatilla, FL: Gentle World, 1983.

Golde, Muriel C. *Vegetarian Cooking for a Better World*. Dolgeville, NY: North American Vegetarian Society.

Hurd, Frank and Rosalie Hurd. *Ten Talents*. Collegedale, TN: College Press.

Kalechofsky, Roberta and Rosa Rasiel. *The Jewish Vegetarian Year Cookbook*. Marblehead, MA: Micah Publications, 1997. (Delicious vegetarian meals for all the Jewish Holidays.)

Katzen, Mollie. *The Moosewood Cookbook*. Berkeley, CA: Ten Speed Press. 1982.

———. *The Enchanted Broccoli Forest*. Berkeley, CA: Ten Speed Press. 1982.

Leneman, Leah. *Slimming The Vegetarian Way*. London: Thorsons, 1980.

———. *The Single Vegan*. New York: Thorsons, 1989. (Convenient, simple, appetizing meals for one.)

McDougall, Mary. *McDougall Health-Supporting Cookbook*. (2 volumes). New Century Publishers, 1985 (Vol. 1), 1986 (Vol. 2).

Robertson, Laurel, et al. *The New Laurel's Kitchen: A Handbook for Vegetarian Cookery and Nutrition*. Berkeley, CA: Ten Speed Press, 1986.

Wasserman, Debra. *Conveniently Vegan*. Baltimore, MD: Vegetarian Resource Group, 1997.

———. *The Low Fat Jewish Vegetarian Cookbook*. Baltimore, MD: Vegetarian Resource Group, 1994. (Over 150 low fat international recipes, based on Jewish traditions from around the world.)

Wasserman, Debra and Reed Mangels. *Simply Vegan*. Baltimore, MD: Vegetarian Resource Group, 1990. (A wide varieties of recipes that are completely free of animal products. Includes a comprehensive section on nutrition, written by nutritionist Reed Mangels, Ph. D.)

Wasserman, Debra and Charles Stahler. *No Cholesterol Passover Recipes*. Baltimore, MD: Vegetarian Resource Group, 1986. (Contains 100 recipes without animal products that are suitable for Passover.)

———. *Meatless Meals for Working People—Quick and Easy Vegetarian Recipes*. Baltimore, MD: Vegetarian Resource Group, 1990. (A wide variety of recipes for people with limited time.)

E. Jewish Teachings on Vegetarian-Related Issues

Fisher, Adam D. *To Deal Thy Bread to the Hungry*. New York: Union of American Hebrew Congregations, 1975. (Excellent review of the world hunger crisis and the Jewish tradition related to food and hunger.)

Hakohen, Yosef Ben Shlomo, *The Universal Jew: Letters to My Progressive Father*. Jerusalem/New York: Feldheim, 1995. (Judaism's universal message, including a discussion of people's obligations to the earth and its creatures.)

Hirsch, Richard G. *Thy Most Precious Gift: Peace in the Jewish Tradition*. New York: Union of American Hebrew Congregations, 1974.

Hirsch, Rabbi Samson Raphael. Horeb, translated by Dayan I. Grunfeld, New York/London/Jerusalem: Soncino Press, 1962. (Wide variety of *mitzvot* are analyzed, including those which teach us how to relate to the earth and its creatures.)

Schwartz, Richard. *Judaism and Global Survival*, New York: Atara Press, 1987. (Application of Jewish values to critical issues such as hunger, pollution, resource scarcity, and the arms race.)

F. Religious/Philosophical Books About Food and Vegetarian-Related Issues

Bernstein, Ellen, editor. *Ecology and the Jewish Spirit: Where Nature and the Spirit Meet*. Woodstock, VT: Jewish Lights Publishing, 1998. (Jewish perspectives on Environmental Issues.)

Berry, Rynn. *Food for the Gods: Vegetarianism and the World's Religions*. New York: Pythagorean Press, 1998.

Dresner, Rabbi Samuel H. *The Jewish Dietary Laws: Their Meaning for Our Time*. New York: Burning Bush Press, 1959. (Fine discussion of the meaning of *kashrut*. Discussion of compassion for animals in Jewish tradition, meat-eating as a concession, and ritual slaughter.)

Kasten, Deborah. *Feeding the Body, Nourishing the Soul*. Berkeley, CA: Conari Press, 1997. (Discussions of spiritual values of the world's religions and traditions related to foods.)

Rosen, Steven. *Diet for Transcendence: Vegetarianism and World Religions*. Torchlight Publishers, 1997.

Sears, David. *Compassion for Humanity in the Jewish Tradition*. Northvale, NJ, Jason Aronson, 1998. (Statements from classical Jewish sources. Some material on compassion to animals.)

Young, Robert Alan. *Is God a Vegetarian? Christianity, Vegetarianism, and Animal Rights*. Chicago and La Salle, IL: Open Court Publishing Co.: 1998. (A Christian analysis on some of the issues in this book.)

G. Books on Vegetarian-Related Issues

Brown, Lester. *Tough Choices: Facing the Challenge of Food Scarcity*. New York, London: Norton, 1996. (Predictions of major food scarcities if current trends continue.)

Diamond, Harvey. *Your Heart, Your Planet*. Santa Monica, CA: Hay House, 1990. (Negative health and environmental effects of animal-based diets and agriculture.)

Rhodes, Richard. *Deadly Feasts: Tracking the Secrets Of a Terrifying New Plague*. New York: Simon and Schuster, 1997. (Powerful analysis of "Mad Cow Disease" and its future threats.)

Schell, Orville. *Modern Meat*. New York: Vintage Books, 1985. (Detailed discussion about many problems related to the production and consumption of meat.)

Spiegel, Marjorie. *The Dreaded Comparison: Human and Animal Slavery*. New York: Mirror Books, 1997. (Foreword by Alice Walker.)

Tansey, Geoff and Joyce D'Silva. editors. *The Meat Business: Devouring a Hungry Planet*. New York: St. Martin's Press, 1999. (Challenging essays on the very negative impacts of animal-based agriculture on hunger, the environment, resources, animals, and human health.)

INDEX